Simon & Schuster
5/9/83
16.50

ALSO BY HERMAN KAHN
(A Partial Listing)

WORLD ECONOMIC DEVELOPMENT
ON THERMONUCLEAR WAR
THE JAPANESE CHALLENGE: THE SUCCESS AND FAILURE OF ECONOMIC SUCCESS
(with Thomas Pepper)
THE NEXT TWO HUNDRED YEARS
(with William Brown and Leon Martel)
THINGS TO COME
(with B. Bruce-Briggs)
THE EMERGING JAPANESE SUPERSTATE: CHALLENGE AND RESPONSE
THINKING ABOUT THE UNTHINKABLE

THE COMING BOOM

ECONOMIC, POLITICAL, AND SOCIAL

BY

HERMAN KAHN

SIMON AND SCHUSTER
New York

Copyright © 1982 by The Hudson Institute, Inc.
All rights reserved
including the right of reproduction
in whole or in part in any form
Published by Simon and Schuster
A Division of Gulf & Western Corporation
Simon & Schuster Building
Rockefeller Center
1230 Avenue of the Americas
New York, New York 10020
SIMON AND SCHUSTER and colophon are trademarks of
Simon & Schuster
Designed by Irving Perkins Associates
Manufactured in the United States of America

1   3   5   7   9   10   8   6   4   2

Library of Congress Cataloging in Publication Data

Kahn, Herman, 1922–
The coming boom.

Includes bibliographical references and index.
1. Economic forecasting—United States.
2. United States—Economic conditions—1971–
3. United States—Politics and government—
1981–   I. Title.
HC106.8.K33   1982   303.4'973   82-5944
ISBN 0 671 44262-7

090941

ACKNOWLEDGMENTS

In addition to recent and, I hope, imaginative thinking carried out in the past several months, this book draws heavily upon work that I have done at the Hudson Institute over the past decade. As Director of Research during this period I have naturally had the benefit of much thinking by the professional staff. I have to acknowledge the help of almost every member.

There are particular sections in which I have collaborated especially closely with various colleagues: many ideas in Chapter 2 were developed in conjunction with Thomas Pepper and Jimmy Wheeler; much of the economic discussion in Chapter 5 was derived from work done with Irving Leveson; Chapter 7 on energy was developed in close collaboration with William Brown, who also supplied ideas for Chapter 6 on unconventional financing; Ernest Schneider helped with the many issues we associate with the phrase "social limits to growth"; and Keith Payne contributed to Chapter 8 on defense issues.

In addition, thanks are due to several "nonstaff" sources. Thomas Chrystie, Chairman, Merrill Lynch White Weld Capital Markets Group, and Chris Andersen of Drexel Burnham Lambert have both been extremely generous in sharing their expertise; the Olin Foundation has been equally generous in supplying us with a grant which made this book possible. Michael Shane helped support the Congressional briefings which were the basis of much of the material included here. I am most grateful to all for their assistance.

Finally, I would like to acknowledge an extraordinary debt to Carol Kahn and Neil Pickett. In more than a courteous sense these two are genuine collaborators in producing the book, not so much in the basic formulation of ideas but in terms of actually selecting and putting many of the pieces together. Carol Kahn is officially the editor. Neil Pickett, my assistant at Hudson for the last two years, did much research. (It was with regret and affection that we sent him off to Oxford to finish his education.) The months of September and October, when the book was nearing completion, were particularly hectic; they especially involved heroic and dedicated—as well as skilled and creative—efforts by Carol. I can only salute her here. A final editing by Erwin Glikes and Marion Osmun of Simon and Schuster was most helpful.

I must also salute Helen Iadanza and Roberta McPheeters for their extraordinary efforts to type from heavily revised manuscripts, and to Marianne Bell, Maureen Pritchard, and Maryellen Pitcairn for doing all the other things that needed doing—and doing them very well. I would also like to acknowledge the support and understanding of my staff and colleagues at Arizona State University, where I held the Goldwater Chair for American Institutions during much of the writing of *The Coming Boom*.

The ideas for the book came out of a series of lectures I gave in late 1980 and early 1981, but the actual project was not finalized until late spring 1981, when I was already fully committed to other projects. It wasn't much more than a few months (June to November 1981) when the book was actually created from my seminar notes, papers, recorded briefings, and assorted dictations. As I noted, the great brunt of the work was actually carried through by Carol Kahn. I am forever grateful for her dedication, wisdom, creativity, and just plain hard work.

Herman Kahn

CONTENTS

SPECIAL PREFATORY NOTE 9

CHAPTER 1
INTRODUCTION AND OVERVIEW 13

CHAPTER 2
HISTORICAL CONTEXT 28

CHAPTER 3
THE BASIC CONTEXT FOR REVITALIZATION 50

CHAPTER 4
THE NEW DYNAMISM OF HIGH TECH 65

CHAPTER 5
CONTROLLING AND ALLEVIATING INFLATION AND ITS EFFECTS 86

CHAPTER 6
UNCONVENTIONAL FINANCING 113

CHAPTER 7
ENERGY: WE MAY WELL LUCK OUT, BUT SHOULD HEDGE 128

CHAPTER 8
U.S. DEFENSE POLICY: THINKING CONSTRUCTIVELY ABOUT THE UNTHINKABLE 146

CONTENTS

CHAPTER 9
GOVERNANCE: MANAGING AN AFFLUENT DEMOCRACY 179

CHAPTER 10
REVITALIZATION: HOW TO MAKE IT HAPPEN AND GROW 203

INDEX 229

SPECIAL PREFATORY NOTE

As I send this book off to the publisher, the Dow Jones average has plunged to its lowest level in about sixteen months. Other more broadly based stock averages have fallen by similar amounts. U.S. long-term bonds are paying about 15 percent interest; the bond futures market (driven by what is often thought of as the "smart money") and some financial experts suggest that high interest rates will be maintained for many years—perhaps decades. Estimates of the fiscal 1982 deficit have more than doubled. In addition, the Reagan tax cuts, coupled with fears of runaway defense spending, seem to many to be likely to force even larger deficits in the future. Some sober concern, if not paranoia, is clearly justified. As far as most commentators are concerned, the bloom is off the Reaganomics rose. It does not seem like a good time to publish a book called *The Coming Boom: Economic, Political, and Social.*

I am reasonably confident, however, that the above phenomena are largely due to temporary pressures and are compatible with the coming boom. Inasmuch as for the first time in almost two decades the Federal Reserve Board and the White House seem prepared to carry through relatively severe, even painful, tight money policies, the consequent high interest rates might even be taken as indications that good health is on the way. They are proof of the government's willingness to persevere, in spite of the lack of faith, particularly among money managers, in the government's real ability to carry out tight money policies in the face of a likely recession that (from the Republican point of view) may affect the Congressional elections of 1982 disastrously. One could argue that this lack of faith is fully justified by the record of the past two decades and the likely pressures on the Republicans. Perhaps so, but our judgment is otherwise. One may also note that tight money policies may not be as effective as they would have been if adopted earlier. The so-called "embedded inflation" now seems to many to have great staying power. Further, changes in the financial system and the economy (e.g., the inflation itself, growth of Eurodollars, introduction of computers, and the rise of money funds), the revision and repeal of state usury laws, and allowing the inflationary component of the interest rates to be fully deductible have all reduced the efficacy of tight money policies and increased the pain of effective policies.

Nonetheless, the fact that tight money policies are less potent and politically more painful does not make them less essential to checking inflation, even at the cost of a recession in late 1981 and early 1982. Many people expect a renewed inflation will automatically come with recovery, but this is by no means inevitable. The administration's basic ideology and policies seem to be appropriate, and barring some perverse combination of bad luck and bad management,* should work. The fact that many in the administration thought an almost immediate and dramatic improvement in savings and investment would be touched off by the tax cuts reflected a somewhat optimistic version of supply-side economics, but one which no longer exists.

The tight money policy will almost certainly be continued, but there are also a number of other ways, as described in the book, to cope better with both the deficit and the lingering (though decreasing) inflation. It would be "bad management" indeed if, as many fear, nothing were done about these problems.

It is now clear that the country was in greater trouble than was generally realized when Reagan took office. The new administration adopted measures to stop a rapidly deteriorating situation—huge unlegislated tax increases, an embedded inflation of 8 to 10 percent that was increasing rapidly, the growth of so-called "uncontrollable" expenditures to more than three-quarters of the budget, the meteoric rise of off-budget items from effectively zero in 1973 to more than $20 billion in 1981, a catastrophic regulatory situation, and so on.

Perhaps the most unusual aspect of the Reagan administration is its willingness to accept measures which are genuinely painful for some important elements of the country. In part this is almost cynical politics: as far as the tax cuts are concerned, the groups losing the most, at least in the short run, are usually those which did not vote for Reagan (mainly the poor and less well off), while those gaining the most, again in the short run, are those which supported him (mainly the rich and better off). But while, as President Kennedy said, "a rising tide floats all ships," it does not float smaller ships more than bigger ones—i.e., it does not help redistribute income from richer to poorer. By now, however, most American voters are essentially against increased redistribution of income, especially if it hampers economic growth or if the income goes to what they regard as "the undeserving poor." This does not prevent them from re-

---

* The phrase "barring some perverse combination of bad luck and bad management" is used several times throughout the book. It is often an essential caveat to some optimistic projection or prediction.

garding Reagan and the Republicans as better for the rich than the poor, but despite distaste for the phrase, most Americans do believe in "trickle down," as Kennedy suggested (see Chapter 10). Further, and perhaps more significant, the tight money policy hurts many in the business community as much as or more than other groups; many of the cuts in entitlements are aimed at the middle class, which the Reagan people feel should not be benefiting at the cost of taxes on rich and poor alike.

At the time this book appears, the United States seems likely to be in a relatively severe recession, but it will very likely be on the way to alleviating, if not solving, the country's stagflation and many other problems. While this is by no means a sure bet, it's a good one. The economic part of the boom may start a little later than mid-1982, as was my original expectation. But whether or not the timing is absolutely correct, unless my prognostications are disastrously wrong, a revitalized America—revitalized in terms of traditional values, of worldwide status and influence, and of citizenship and morale, as well as of economic improvement—seems to me very probable, and with sensible social and economic policies, a near certainty.

CHAPTER 1

INTRODUCTION AND OVERVIEW

Talk of an expansive new decade dominated discussions of the early 1970s; few people anticipated the enormous economic, social, political, and military dislocations that in fact occurred. The sudden end to an extended period of high economic growth in both capitalist and communist developed nations was marked by the emergence, among other things, of a (nominal) tenfold increase in world oil prices, double-digit inflation on a global scale, sharp declines in productivity, and the large-scale erosion of traditional social values. Opposition to America's involvement in the Vietnam War, and by extension, to the entire U.S. defense effort, grew substantially as U.S. defense spending (except for the operational expenses of the war) remained more or less constant in fixed dollars but declined steadily as a percentage of its GNP. At the same time the Soviet Union was steadily increasing its defense spending and procurement in a (largely successful) effort to overcome its substantial inferiority in strategic delivery systems and to increase its lead in other aspects of military power. All of these events were the results as well as the causes of a national and world climate dramatically different from that of the previous twenty-five years. Under their influence, U.S. status in the world dropped to an unprecedented low.

Except for a brief period of euphoria early in the Reagan administration, most discussions of the early 1980s assumed that the decade would very likely continue to experience the negative trends of the recent past, i.e., continued rapid erosion of traditional values and institutions, low economic growth, upward pressure on energy prices, double-digit inflation (or something close to it), growing confusion and erosion of unity in NATO, and a generally pervasive low morale.

It is now increasingly clear that most of these projections may be wrong. Although we do not expect instant happiness, we do expect a revitalization—a boom—in America.* We do not anticipate a return to the conditions characteristic of the 1950s and 1960s. We do, however, foresee a good possibility for substantial improvement in the economy and the global standing of the United States, with economic growth averaging about 3 percent or more over the next two decades—i.e., the GNP about doubling between 1982 and 2002. We expect a high degree of synthesis of old and new values, involving at least a limited revival of traditional values (initiated more by the middle than by the upper and upper-middle classes). Further, we believe the United States will respond reasonably successfully to the problems of inflation, defense, energy, governance, and changing values, resulting in a relatively high-morale country guided by constructive, positive, and realistic visions of the future.

Our prognosis, therefore, is for a renascent United States. We anticipate both a boom and a revitalization which are more than economic; the revitalization, in particular, should range from work and family values to U.S. prestige and influence at home and abroad. If the proper new initiatives and policies are developed and carried through by the Reagan administration and Congress, the revitalization could extend well into the next two decades, perhaps even beyond.

Barring political problems in the Middle East (and maybe even with them), we do not anticipate a significant—or even insignificant—rise in world oil prices. It is probable that average world price for oil peaked at under $40 a barrel in 1980 and will not exceed that figure in real terms—at least not in the next two decades. Indeed, world oil prices have been declining in real terms and are likely to decline further over the next few years. Even more important is that inflation rates are beginning to decline, at least in most of the developed countries. Accordingly, we believe

---

* Throughout this book the author uses the term "we" to indicate that most of his colleagues at the Hudson Institute (where he is Director of Research) share the outlook in question and contributed to forming it; when the author uses the first person singular, he is stating a more personal position. There is often disagreement and dissent on "we" positions as well, but there is also enough consensus to make the use of "we" reasonable.

that these adjustments, together with other positive trends, will exert a beneficial cumulative influence on the upcoming course of events. The result will be higher growth rates than the United States experienced in the 1970s and at the beginning of this decade.*

Several of the reasons we expect a boom are summarized below. A fuller discussion occurs throughout the book.

1. *Cyclical recovery.* Eventually the high inflation and interest rates will trend downward; the normal adjustments that happen in every "abnormal" situation will occur and a more or less standard recovery will take place—assuming that current tight money policies are basically continued and not relaxed prematurely, as happened in all recent recessions.

2. *Adequate control of inflation.* I expect policies will be followed that will bring inflation down to less than 5 percent by the mid-'80s. This is optimistic compared with most estimates but I believe it can and will be achieved, though with some pain and at the cost of a relatively severe but fairly short-lived recession (which should bottom out by mid-to-late 1982).

3. *Reduced costs of coping with residual inflation and the expectation of inflation.* It is important that contracts, particularly loans, not be distorted by factoring in an excessively high premium to correct for inflation or to guard against its changing unpredictably. One way to do this is for the administration to change inflationary expectations; another (as described later) is to use appropriate indexing and what we call "unconventional financing."

4. *Improvement in indexing.* The consumer price index (CPI) is a bad index. It exaggerates the inflation by including technical mistakes (such as using old market baskets and incorrectly defining costs of home ownership and mortgages) and because it gives full (or even excessive) weight to "impoverishing events" which we believe should be considered separately from a pure monetary inflation (see Chapter 5). As such, the current CPI is unsuitable for indexing long-term contracts, for long-term instruments such as twenty-to-thirty-year bonds, and for many other kinds of "agreements" (e.g., Social Security)

* For a detailed discussion of the view that the adjustment process itself could be the dominant influence on the world economy in the 1980s, see a recent Hudson Institute report: Irving Leveson and Jimmy W. Wheeler, eds., *Western Economies in Transition: Structural Change and Adjustment Policies in Industrial Countries* (Boulder, Colo.: Westview Press, 1980).

which attempt to prevent one group in society from being affected more severely by inflation than another. The administration has indicated that it will improve this situation in the near future. We anticipate other related improvements as well, such as indexing the principal of loans and not the interest (see Chapters 5 and 6).

5. *Energy success.* Energy should no longer be a depressing influence on the economy. Instead, as described in Chapter 7, energy costs should go down, its reliability should go up, the low morale caused by a continuing "energy crisis" should begin to dissipate; and the energy industry should contribute greatly to the long-term capital boom we expect.

6. *A long-term capital boom.* This is partially propelled by resource development, by making up for the underinvestment in the 1970s, by tax incentives (including the stimulation of the lower rates for individuals), by new technologies including the computer and advanced communications (and their extraordinarily diverse and revolutionary applications in the service economy), by a likely housing boom (based on the baby-boom generation's coming of age), by new programs in defense and space, and by massive developments via high technology in areas ranging from pharmaceuticals to plastics to commuter aircraft.

7. *Increased savings and cash flow.* Many aspects of Reaganomics, increased real interest rates, the lessened protection against financial disaster due to increased and inflated housing values (where second mortgages once substituted for savings), should all contribute to and help support 6 above.

8. *Improvement in productivity.* This will result from a more experienced work force, a high rate of application and exploitation of new technologies (especially in the service industries), much better industrial relations, an improved regulatory situation, and some return to the traditional values that have been so helpful to economic development.

There are likely to be synergistic effects among these diverse forces, so that the total impact on revitalization will be greater than the simple impact of the individual components.

Our expectations of a boom notwithstanding, there are a variety of more forbidding scenarios which are also conceivable. Bad luck and bad management are always possible. How the United States either avoids this possibility and/or meets various other challenges will, in large measure, determine both its role in world affairs for the remainder of the century and its potential for long-term revitalization. Alternatively, the measures promulgated by the Reagan administration, while mostly desirable, may not work well (at least in the near future), and there may be an extreme backlash in the Congressional elections of 1982—particularly if the recession doesn't seem to be easing up by the third quarter.

There is also the possibility of what we used to call a "technological crisis" in the next decade or two,* or what we now call the "growing pains" of the "emerging problem-prone super-industrial world economy." We are dealing with new technologies and products and other innovations on a scale and with a variety of possible effects that is genuinely frightening. We feel it is safer to go ahead, to suffer the growing pains of technological advancement, than not to, but we may be wrong in our basic estimate of the problems that new technologies will present. Therefore, though we are indeed optimistic, our optimism has elements of deep concern. But such remote—even if potentially disastrous—problems are not the subject of this book. We discuss these problems only when they are of special interest or relevance, but because our focus is elsewhere we do not dwell on them at length. In addition, we believe that many scenarios which are sometimes discussed (north-south world war or race war) are quite improbable and therefore don't warrant lengthy discussion here (or perhaps anywhere).

In fact, throughout the 1970s, most of us at Hudson Institute argued that the long-term economic and technological prospects for mankind were probably favorable, or at least more likely to be favorable than not. This position was in sharp contrast to such widely publicized studies as the book sponsored by the Club of Rome, *Limits to Growth,* and the *Global 2000* report prepared for President Carter, both of which were basically pessimistic about the prospects for the human race. These studies held that the world is running out of resources, that pollution and other destruction of the environment is nearly out of control, and that management of human society is becoming impossibly difficult. It was argued that the future would in many ways not be as good as the past. In two Hudson studies of worldwide economic prospects,† however, we took a very different "guarded optimist" position, arguing that while various problems would occur, there were practical measures that could—and probably would—be taken to deal with them reasonably effectively.

* See Herman Kahn and B. Bruce-Briggs, *Things to Come* (New York: Macmillan, 1972).
† Cf. Herman Kahn et al., *The Next 200 Years* (New York: William Morrow, 1976); and Herman Kahn, *World Economic Development* (Boulder, Colo.: Westview Press, 1979).

To be sure, much of our current optimism depends on a restoration of the ability of the United States to play a genuine leadership role. The longer the economic, military, political, and social recovery is delayed, the less optimistic we become—in part because of the increasing probability that significant challenges to the international system and to U.S. values and programs will occur. In that event, the problems we do not discuss may turn out to be dominant.

Take, for example, the general world reaction to the failed U.S. rescue mission in Iran. Or the reaction to the Olympic boycott against the Soviets, which can be judged only a limited success at best; the same can be said of the U.S. grain embargo that was lifted in May 1981. Each of these events occurred in a context of a general U.S. and West European malaise* and a relative decline in U.S. and NATO military power. Thus we have had to ask ourselves what might happen if the United States continues to pursue military and political policies that make it almost impossible for it to resume the leadership role it held from 1945 to the late 1970s. Indeed, unless something changes soon, a "guarded pessimist," or even pessimist, position would become increasingly justified. The current administration appears to recognize this fact and is taking steps to restore American status and power, thereby improving the nation's ability to choose and execute various options, and, perhaps more important, to discourage the Soviets from doing so.

We believe that the Reagan administration has the ideology, motivation, and attitude—and solid enough leadership and support—to be adequate (or better) in meeting many domestic challenges. The American voter has been looking for a president to do many of the kinds of things we expect the current administration to do. In the last twenty years a new intellectual structure has grown up which is now replacing the liberal consensus on the economic, social, and defense issues which so dominated national discussions from 1930 to 1980. To a large extent, the present administration reflects this change.

In the economic area, the role of Milton Friedman has been central—not just his monetary theories, but his whole emphasis on the free enterprise system and the use of market forces. A number of young (mostly

---

* When we first began to use the word "malaise" to characterize the American condition, it was a perfectly valid term meaning a state of not being really sick but also not being totally healthy. In the meantime the word has been discredited and the condition significantly alleviated. Nonetheless, it is still a useful term to describe a particular kind of societal discomfort, and we shall continue to use it.

under forty), more or less conservative economists are also becoming increasingly important in determining or influencing attitudes and proposing solutions to various problems. They are focusing on issues of increased savings, economic efficiency, market incentives, rationalized taxation and expenditures, reduced and more appropriate welfare, and so on. They are competent, hardworking, and inspired, and easily win most of their debates. There has been a corresponding revision in debates over social and defense issues, but the revisions have been less dramatic and their influence less effective than in the economic debate.

These factors buttress our feeling that the kinds of changes President Reagan proposes may have long-term staying power in that they represent a new intellectual consensus and a new role for both traditional conservative and neo-conservative concepts. And even the New Right, despite the widespread apprehension it has generated, is likely to play a most constructive and helpful role, though not necessarily according to the program it has laid out or according to the fearful nightmares it has generated among some liberals.

This book therefore outlines, from a "guarded optimist's" point of view, an economic, political, social, and national-security context in which to consider U.S. policies and prospects in the 1980s. It is our firm belief that such analysis must consider both present-day realities (subject as they are to varying interpretations and rapid and confusing change) and the many possibilities for the medium and long-range future. Even if the contexts and scenarios turn out to be imperfect, they can still provide a valuable frame of reference for looking beyond current assumptions and bureaucratic requirements. It is our belief that the better one understands the new coalition of economic, social, and political forces now at work, the better position one is in to benefit from the opportunities of the coming boom (and to guard against the dangers) which these forces will help to create.

LEVELS OF BELIEF AND CERTAINTY

To some degree this book deals with uncertainties—areas in which there are severe limitations to our evidence and analysis, and in which rigorous studies and documentation are usually not available. As a result, much of what we discuss must be taken at the level of what we call a "Scotch verdict."*

In criminal proceedings in Scotland, the jury need not choose only between "guilty" or "not guilty" (the only two verdicts in most Western judicial systems) but may decide on a third outcome, "not proven." This means that the case against the defendant is very persuasive, and that for practical purposes (i.e., lending money, hiring or firing, etc.) most laymen would accept the case presented by the prosecutor even though it has not met the legal requirement of "beyond any reasonable doubt."

The Scotch verdict often denotes what might be called a "good enough for our purposes" case: we have information that is considered valid enough for immediate decisions and yet would not satisfy rigorous academic standards. Indeed, it is rare for public discussions to be informed by or based upon information and theories that are of much greater certainty than this "not conclusively proven" basis. The issue is whether or not one is willing to act on this basis; in either case the position is simply too plausible for opponents to argue that it is clearly false. This is an important aspect of the "Scotch verdict" concept: while neither side may be able to force the other side to accept its position, opponents of a Scotch verdict cannot dismiss the opposing views out of hand.

The Scotch verdict is closely related to another concept we have found extremely useful at the Hudson Institute, the "surprise-free scenario." By that we simply mean that it would not be surprising to some relevant group if a particular prediction turned out to be valid, or if a given event occurred. Two surprise-free projections can be inconsistent; it would not be surprising if one *or* the other occurred (but not both).

A different level of certainty is operative when decisions are based on a position accepted by a professional group, academic community, public body, or even the general public. This could be either a "conventional wisdom" position or an ideological or religious stance held only by a limited group of followers. Acceptance of concepts, theories, facts, or other information in these instances does not necessarily imply validity, only that the group concerned does not question them—i.e., there is a high degree of consonance with the values, ideology, or even prejudices of the

* For a discussion of eight levels of belief—atheism, agnosticism, skepticism, deism, Scotch verdict, acceptance, scientifically valid, and "divine revelation" (or ideological certainty)—and the use of this methodology, see Kahn, *World Economic Development*.

group. This acceptance is usually so immediate and widely shared that it is almost unperceived as being a "position."

Because of inadequate data or theory, and to prevent endless delays while pursuing additional information or documenting observations based on personal judgments, much of what we discuss in this book should be taken at the level of a Scotch verdict and/or a surprise-free projection—i.e., for practical purposes, we have done our best. Often our views coincide with the emerging (post-Keynesian and post-LBJ Great Society) "conventional wisdom," but often they disagree, at least in particulars. While we are not dyed-in-the-wool Reaganites, we often concur in the positions taken by the administration. But not always.

THE SPECIAL BUDGETARY SITUATION OF THE UNITED STATES

One example of our divergence from the commonly accepted wisdom concerns the budgetary situation of the United States: we do not believe in the widely discussed "budget deficit"—at least not in some of the implications that this phrase normally conjures up.

If one looks at the problems of various advanced European industrialized countries, one finds that a very high percentage of their gross national product (40–60 percent) goes through the hands of the government, and that these countries have long run genuine deficits, thereby increasing their national indebtedness (as measured in a currency of constant value). The rhetoric in the United States could lead one to believe that this is true here too, but it is not at all true for the deficit and not completely true for the share of the GNP. Thus, if we look at Figure 1-1, which covers the last twenty-eight years, it turns out that *the United States owes only slightly more today in constant dollars than it owed twenty-eight years ago*—as opposed to the situation in almost every other country in the Organization for Economic Cooperation and Development (OECD). This is true whether one is looking at the net or the gross national debt.

The explanation is very simple. During most of this twenty-eight-year period the interest on the U.S. national debt was close to or even less than the inflation—i.e., the real interest was much less than the nominal rate, sometimes even negative. Thus in 1980 the average nominal interest rate

Figure 1-1

**GROSS FEDERAL DEBT, CURRENT AND CONSTANT (1972) DOLLARS
1954–1985
(DEBT OUTSTANDING, END OF FISCAL YEAR)**

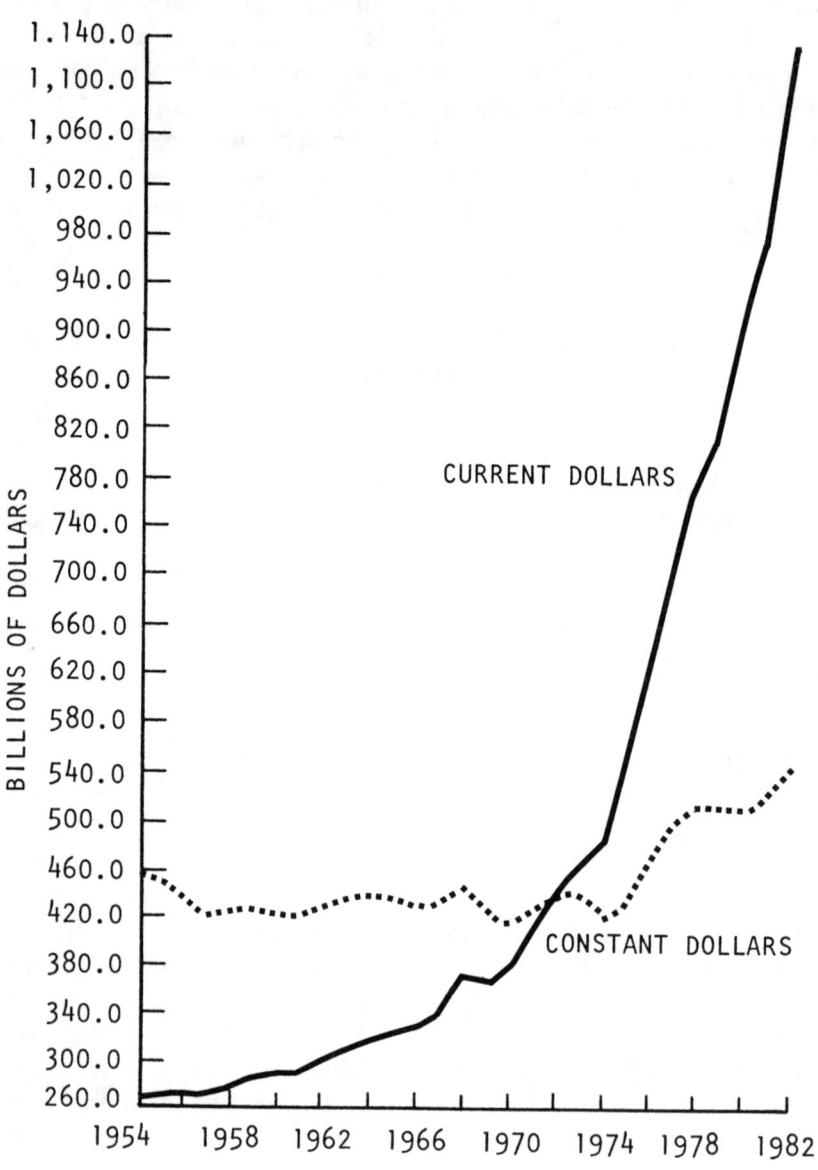

INTRODUCTION AND OVERVIEW ■ 23 ■

was about 10 percent and inflation was about 11 percent (in terms of the GNP deflator; in terms of the CPI, it was even greater—a misleading 14 percent). The real interest on the national debt was therefore negative. But $85 billion was allocated in the 1980 budget to pay interest on that debt; in fact, this amount represents a repayment on capital or on principal. In effect, the United States was borrowing money for a turnover of existing debt, not to pay real interest. In 1980 this payment did not quite compensate debt-holders for the decrease in the purchasing power of the bond. On average there was, therefore, no payment for borrowing the money—i.e., no interest in real terms. (This point that the inflationary component of the interest is a payment on principal and not really interest is an important one and will be used in later discussion of inflation issues and unconventional financing.) In terms of constant dollars, therefore, the U.S. national debt has been relatively stable for the last twenty-eight years, or, put another way, the United States government has not truly had many deficits—at least as far as the official budget is concerned.

We are here defining deficit in a very straightforward fashion—since U.S. debt has not increased, the government is not truly spending more than it is taking in. We are not arguing that a large deficit, even if only nominal, does not cause serious problems or that the presence or absence of a deficit in the official budget, whether in real or nominal terms, is the only way to characterize the nation's financial position. We simply wish to note that if the term "deficit" is used reasonably (i.e., an increase in real debt), the United States is running a balanced budget. In terms of constant dollars the United States has not been passing on an ever-increasing debt for future generations to pay. In terms of its ratio to GNP, the U.S. debt has gone down more or less steadily for the last thirty years—a trend which is not true for almost any other OECD country.

That this almost self-evident fact is not widely understood is indicative of the low level of discussion of inflation problems in the United States, even by experts. It would probably hurt the morale of those working to reduce federal expenditures to know that they have not really been fighting a current deficit. But U.S. government expenditures should be controlled, partly because they were too high, and partly because they were growing too rapidly. Even if the strongest single political argument for putting government expenses under control, that we are "spending much more than we are taking in," was not quite accurate, its acceptance is an important political fact and is therefore unlikely to be abandoned. This is also probably the reason so many economists fail to understand that the U.S. federal budget has been more or less in balance (in fixed dollars). The fallacy is too widely accepted to be discredited or discarded easily. And, of course, the current projected deficit is about half real.

Further, while the amount of money expended by the U.S. federal government in constant dollars about doubled in the last thirty-five years, the GNP about tripled. (The big increase in U.S. government spending has been at the local and state level.) In the last two decades, the total spent (including transfer payments) at all levels of government has varied from 30 to 35 percent of the GNP and in 1981 will be about 32 percent. In most developed West European countries, this number has about doubled, going from a range of 25–35 percent of the GNP to 40–65 percent. Thus in terms of the proportional flow of resources between public and private channels, unlike most other OECD countries, the United States does not have much more of a problem today than it did twenty years ago. In contrast to other OECD countries, the role of government in the United States, when measured by the percent of the gross national product that goes through government hands, has not increased greatly. (While much of this money is probably better spent—i.e., more acceptably to a larger consensus—in Europe, Japan, and Canada than in the United States, it's probably not spent much better.)

THE U.S. INFLATION/BUDGET/STAGNATION VICIOUS CIRCLE

The above indicates that the United States is, from the viewpoint of excess (real) deficits or percent of GNP that goes through the government, much better off than most advanced capitalist nations (ACNs). But there is a vicious circle in the United States. The high level of inflation causes a high level of interest rates; high interest rates can by themselves cause deficits. If there is also a low level of economic activity (i.e., stagflation), then this nominal deficit is exacerbated by extra costs and lower tax receipts. A high deficit, whether real or nominal, must be financed. Depending on how it is financed, the deficit causes either inflation or "crowding out" of private borrowing, and either of these leads, at least temporarily, to high interest rates. This situation, plus "social limits

INTRODUCTION AND OVERVIEW ■ 25 ■

to growth" and certain structural problems,* leads to more stagflation—i.e., higher interest rates, lower levels of economic activity, greater deficits. It's the vicious inflation/budget/stagnation circle.

If the United States could momentarily eliminate inflation and expectations of inflation but leave everything else the same, there would be an immediate and enormous "revitalization," particularly if the regulatory process were also rationalized so that government would no longer be "on the backs of business." If the same trick were tried in almost any other West European country it wouldn't work; in order to restore most pre-inflation relations in terms of debt ratios and proportional resource flows, one would have to significantly cut the amount of money spent or transferred by the government, and to a lesser degree to cut taxes. This would not be necessary in the United States. The structural problems and social restraints on growth (assuming reasonable regulatory reform) are not bad enough to exert particularly strong inflationary pressures. The greatest inflationary pressures in the United States at present basically derive from the ongoing inflation itself.

Nonetheless, a large deficit—even if nominal—can be very harmful. If the nominal deficit (actually the turnover of existing debt) is financed through the Federal Reserve and the banking system at low interest rates, then the government is creating the money (credit) with which the banks buy the bonds. This is sometimes called "monetizing the deficit" and is just as inflationary as printing money. On the other hand, if the nominal deficit is financed by borrowing from the general public, then high interest rates must be paid. This may or may not be inflationary; it may even be deflationary. But the high interest rates that accompany this method of financing tend to crowd out private borrowers and therefore can hurt investment; inadequate investment is one reason for low productivity and stagflation. So whether or not the government finances the nominal deficit by artificially low interest rates (which is inflationary) or by high interest rates (which crowd out private borrowing), the economy is hurt.

The nominal deficit, therefore, is very important; but it is part of the entire inflation syndrome and not an independent driving force. For the

---

* We define a structural problem as any economic problem that cannot be fixed primarily by fiscal or monetary policies (though they are often strongly affected by these). Structural problems can involve institutional and value issues as well as structural imbalances in industries or the labor force. See Edward M. Bernstein, "Structural Problems and Economic Policy: The U.S. Experience," in Leveson and Wheeler, *Western Economies in Transition,* pp. 163–82.

United States today it is not accurate to argue that deficits caused the inflation. Rather, inflation caused the deficit. It is this vicious cycle which must be broken or evaded.

As will become clear, we often disagree with Reaganomics on theoretical details but tend to support most of the administration's actual economic policies to one degree or another. The basic instincts of the administration are often better than its theories, and its theories are usually more defensible than their own defenses would indicate. For example, the idea that there may be more money collected in taxes if the tax rate is reduced has been around for literally millennia. It is neither voodoo economics nor an idea which is particularly difficult to justify—at least in principle. For example, someone in the 70 percent bracket would clearly prefer a municipal bond yielding 10 percent which is tax-free to an investment which yields 30 percent but leaves him only 9 percent after taxes (21 percent goes to the government). At present, the system is so dominated by legal tax avoidance and illegal tax evasion that the government collects only a fraction of what it ought to collect. Most taxpayers, as well as the government, are likely to gain from a drastically revised system which collects approximately the same amount collected today, but at much lower rates. Until fairly recently it was widely accepted in this country—and oppressive governments have always known it—that if the government presses too hard, tax collections go down. But the situation is very complex, and while most recent studies do not show any significant income effects to be achieved by reducing taxes, these studies seem to be misleading. Simple common sense indicates that a great deal could be achieved. For example, recent tax rates running as high as 70 percent for unearned income managed to collect only 11.7 percent of the national income and presumably distort the economy and reduce the national income. Milton Friedman has suggested that a simple tax of 10 percent across the board might, at least eventually, net as much or more (see Chapter 10) as current income taxes do.

On the other hand, we would argue that it is most implausible that the tax cuts of 1981 are likely to result in much increased revenue in 1982 and 1983 (with the exception of those affecting capital gains and the 70 percent on unearned income). But in the long run, we expect the lessened tax rates to have very beneficial results—including increased incentives for many economically virtuous things. So far, however, we do not have good quantitative theories or data for estimating how beneficial the tax cuts may be.

However, we believe that there are many possibilities for flexibility, ingenuity, and creativity (as well as for basic reforms) in dealing with the 1980s and 1990s. This is true in economics, defense, technology, and ideology—all areas where the administration is taking new initiatives. To these new policies, trends, and inevitabilities we will offer some insights and suggestions of our own. All told, we seem to be on the threshold of a unique American opportunity and should use it to the utmost.

CHAPTER 2
HISTORICAL CONTEXT

THE GREAT TRANSITION

A long-term perspective on mankind's economic past and present includes two watersheds. The first was the agricultural revolution that occurred some ten thousand years ago and essentially created civic culture. Man ceased to be a wandering nomad and created communities tied to a particular area of land. The agricultural revolution took eight thousand years to spread around the world. While it marked a basic change in the condition of mankind, it never produced sustained levels of economic growth or affluence. Comparisons of GNP per capita across cultures and time spans are difficult to make, but one can reasonably argue that most cultures varied between $100 and $500 (1980 dollars) per capita; none got much above $500 for any sustained period of time.

The second watershed is what we call the "Great Transition" and is what we are living in today. The transition began two hundred years ago when human beings were almost everywhere comparatively few, poor, and at the mercy of the forces of nature; it will basically end within the next two centuries when, barring some "perverse combination of bad luck and bad management," human beings should be almost everywhere numerous, rich, and largely in control of the forces of nature.

This four-hundred-year period comprises three overlapping phases: the Industrial Revolution, the current emergence of a super-industrial (technological) world economy, and a future post-industrial world economy and society. There may be other watersheds yet to come, such as a massive movement into space with settlements on other celestial bodies and/or in man-made space colonies. This possibility, which we think is likely, could lead to the development of new kinds of economic and social activities which would differ radically from previous earthbound experiences. For the moment, however, we consider the Great Transition in the context of economic growth on earth* and leave out any great transition in man's spiritual nature or planetary domicile.

We do not argue that the Great Transition is inevitable, only that it is likely and plausible, given the data and trends that are known today. Growth rates for world population and gross world product began to increase extraordinarily in the seventeenth and eighteenth centuries. This growth, along with steady advances in science and technology, produced the vast material progress made in the past two hundred years. Pessimists argue that if these growth rates continue much longer the world will exhaust or overwhelm its physical resources in the next century or so. We doubt this but believe the argument is in any case irrelevant. We believe that rates of growth of world population, and probably of world economic output, have peaked (or soon will) and that the next phase will be a gradual leveling-off process which will stabilize at high but sustainable levels of population and economy between the middle of the twenty-first and the middle of the twenty-second century.

This trend of sudden rapid growth followed by a peak and then a return to long-term stability is dramatically illustrated by the "spike" graph below (Figure 2-1). The figure exaggerates the width of the curve; it is only about one hundred years wide at the 1 percent point and, if drawn to scale, would look like a single straight line up and down. In effect, this "straight line" defines the Great Transition, though with perhaps excessive precision. Surprisingly, even though the curve is considered reasonable by most demographers, and the data on which it is based has received substantial press attention, neither the curve nor its implications are widely recognized. It depicts the long-term perspective—that for most of the past ten thousand years the smoothed-out annual population growth rate was less than 0.1 percent; the narrowness of the spike emphasizes the unique and dramatic quality of the Great Transition period in which we now live.

---

* Cf. Herman Kahn et al., *The Next 200 Years* (New York: William Morrow, 1976).

Figure 2-1

THE DEMOGRAPHIC TRANSITION

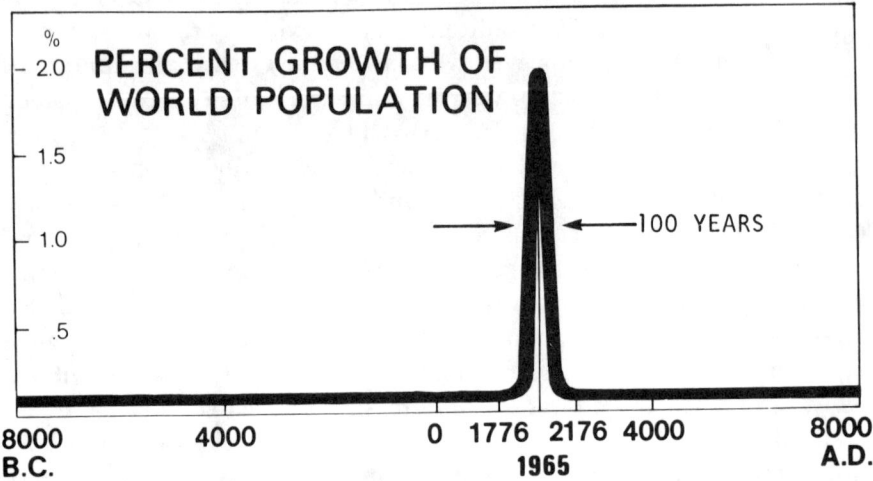

The dramatic increase in the growth rate which began in the seventeenth century became almost explosive during this century. It is believed to have peaked at around 2.1 percent during the mid-1960s, and is now at about 1.7 percent and rapidly declining. Barring some great change in current and likely trends it should ultimately produce another more or less static growth situation—a rough prototype of many current long-term growth trends.

We believe the coming slowdown in growth of world population, gross world product, and other measures of rates of development will stem less from physical limitations on resources than from changes in social priorities, values, and tastes. These affect both demand and supply adversely. Demand will change as people are affected by high levels of technology, affluence, and the law of diminishing returns of affluence—i.e., the spread of higher standards of health, safety, literacy, and material goods to all people. Perhaps the most striking evidence of these social limits to growth—of this impact of affluence on social priorities—is the strong steady downward trend from 1800 to 1945 of the fertility of women in the United States (well before the development of birth-control pills, IUDs, and other contraceptive devices). It went from an average of 8 children per woman to 2.1. Similar declines in birth rates have occurred in other countries and regions as they have become more urbanized and/or affluent. The basic forces behind the decline have traditionally been economic, though other factors, especially religious and cultural ones, have played a role. In effect, children in affluent or urbanized nations are consumers. In earlier days they were producers and a source of wealth and social security. Benjamin Franklin observed that one good way for an ambitious young man to become rich was to marry a widow with many children; this once sane advice seems ludicrous when applied to contemporary America and many other countries today.

New generations of more affluent children take affluence and welfare for granted, and as a result tend to be less motivated than their parents in acquiring material goods. They are also less willing to accept what the Austrian economist Joseph Schumpeter called "creative destruction"—the notion that rapid economic growth often destroys the old (from historic buildings to biological species to traditional ways of life) when introducing the new. Opposition to creative destruction has become a very important social limit to growth.

As the rate of increase in economic growth tapers off, new noneconomic demands and activities arise. This phase, which we label "post-industrial" because of society's deemphasis on industrial and agricultural activities (but not on agricultural and industrial products), marks the end point of the Great Transition and will probably cause a permanent change in the condition of mankind. It should be noted that the de-emphasis is possible precisely because the productivity of agriculture and industry is so great that the society can afford to turn its energies elsewhere; it takes only a few people to produce and distribute almost all the goods and many of the services that society needs. One example of this is the United States and agriculture. Ours is a super-agricultural society with respect to the variety and volume of agricultural products; it is post-agricultural in that agriculture involves less than 3 percent of the work force.

Just as there are many pre-industrial and industrial cultures, it is probable that there will also be many post-industrial ones rather than one huge deracinated cosmopolitan culture. Moreover, the movement toward post-industrialism will take place at different rates in different places, but at least 90 percent of the world's population lives in countries now moving in this direction.

In a post-industrial United States the advantages of being upper-middle-class as opposed to middle-class will not be great, in part because even the so-called lower classes will have most of the essential benefits of social welfare and material growth and many of the nonessential luxuries as well. Further, the "lower classes" will no longer be as available to work as personal servants, or to carry out poorly paid service occupations. In fact, in many ways the quality of life and the standard of living for the upper-middle class may decrease as compared to fifty years ago. (One distinguished couple visiting England was told that fifty years earlier the average English middle-class family had three live-in servants. The American wife said, "Gee, that would be wonderful." Her husband corrected her: "No, you would probably have been one of the servants.") While it still is fun to progress from middle class to upper-middle class it is not as much fun as it used to be. The "perks" of that status are fewer and the "exclusive turf" much narrower. The "lower" classes now have virtually the same access as the "upper" classes to schools, cars, travel abroad, and so on.

WORLD ECONOMIC DEVELOPMENT

Economic growth in the twentieth century should be considered from the broad perspective of long-term growth rates and their meaning. This century has seen the industrialized nations attain unprecedented levels of affluence and also, for the first time since World War II, the spread of industrialization and affluence (and the potential for affluence) to the Third World. A basic overview of this process is important for understanding our present economic problems and prospects.

Economic growth in the twentieth century can be divided into four phases:* (1) moderate but unprecedentedly dynamic (1890–1913), a period often known as La Belle Epoque; (2) disastrous (1914–1947), a period we sometimes call La Mauvaise Epoque; (3) highly dynamic (1948–1973), a period we sometimes call La Deuxième Belle Epoque; and (4) a troubled period, most of which lies ahead and which we label a period of malaise (1974–   ), though its prospects for success and failure are

* An earlier takeoff period, which we usually call the Industrial Revolution, is not included in this discussion.

Figure 2-2

AGGREGATE GDP OF THE 16 ADVANCED CAPITALIST NATIONS (1870=100)

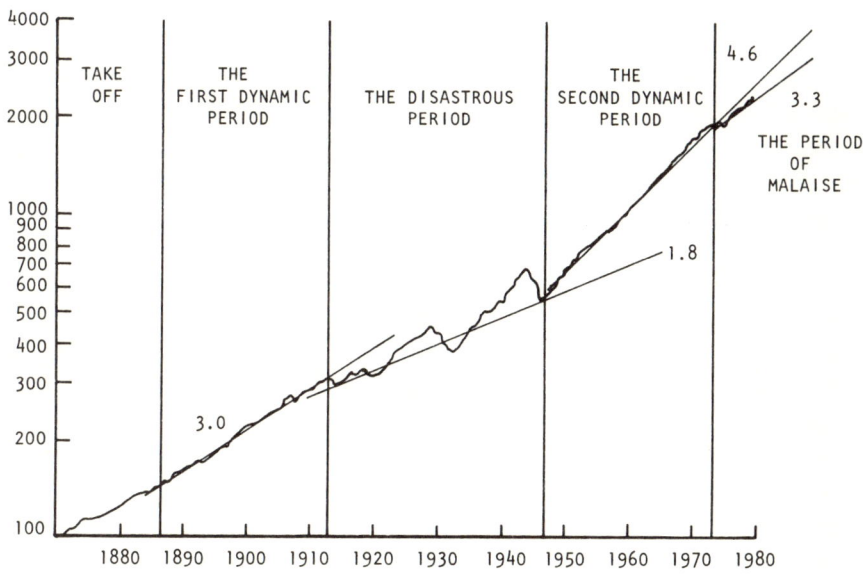

HISTORIC DATA BASED ON THE WORK OF ANGUS MADDISON.

more or less equally great. Figure 2-2, mostly based on data compiled by Angus Maddison, shows these four periods in terms of the aggregate output of sixteen advanced capitalist nations (ACNs).*

From the viewpoint of economic growth, the twenty-six years from 1948 through 1973 (the highly dynamic or second dynamic period) were an extraordinarily creative and productive period. Growth rates of the ACNs averaged about 5 percent annually—the first time in history that such high and sustained growth was achieved. Furthermore, the rest of the world, also for the first time in history, began to industrialize rapidly.

* Cf. Angus Maddison, "Phases of Capitalist Development," *Banco Nationale del Lavoro Quarterly Review,* No. 121 (June 1977). The terminology "advanced capitalist nations" is also drawn from Maddison's work.

While the ACNs grew at an unprecedented rate between 1890 and 1913 (the first dynamic period), that rate averaged only 3 percent a year, or 60 percent of that achieved in the second dynamic period. Except for Russia and a few primary producing countries, the economic growth rate in the rest of the world was almost negligible, often not even keeping up with the population growth rate.

However, even the "good" growth years of the second dynamic period were not without some bad times for various countries. Indeed, as discussed later, in some of the ACNs (and especially in the United States) a deterioration in economic and social conditions—a kind of malaise— started in the early and middle 1960s; in other places, somewhat later. By the early and middle 1970s much the same syndrome had begun to affect almost all advanced capitalist nations, and a similar malaise affected the Soviet Union as well. For this reason, the period beginning with 1974 may justifiably be referred to as a "bad" era, at least in the sense of being considerably less prosperous and less dynamic than the preceding "good" years.

Both the slowdown and the letdown of the current period of malaise is more characteristic of rich capitalist nations than of what we call middle-income countries (countries with a per capita income between $500 and $4,000—i.e., rich compared to the past, poor compared to the current rich; about two billion people now live in middle-income countries). Even with these reversals the growth rates of the middle-income countries have ranged mostly between 5 and 10 percent and averaged more than 6 percent. We expect this to continue for a while. As far as the poor countries of the world are concerned, their performance will vary even more. In general, however, they will be weaker than the middle-income countries, but comparable, on the average, with the rich countries.*

Perhaps the single most striking characteristic of these "years of malaise" is the combination of relatively high unemployment, excess industrial capacity, and inflation, all of which affect the ACNs to at least some degree (but Japan least of all). The term "stagflation" has been coined to describe this condition, which is increasingly thought of as more or less chronic. A decade ago, many observers would have denied that such a widespread and persistent combination of difficulties was even possible. We attribute the persistent stagflation of recent years partly to structural

---

* For details on all of the above, see Herman Kahn, *World Economic Development* (Boulder, Colo.: Westview Press, 1979).

(including institutional) factors, but mostly to a prolonged period of unwise or inadequate fiscal, monetary, and regulatory policies. We are beginning to learn how to deal with these issues, in addition to which it seems that many of the basic trends are changing or being changed, thereby creating conditions which are far more conducive to renewed growth and prosperity.

KONDRATIEFF CYCLES AND ECONOMIC GROWTH

Some readers may associate this "good era/bad era" view of twentieth-century economic history with the Russian economist Nikolai D. Kondratieff, who studied long-term cycles of price movements, interest rates, and wages in Western economies going back to about 1790. Kondratieff noticed two and a half long-term waves between the late 1780s and 1922, when he published his observations. He suggested that the third wave had already peaked and would be followed by a depression during the late 1920s. Partly because of the subsequent accuracy of this prediction he was taken very seriously by Joseph Schumpeter and other noted economists. Figure 2-3 indicates both the regularity of the observed cycle until about World War II and the quite different nature of the phenomenon since then.

After enjoying a certain vogue, Kondratieff's ideas gradually dropped out of favor. Interest in Kondratieff's long waves has, however, revived in recent years, modified by new research and information. In particular, economists associated with Wall Street firms and New York City banks again began to discuss Kondratieff concepts about ten to fifteen years ago. In addition, economic theorists have revived them, so that there are now at least five versions of what might be called Kondratieff theories: (1) that of Jay Forrester of the Massachusetts Institute of Technology (interaction of durable and capital goods sectors); (2) that of Walt Rostow of the University of Texas (interaction of commodities with manufacturing sectors); (3) that of Schumpeter or Gerhard Mensch and others (various theories of impact of innovation); (4) population-based and demographically based spin-offs; and (5) Kahn's concepts of an archetype scenario. These five versions—while not really useful for predictive purposes—are quite useful for giving insights into and explanations of what has already happened.

■36■ THE COMING BOOM

Figure 2-3

WHOLESALE PRICE INDEX 1750–1976
(1967=100)

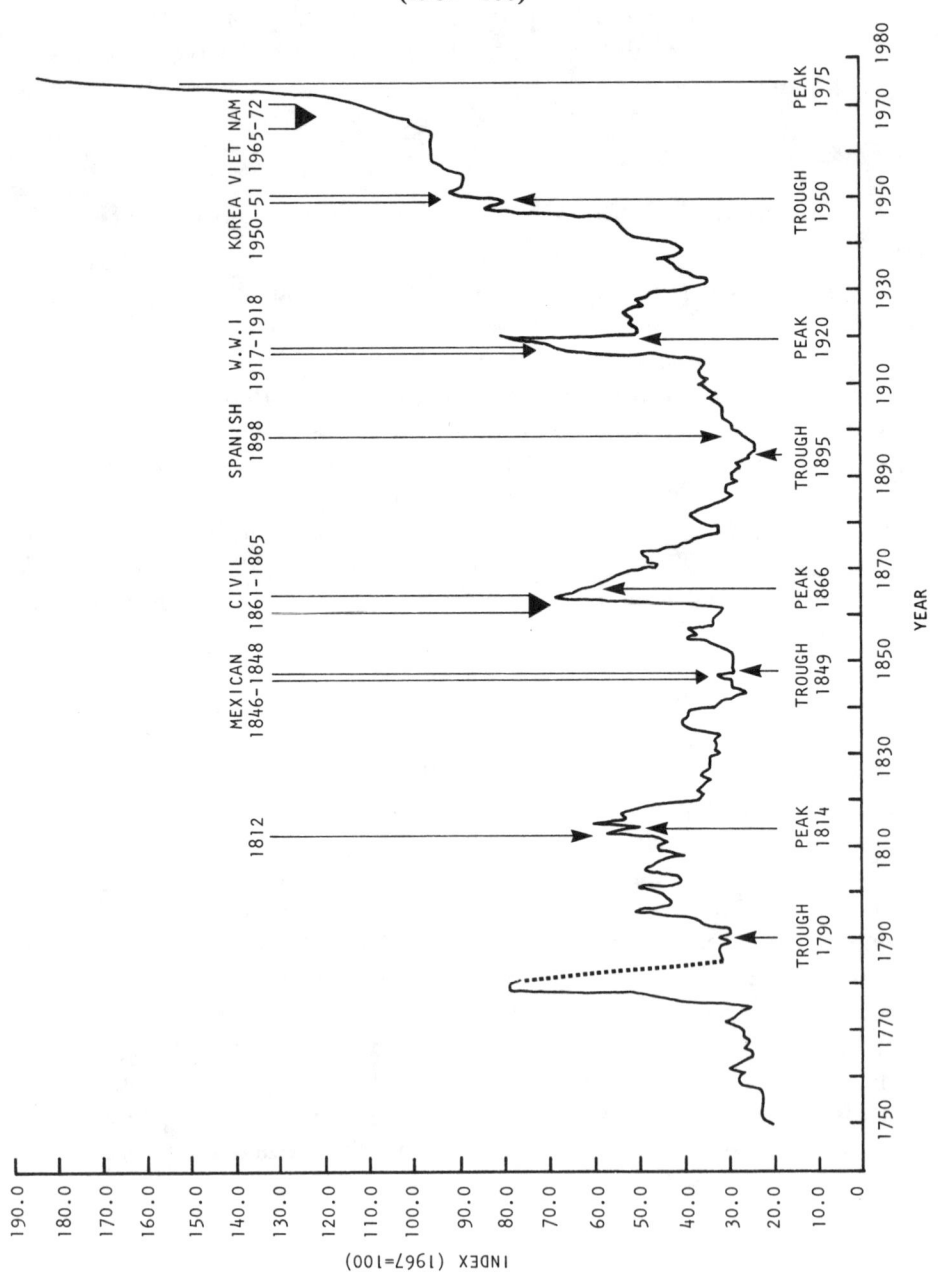

Jay Forrester focuses on leads and lags generated by the interplay between capital-goods industries and consumer-goods industries; Rostow concentrates on the leads and lags caused by the interplay of commodities and industrial products. Both make dire predictions about the immediate future, but for different reasons.

Forrester argues that the capital-goods sector has been overbuilt worldwide and therefore foresees a long period of excess capacity and deflationary pressures—in effect, the fourth Kondratieff downswing. (We argue that there is almost no question that something like Forrester's analysis applies, for example, to the world steel industry today. Many other industries have also built up a huge excess capacity in exactly the way he describes and may have to work it off in much the way he suggests.)

Rostow argues that contemporary Kondratieff theorists have been misled by the pervasive inflation and that the proper index to look at is not the *price* of commodities but the *ratio* of the price of commodities to manufactured goods. This ratio became depressed in 1950 but was reversed in the early 1970s. In effect, Rostow is arguing that the fourth Kondratieff downswing started thirty years ago and the fifth upswing is now starting; that because of their relatively low prices there had not been sufficient expansion in commodities production; and that it takes about two or three decades to get enough investment into commodities production to correct this imbalance. Thus Rostow believes that the lack of investment in commodities production brought about various resource scarcities and presumably high commodity prices and inflationary pressures. (We agree that something like this has clearly occurred in the energy and some other resource areas.)

An earlier interpretation of Kondratieff cycles was suggested by Joseph Schumpeter, who associated the cycles with the clustering of technological innovations. He argued that the coincidence of several major innovations triggered the adoption and use of new production systems; linkages throughout the economy then stimulated the long upswing. We discuss in Chapter 4 our belief that the 1980s and 1990s will see an extraordinary technological development in a number of areas with great potential to stimulate pervasive growth and change (e.g., the microprocessor). We also note that the continued growth in the middle-income countries seems to be largely spurred by this force and will therefore take decades before being (temporarily) halted.

Dramatic shifts in the demographic profile of a country that occur over a relatively short period of time—major changes in fertility, mortality, or migration—could also initiate investment and capital growth. Analyses of such forces (still relating to Kondratieff) have been done by Simon Kuznets, Richard Easterlin, and others. Based on their studies, it is clear that the baby-boom generation is now entering a period of maximum productivity and will contribute much to the coming boom in the United States.

Kondratieff cannot comment on the various versions of his theory. In fact, he did not even comment on the price movements he described but simply argued that the empirical evidence was sufficient to prove their existence. He also noticed a connection between the troughs and peaks of the waves and various European and American wars. In particular, the bottom of each wave often seemed to coincide with a relatively small and profitable war that helped get things started again, followed by a twenty- or thirty-year period of rising prices during which almost everything worked well. In time, however, a number of stresses and strains built up, the system got overconfident and ruthless, and finally a "peak war"—coinciding with the top of the wave—was precipitated. These wars were extremely destructive and divisive, almost as if the society had an excess of energy, dynamism, and ruthlessness that it could not contain.

The extreme exacerbation of the peak war damages the system. Prices are pushed to extremely high levels, leading to subsequent collapse and deflation which generates a period of declining or low (stable) prices for the next fifteen to twenty-five years. However, as discussed in *World Economic Development,* World War II does not fit into Kondratieff's scheme and may be partly responsible for the anomalous recent behavior in the curve as shown in Figure 2-3.

The behavior patterns of a typical long cycle of activity, incorporating various interpretations of Kondratieff's hypothesis, contribute greatly to understanding the way in which the world economy is presently evolving. We believe that for analytical and descriptive purposes (but not for predictive purposes) the cyclical theory is quite useful. There are clearly still repetitive aspects of the cycle, even though the basic economic system has evolved so much during the first 150 years of industrialization that the cycles themselves will no longer be replicated exactly. The long-cycle forces today have different characteristics among different advanced capitalist nations, but they continue to interact and feed on one another. Consequently, social, political, and psychological (as well as economic) trends might still be described according to an archetype Kondratieff long cycle. I have chosen an archetype that fits the more recent cycles better than the earlier ones:

*ARCHETYPE LONG CYCLE**

1. *A sobering context.* The cycle begins with stagnation and very slow growth, deterioration of plant and equipment, and little or no exploitation of new technologies or other innovations. This creates or encourages competitive situations, and most wages and other costs tend to become more competitive. (Overall, a pretty good description of the United States in the late 1970s and the early 1980s.)

2. *Relatively cautious, disciplined behavior.* Businessmen begin to think about opportunities, but invest mainly in low-risk ventures. Since getting a job is difficult, having a job is prized. High rates of saving are induced, and these may become more valued because of deflation. (This last effect may just be starting and should be facilitated by the Reagan tax cuts and current high real interest rates.)

3. *A turning point.* After a long period of low investment in capital facilities and continued slow obsolescence of existing plant and equipment, opportunities for new investment and expansion eventually open up. A slow but general revival of confidence in longer-term prospects begins to make possible long-term investments. (This is beginning to happen in the United States but not yet in Europe. Chapters 5, 6, and 10 describe some of the issues and possibilities.)

4. *An expansion psychology begins to develop and full confidence is restored.* New technologies and opportunities which have been ignored are now exploited. Indeed, there begins an intense search for more new technologies and new opportunities, and a general willingness to replace even marginally obsolete equipment. A competent, dedicated work force is still available, along with wide public and private support for economically and technologically oriented projects. There is a search for areas where investment can expand and where a long-term view is possible. The "creative destruction" produced by these ventures is almost always judged to be more creative than destructive. (Our view of the mid-1980s to the mid-1990s or later—i.e., this is the economic boom I am predicting.)

5. *A "good" era psychology emerges.* Self-fulfilling prophecies begin to play a very important role in inspiring business investment and economic growth. People begin to take affluence and prosperity for

* We are grateful to Thomas Pepper and Jimmy W. Wheeler of Hudson Institute for their contributions in the development of this concept.

granted, and the atmosphere begins to become relatively relaxed, even careless. Discretionary, odd, and relatively extreme behavior begins to emerge. There is a limited emergence (or a re-emergence) of anti-bourgeois, anti-business, and anti-materialistic attitudes and movements. Priorities and values begin to change. "Creative destruction" begins to look more destructive and less creative. Welfare and other government transfer payments increase rapidly. (Chapter 10 suggests ways in which this latter phase might be restrained and/or postponed in the coming boom.)

6. *Confidence peaks even while extraordinary strains and excesses appear and extremist discretionary behavior and polarization characterize society.* Demand for all kinds of commodities grows and prices rise rapidly, particularly if government officials and monetary policies encourage (or simply permit) inflation. There is a boom in capital-goods industries. Speculation becomes rife, increasingly based on fashion, self-fulfilling prophecies, "discounting the hereafter," and "Ponzi schemes" (i.e., illusory profits paid out of capital or by income transfer). "New Class" values,* especially among upper-middle-class youth, appear ascendant. A peak war occurs, or a similar event that goes badly. However, there is no attempt to cut losses (the dynamism and energy of society is too high). Eventually, various self-styled idealistic groups drawn from the more affluent classes mobilize in protest against materialism, creative destruction, and various real and imagined defects of the society. This protest can be carried to the point of promoting extremist but still discretionary behavior; or it can simply go too far. In any case, being anti-establishment becomes so popular and acceptable that in many situations the roles of the pro and con forces may be reversed—i.e., protest becomes an "establishment" value. (It is during this phase that the difference described in Chapter 9 between what we call "natural and inevitable" and "creeping stagnation" is crucial.)

7. *Eventually a day of reckoning.* One or two increasingly serious recessions, or a depression, occur. Recovery is slow because of excess capacity, many new rigidities, and high social overhead costs. There is great caution among businessmen and investors, and a tendency to invest mainly for the short run (e.g., to patch up old buildings rather than build new ones).† Eventually, either a "bad" era or collapse of

---

* The "New Class" concept is explained later in this chapter.

† In the United States today, business has typically shortened its investment horizon from a more or less traditional twenty- or thirty-year framework to a time span of approximately five years, except in instances of obviously defensive investment. This lack of a long-term perspective is both an effect and a cause of current economic problems.

the system (and normally prices as well) occurs. (The big problem here is not to exacerbate the problem by making any disastrous mistakes—e.g., the Federal Reserve letting the money supply collapse by one-third during the Great Depression.)

8. *Recovery proceeds, but erratically, with a troubled period of transition and sobering up.* Residual anti-business attitudes and institutions persist and greatly handicap the revival of the system. Subsequently, new moods of both seriousness and cynicism, as well as pessimism and hope, spread. There is much disillusionment with the values and attitudes, both old and new. As a result a synthesis between old and new emerges. Some degree of counterreformation and a "balanced," or even perhaps excessive, emphasis on economic growth comes back. But it takes a long time to sober up and reestablish the priorities and discipline necessary for economic growth. (We are to some degree in this phase right now.)

This typical long swing in economic activity suggests that there is a way out of the myriad problems that seem to have been the legacy of the 1970s. We do not believe that there is a particular process through which these cycles inexorably play themselves out, or that each cycle must follow rigidly the pattern of the previous one. The mechanisms at work are very flexible as society is constantly evolving, accumulating new knowledge, new technologies, new institutions, new markets and producers, new levels of affluence, and new problems. However, we do believe that the long-cycle theory supports our contention that the United States is on the road to recovery and that near-term prospects are promising. We claim here a Scotch verdict. Our contention is not entirely provable, but it's based on more than sheer speculation.

We will deliberately not use the currently popular term "reindustrialization" to describe this process, partly because we include in our outlook a good deal of "de-industrialization"—a moving away from certain industries (e.g., consumer electronics) in which the value added, or the productivity, is not high enough to support a high standard of living for its workers. To some, the policies of de-industrialization appear to be relatively harsh, as they include the reassignment of human and material resources to more productive activities. They involve the concept of creative destruction, of getting rid of the less workable old for the sake of the more efficient new. In this case one uses the old—the personnel and the capital—for new ventures. If a nation can do high-quality work, why do low-quality work? If it can provide interesting, well-paid jobs, why provide uninspiring, poorly paid jobs? This is the key to de-industrialization.

But not everybody who is "reassigned" will gain by the change; many people will lose. Skilled workers often do not have the flexibility to pick up new skills; capital that becomes obsolete often cannot be transferred and has to be junked. But on the average, there will be a gain. The government might have to intervene (moderately) so as to alleviate some of the costs of the shift.

The Carter administration in its last year became concerned with this task of revitalization, or rather with a less ambitious task, the so-called reindustrialization of the United States. In the implications of reindustrialization, the Carter people seem to have been greatly influenced by their concept of Japan. They envisaged a kind of coalition between management, labor, and government, all working together in a harmonious consensus to increase productivity and to improve the operation of the American industrial system. This vision was based pretty much on a misunderstanding of how the United States works—and, to some degree, of how Japan works. It also failed to take into account that very important cultural differences exist between these two nations. While many things that work in Japan will also work here (in fact, a number of "innovations" such as quality control were copied from the United States), many won't (mainly because the United States is not a homogeneous society). In particular, collusion among management, labor, and government does not seem likely to be a creative, productive, or constructive option in the United States. This is not to say that the government should continue the almost adversary relationship that it has had with business in the last decade or so, but only to argue that there is a big difference between the government's trying to be helpful—to be part of the solution rather than the problem—and getting into bed with management and labor.

Take, for example, the enormous difference in Japanese and U.S. commercial psychology. If the Japanese government took two Japanese companies and gave one of them exclusive jurisdiction over the territory east of the Mississippi and gave the other rights to the territory on the west, each company would absolutely kill itself to show that it could do more with its territory than the other company. If two American companies were given the same divided jurisdiction and knew it was safe to take it easy, they would. Neither the managers nor the workers would feel the

Japanese competitive sense of honor to do better than the other. This difference in psychology is part of the reason the Japanese system works so well—in Japan.*

We should also note that Japan itself is in fact not as much "Japan Inc." as is assumed. The bigger and more affluent Japan becomes, the less secure and effective the once-tight system is. There is, and always has been, an incredible amount of factionalism and infighting both within and between companies. Increasingly, the big Japanese companies are operating very much like American transnationals. What we need is less the Japanization of the United States than the re-Americanization of America, in many cases taking back or reviving that which we taught the Japanese. Americans, for example, have always understood that quality control requires the active participation of everybody, including direct, hands-on experience by executives. Indeed, the so-called quality-control circles which we are now copying from the Japanese were originally transmitted to them about twenty-five years ago by Edward Deeming, an American expert on quality control. In fact, the Japanese have estab-

---

* There are many other ways in which the Japanese culture is more or less unique. In 1963 Hudson did a study for the U.S. Air Force looking at the future growth rates of the big powers. We decided that the growth rate of the Soviet Union and West Germany would not continue with anything like the dynamism they had had, but that of the Japanese would continue (actually it increased). As a result, we did a separate study for International Security Affairs, Department of Defense, on Japan alone. We concluded in 1965 that until the end of the century, Japanese growth rates would be very high on the average. This meant that they would pass the United States in per capita income about the year 2000, give or take a decade, and it was even conceivable that they could pass the United States in total GNP. We took the conclusion to Japan and found that they were quite shocked, though eventually many accepted the concept. Most of the analysis was based on the idea that the Japanese culture was very special; that while much of what they were doing was copied from the United States, one of the ways in which they were special was their extraordinary ability to copy as well as to originate.

It should also be noted, for example, that only the Japanese and the South Koreans have been able to create the large trading company of the kind that plays such a special role in both countries. Such trading companies are extremely useful to rapid economic development, and the Taiwanese and Hong Kong Chinese have also tried to create such organizations, but have simply failed. The difference seems to be in the ingrained capacity for loyalty which is inculcated in Japanese and South Korean children at a very young age. They transfer this sense of loyalty to the trading organization. If this kind of organization is what is wanted, then training of children must start long before the age of six. We can learn much from the Japanese, but there are many things we cannot learn and should not try to. For a description of this study and of the importance of its unique culture in Japanese development, see Herman Kahn, *The Emerging Japanese Superstate: Challenge and Response* (Englewood Cliffs, N.J.: Prentice-Hall, 1970).

lished the Deeming Award, an honor which is given to those who best carry out these American ideas.

However, the most important point is that the reindustrialization concept focuses too much on big business. Big business, of course, is important. But important as it is to the revitalization process, it is likely to be less important than smaller business. It should be noted that from 1909 to 1969 the number of people working for Fortune 500 doubled; from 1969 to 1979 the number of employees stayed constant. All of the extra twenty million jobs or so created during the second period were created by smaller businesses. We expect that both segments of the economy will become more dynamic, but that the relative importance of smaller businesses will increase, not decrease.

THE SUPER-INDUSTRIAL WORLD ECONOMY

Mankind's socioeconomic development is now often thought of as a progression from pre-industrial to industrial to post-industrial. Yet many of the problems of the next decade are likely to be those of an emerging worldwide *problem-prone* "super-industrial" economy. The term "super-industrial" refers mainly to the high rate of innovation in a modern economy that involves badly understood risks of various sorts, to the very large scale of many of the projects which are undertaken, and to the various unintended side effects—externalities, as economists call them—which are sometimes of greater consequence than the intended effects. These issues can pose urgent and dramatic problems for modern societies.

In particular, an emerging super-industrial economy poses major problems in three ways: (1) it confronts societies with the specter of many new technologies, some of which cannot immediately be fully or even adequately controlled; (2) it presents many problems of scale which are unprecedented, and (3) since some of these problems may grow exponentially (at least for a while), societies may not become aware of them until they are already critical. For example, super-industrial growth could conceivably bring:

—an ecological catastrophe from large-scale interference with the biosphere;

—a genetic calamity from thousands of new chemicals about whose long-term effects we know practically nothing;
—worldwide epidemics or "pandemics" owing to increased travel;
—the large-scale appearance of drug-resistant pests and viruses because of an excessive use of drugs and antibiotics; and
—the danger of an Armageddon as an increasing number of smaller countries come to possess nuclear, thermonuclear, or biological weapons, and as the superpowers develop increasingly destructive weapons systems.

Indeed, there is no way that a super-industrial economy can come into being without endangering the environment and the general quality of life to some degree. Defective bolts in DC-10 aircraft, oil blowouts that pollute the sea and beaches, PCBs in the food chain, and the fall of Skylab are recent examples of problems of a super-industrial society. In the future, the ozone layer might be depleted; a new ice age might be caused by putting an excessive number of particles into the upper atmosphere—or there might be excessive carbon dioxide put in the atmosphere and a disastrous warming of the earth; lakes and streams might turn acid as a result of insufficient pollution controls. Such events, though highly unlikely, cannot be considered impossible.

Enough problems of a super-industrial nature have already arisen to necessitate a redefinition of the very process of economic decision-making. New perceptions of what is rational and acceptable have greatly affected business decision, government (including defense) policies, and political processes in all advanced capitalist countries. For example, new attitudes toward the environment have changed the manner in which public utilities operate and have led to much tighter regulations over the automobile industry. Opposition to the MX missile is based in part on the size of the project and the possible environmental disruption it would cause.

In general, these new priorities have lowered the aggregate volume of investment, causing delays, increasing costs (such as high pollution-control expenditures), and, most important of all, greatly increasing risks and uncertainties. For example, throughout the ACNs, so-called public-interest groups have more and more sought a voice in decisions such as those that involve the siting of nuclear power plants and the construction of superhighways. Here again, opposition to the MX is indicative of this trend and highlights the need for even military planners of high-priority projects to be aware of the policy implications of public input.

Yet new technologies solve problems as well as cause them. Indeed, it is often said that there are no intrinsic tendencies in technology, that by itself it is neither beneficial nor harmful. We prefer to take the position that some technologies are more likely to be harmful than others, and that intrinsic to the concept of technological progress is the possibility that it may get out of control.

But the key determinants are still how technology is used and what one's values are. One can probably say that most potential technological problems can be prevented by a relatively small degree of self-restraint and a fairly large dose of appropriate new technology and better design. Take, for example, the automobile. One could easily imagine that the exercise of self-restraint could cut pollution by a factor of 2. One could even more easily imagine that new technology could cut pollution by a factor of 100 within a decade. For those who are hostile to the automobile as a symbol of everything they dislike about modern societies, this projection will make no impression. But for those who appreciate cars for the freedom, privacy, and mobility they provide and wish only to alleviate their costs, this projection is impressive indeed. For the first group, some of the harm they claim the automobile causes (accidents, suburban sprawl, the breakup of family life) will actually be aggravated by the car's becoming more acceptable as it becomes less polluting. Thus the key to whether any particular technology will benefit rather than harm society lies not only in how it is used, but also in the value systems and criteria by which it is judged.

As industrialization spreads to more and more countries and as the world economy as a whole becomes super-industrial, the system at first tends to become "problem-prone" simply because of the scale of and lack of experience with the new technologies. The external effects are initially unclear and difficult to control. But once the externalities are satisfactorily understood they will presumably be properly controlled, turning a problem-prone super-industrial economy into a *largely problem-controlled* one. We expect the super-industrial society to be largely problem-controlled sometime early in the next century, at which time the transition to a post-industrial economy can begin in earnest.

SOCIAL LIMITS TO POPULATION AND ECONOMIC GROWTH

Economic decision-making, in addition to being redefined by the problems of a super-industrial society, will also be affected by the slowdown in population growth. Birth rates are going down; and migration, immigration, and the use of guest workers are increasingly becoming controversial social and political issues in the developed world.

In general, rapid economic growth, like rapid population growth (which is nevertheless slowing down), is a relatively recent phenomenon. It was first achieved by Western culture only two centuries ago. For the previous ten millennia, no civilization had attained the kind of sustained economic progress that is now taken for granted. Ancient China, Greece, Rome, and India all had technology of a relatively high order. Their failure to attain sustained economic progress stemmed from societal or cultural attitudes which constituted social limits to economic growth. In particular, these ancient societies rejected Schumpeter's concept of "creative destruction." Rapid growth was not permitted if it meant destruction of the old to make way for the new—or if it meant a change in ruling ideologies or the balance of power. Such social (and political) limits have always been dominant and could be so again.

Thus, many attitudes that have emerged in the ACNs in recent years could bring to a close the kind of sustained economic growth experienced since the Industrial Revolution. The explanation of these new trends lies in a profound change in value systems in affluent countries, countries which have both the technology and the wealth required to satisfy their new values. If economic growth were to stop or slow drastically, it would mainly be the result of various social limits. (See Chapter 9.) Indeed, it is difficult to think of any intellectual change in the second half of the twentieth century that is likely to have greater consequences on material growth than these noneconomic factors. While these forces are temporarily in abeyance in the United States, they will resurface eventually; how and when is of the greatest importance.

During the last decade we have been confronted with an entire literature of pessimism. All of the books reflect a startling loss of confidence in the traditional premises and values of economic progress, specifically the acceptance of material advancement as a sign of intellectual and moral growth. As a result, a shift has occurred in public policies. The new policies often encourage an unwise distortion of market forces for nonmarket purposes, and generally urge an interference with and undermining of the social patterns that once supported economic growth. The policies have been encouraged most strongly by certain sectors of the upper-middle class, described by Irving Kristol, B. Bruce-Briggs, Daniel Bell, Daniel Patrick Moynihan, and others as the New Class.*

We prefer to think of the New Class as a socioeconomic group rather than a political category. The political persuasions of upper-middle-class elites, even if we restrict ourselves to those in similar occupations, are very divergent. There is a special group among them which we call the symbolist class, defined (as per Karl Marx) by their relationship to the means of production. They earn their living by dealing with symbols—producers, editors, entertainers, most of the media and literary worlds, analysts, writers, academics, and so on. They are not directly involved in primary and secondary activities, i.e., they do not use their hands and/or equipment to extract from nature or to manufacture or construct various goods and buildings, nor do they have many line responsibilities.

As part of the "upper-middle class," the members of the neo-liberal symbolist or New Class are likely to have annual family incomes between $25,000 and $100,000, to have attended a university, and to be engaged in white-collar occupations. For example, a large part of academia, the media, and most members of so-called "public-interest" groups are symbolists. Their work is often associated with a lack of practical experience that can all too easily convert the most well-intentioned goals into counterproductive policies.

Typically, members of the neo-liberal New Class deny that they exert themselves on behalf of their own interests. They feel, often unconsciously, that since they are so well educated they should set the standard for others. Many see themselves as the "progressive" force overturning the "oppressive" dominance of "selfish" profit-oriented business values, "dehumanizing" organizations, "blind" technology, "crass" materialism, and "commercialized" vulgarity. These same phenomena are seen as liberating, useful, enjoyable, and admirable by virtually any middle- or

---

* See, for example, Irving Kristol, *Two Cheers for Capitalism* (New York: Basic Books, 1978); B. Bruce-Briggs (ed.), *The New Class?* (New Brunswick, N.J.: Transaction Books, 1979); Daniel Bell, *The Cultural Contradictions of Capitalism* (New York: Basic Books, 1976); *Society,* A Symposium, "Is There a New Class?" Vol. 16, No. 2 (January/February 1979), pp. 14–62; and James T. Barry, "Welcome to the New Class," *Commonweal,* Vol. 106 (February 16, 1979), pp. 73–77.

lower-middle-class person who seeks to improve his or her position over the course of a lifetime.

While it is probably true that members of the symbolist class in particular feel relatively worse off as economic growth proceeds, the upper class may also be "adversely affected" to the extent that they take their wealth for granted and consider inconveniences or infringements upon that wealth to be intolerable. Being preoccupied with their own conditions, both classes wrongly assert that society *as a whole* will suffer from further advances. Most writings on the pros and cons of growth almost completely ignore this tendency of New Class authors to confuse their own values with those of society in general. This confusion contributes to the extreme positions taken by some of the neo-liberals against economic growth and other manifestations of progress, as that term has traditionally been understood. (We will return to this unique breed in Chapter 9.)

The more conservative sectors of society, specifically social and economic conservatives, also suffer from frustrations and hostility engendered by continued economic growth—and even more from the actions of the "left." We argue (in the next chapter) that their frustration is causing counterreactions and responses that are mostly but not totally constructive, while the frustration of the left is being discredited because it simply went too far. This does not mean that there is a pronounced movement of the country to the right, just that the dominant intellectual, political, and cultural milieu has changed dramatically.

One result is the Reagan administration. It may no longer be true, as it was in Coolidge's day, that the "business of America is business," but it is certain that there will be much more emphasis on the needs of business and on the perspective of what we call supply-side orientation (whether or not the specific concepts of Laffer or of Kemp-Roth on savings and investment are widely accepted or implemented). There is also—and this may be extraordinarily important—much practical learning going on about how to deal with our problems. This ranges from learning how to conserve energy so that we use less and live better with its high price, to learning how to control as well as to work with inflation. The fact that the country as a whole is learning to deal with many current problems is, in addition to normal cyclical and countervailing forces, one of the primary reasons we believe that many corrections—leading to a boom—are on the way.

CHAPTER 3

THE BASIC CONTEXT FOR REVITALIZATION

The coalition of social, economic, and defense conservatives which President Reagan was able to bring together in the 1980 election is likely to stay coalesced for some time, even though it is already showing signs of strain and disillusionment, e.g., the David Stockman crisis touched off by the interview published in the December 1981 *Atlantic*. It is clear that the alliance will not remain static; some adherents will drop out (currently disenchanted Wall Streeters) while others drop in ("Boll Weevil" Democrats). But the essential conservative core, while not yet well enough established and coordinated to become a long-term reality in American political life, will clearly play a predominating role in the near future.

Most of this book focuses on ways in which a combination of current trends, conservative concepts, and technical fixes can be used to correct the excesses, failures, and general malaise of the last two decades, most of which (including Vietnam*) were more the result of permissive,

---

* Eisenhower carefully limited intervention in South Vietnam to a few hundred advisers, an intervention which could easily be withdrawn and which did not involve U.S. status and prestige. President Kennedy decided to increase this number to about 14,000. It was this increase by a liberal president that made the U.S. commitment so firm. The commitment was made for a number of reasons, but one of them was a concept held by many liberals (at that time) and by Kennedy himself, in which the U.S. would compete head to head and toe to toe with the communist world in capturing the hearts and minds of men and in fighting insurgency warfare.

The Basic Context for Revitalization ■51■

progressive, "enlightened," and radical forces than of the "bigoted right" (though the right, of course, also made characteristic mistakes—they just weren't as influential). There are some quick fixes, but most of the administration's new initiatives must be given time to work—as transitions of this magnitude are rarely fast or easy. But from all indications—and in spite of the current forecasts of doom and gloom coming out of Wall Street—confidence and optimism will be very much in order as the decade progresses. Indeed, many of the doubts and criticisms arise out of therapeutic measures—the tight money policy, the financial difficulties of many localities and states, and the recession in late 1981 through early and middle 1982.

President Reagan is not a scholar but a politician. He will probably take credit for whatever progress occurs, even for certain favorable trends which are simply coming due. The postwar baby boom, for example, a generation which flooded the labor market in the 1970s, is entering its most productive years. Output per worker should grow steadily because of increased experience, and because of additional capital investment which will be justified as inflation declines or unconventional financing (see Chapter 6) is used, as new technologies appear, and as a relative shortage of low-paid labor becomes apparent. In addition, as "young" earners get older they tend to become more conservative (entering what we sometimes call the "nesting age"). They spend more on big-ticket durable goods like housing and major appliances, and politically become more concerned with "establishment" values, though perhaps not as much as their parents were at the same age. The "baby-boom" years helped create inflationary pressures; their "coming of age" should help reduce them.

One negative is the low rate of growth of the labor force. The U.S. Department of Labor expects the work force to increase by only 17 percent by 1990, and expects the number of new workers (age 16–24) to decline by about two million. It also expects a significant slowdown in the number of women entering the work force. But the negative has a positive aspect: some of the main reasons for the high unemployment of recent years—the changed composition of the work force to include more young people, more minority groups, and more women (all of whom increased the "natural" unemployment rate, as did the high price of energy)—will be minimized in the '80s and '90s, because of the decline in participation of these various groups in the work force. There will consequently be lower unemployment and therefore less pressure to reduce unemployment. On the other hand, we anticipate a secular trend toward higher unemployment, caused mostly by the fact that the unemployed are less motivated to look for jobs or to accept the kinds of jobs actually available.

We also feel that there will be much more movement in and out of the work force. The automatic classification of a person who leaves the work force as a "discouraged worker" is no longer accurate. In fact, the classification probably applies to less than half the people who move out of the labor force. The term, which came out of the depression and raises the image of an individual who was desperately looking for a job, is not representative of today's teenager, student, wife, or part-time worker who goes into or out of the work force for personal reasons.

In any case, we believe that a 6–7 percent rate of unemployment will come to be recognized as acceptable and that it will be relatively easy to hit this target. Aiming for a rate less than this will be seen as inflationary. That we consider 6–7 percent unemployment to be "acceptable" does not, however, imply that nothing needs to be done about unemployment problems. It may well be desirable to have programs targeted at making specific sectors of employed people more employable, or generally upgrading the skills of both employed and unemployed alike. It is just that we should not initiate inflationary programs to deal with the problems.

Other deflationary trends which should lead toward increased productivity and capital investment include the more efficient use and conservation of energy, the rationalization of regulations, and the administration's emphasis on economic efficiency over social programs. New tax incentives and liberalized depreciation allowances similarly account for part of our economic optimism. But probably one of the major components of the coming boom—and one which is being nurtured by many both in and out of the administration—is the creation of a more positive vision of the future. A revised outlook is needed to reflect the more upbeat reality of changing policies, practices, and trends. One need not be a total disciple of Reaganomics to accept this new vision of reality.

Realistic scenarios (of reduced oil prices, abundant domestic energy sources, decreased unemployment, a stronger U.S. dollar, a revitalized global standing) can be developed to replace the essentially negative and pessimistic views the United States has come to hold in the last two decades. "What is important for us now," President Reagan told an audience in September 1981, "is not to be tempted again by those promising a quick fix or something for nothing. We'll come out of our current finan-

THE BASIC CONTEXT FOR REVITALIZATION ■ 53 ■

cial difficulties because, like every generation before us, we're going to knuckle down and work our way out."

We agree. But we also believe there must be a longer-term frame of reference to help us *want* to work our way out, and to help supply a rudder for the transition toward a post-industrial society. The transition—which is already beginning in the United States—has to be supported, guided, and analyzed according to an overall ideology. Properly formulated concepts can help set achievable goals, decrease avoidable conflicts, restore the more or less traditional values of many alienated members of our society on both the left and the right, and solidify the resolve of the new coalition to stay on course.

Part of the revitalization is a cyclical phenomenon, a normal and almost inevitable recovery from a period of recession and from a period of very tight money policies, which will presumably be less onerous as the inflation, interest rates, and nominal deficits—what we call "the vicious circle"—goes into reverse, aided and supported by various other policies (see Chapters 6 and 10). We believe, then, that the United States is now coming out of the period of malaise it entered in the early 1960s. (Western Europe experienced a similar malaise in the early 1970s, but doesn't seem to be getting out of it yet. One suspects it will take them about the same fifteen to twenty years it took the United States—i.e., they'll probably emerge from it in the late 1980s or early 1990s.)

Still, the United States will not exceed (or even return to) the relative dynamism of the 1950s, when it was less dynamic in terms of its rate of economic growth than it had been in its first "good" era (1886–1913), and did not even show any catch-up phenomena to make up for the "bad" years (1914–1947) as almost all other advanced economies did. This peaking out of the S-shaped curve of economic growth seems already to be happening in the United States and is likely to occur eventually in all countries.

The United States is now rich enough, and "post-industrial" enough, that long-term social limits to growth are beginning to take effect. Even if it has a successful revitalization, its potential for long-term economic growth will still begin to slow down (see Chapter 10). The relative "stagnation" which results from this is due less to physical constraints than to specific acts of mismanagement, to new emphases (see Chapter 9), to growing hostility to "creative destruction," and to other social limits. But despite these likely long-term trends, and barring major setbacks (whether originating in the Middle East, the Soviet bloc, the OPEC countries, or the United States), we think domestic revitalization—a boom—is a matter of when, not if.

THE REAGAN ADMINISTRATION AS A WATERSHED IN U.S. POLICIES

"In this election we have brought together the elements of a new coalition. The cementing of that coalition depends on our performance in office." This assessment was offered by Republican National Committee Chairman Bill Brock on the day after President Reagan's dramatic election victory. We agree.

In fact, we believe that the president has the opportunity to forge the most important new coalition in fifty years—the "free market/ free enterprise" *economic conservatives,* the "strong America" *defense/national security/foreign policy conservatives,* and the "traditional values" *social conservatives.* The potential for a new political coalition has existed since the mid-1960s, but because the process was greatly disrupted by Vietnam and, more significantly, by Watergate, the New Deal/ Great Society coalition originally put together by Franklin D. Roosevelt in the early 1930s and sustained by Presidents Truman, Kennedy, and Johnson continued to hold together and to dominate American politics until President Reagan's election. Many of the political forces which kept that coalition going for fifty years are the same ones that make the new conservative coalition possible.

In the midst of the Great Depression, Franklin Roosevelt was able to unite a disparate array of groups which included the traditionally Democratic South, a majority of the small farmers (who had previously voted Progressive), blue-collar union workers, big-city Catholics (the Irish, Polish, and Italian "ethnics"), and liberal Jews, as well as the large majority of the black vote (which had traditionally voted Republican). In the broadest sense, Roosevelt united the "have-nots" into a party to oppose the Republican "haves," i.e., the establishment business community which opposed government intervention into the economy, especially when intervention was motivated by "social-justice" and "social-welfare" considerations. H. L. Mencken described the Democratic Party of his day as "gangs of natural enemies in a precarious state of symbiosis," which indeed seemed to be the case. But the "New Deal" coalition lasted beyond the Depression and produced a whole new generation of voters who basically identified with the Democratic Party. The Democrats have relied on this electoral advantage ever since.

The ideological foundation of the New Deal—the idea that government must use its power to protect individuals against economic catastrophe, and that a relatively unregulated free enterprise system could no longer be counted on to provide for the welfare of the average citizen—produced a gamut of corollary theories: guaranteed full employment; support of union organization; regulation of consumer products; central economic planning to control the vagaries of the business cycle. This philosophy more or less dominated American economic and social policy up until 1980. (Dwight Eisenhower's Republican electoral victories were more personal than philosophical; Richard Nixon's presidency did not announce any fundamental ideological changes.)

The election of John F. Kennedy, and especially that of Lyndon Johnson, resolidified the New Deal coalition and tried to carry its program even further, and, indeed, in the opinion of many, much too far. Johnson, a basically conservative Southern Democrat with liberal views on racial issues, was able to draw support from all of the voter blocs which had become "traditional" Democrats since Roosevelt. Johnson also benefited from the negative reaction to the outspoken and controversial conservative views of his opponent, Barry Goldwater (whose position, as represented by Ronald Reagan sixteen years later, was hardly radical).

Johnson used his electoral landslide to push through the program designed by President Kennedy—a "basic attack on the problems of poverty and the waste of human resources." Johnson's Great Society created some five hundred social programs between 1965 and 1968. He sought to use America's postwar prosperity to finish the job of ensuring the economic and social well-being of all Americans, of completing the social net and the regulated society started thirty years earlier by his political idol, Franklin Roosevelt. While some of the Great Society programs (most notably Medicare and the Voting Rights Act) basically achieved their goals, most did not (e.g., Model Cities and community action programs). All of them helped create a swollen and almost uncontrollable federal bureaucracy. Despite some impressive beginnings, the question of whether Reagan can stem the tide is still open.

Following the 1968 election, a young Republican voting analyst named Kevin Phillips wrote a controversial book entitled *The Emerging Republi-*

can Majority.* He argued that the party's base of support would be "the Heartland, the South (including the Southwest) and California"† (now known as the high-growth suburb-oriented "Sunbelt" states), and that the more liberal Democratic Party would be able to rely only on the Northeast and Pacific Northwest for regular support.

Phillips' projection turned out to be remarkably accurate; it was simply delayed by the legacy of Watergate, which is what ultimately defeated Gerald Ford in 1976. Long before that time, however, the New Deal coalition had in fact been loosened by growing ideological gaps among its constituent groups, but it was not really shaken until the takeover of the 1972 convention by the New Left and the nomination of George McGovern. McGovern's disastrous defeat indicated that perceived extremism on the left was just as likely to alienate the general electorate as perceived extremism on the right (Barry Goldwater). McGovern won only one state (Massachusetts) and the District of Columbia; nonetheless, Democrats retained control of both the House and Senate.

The election of Jimmy Carter in 1976 appears to have been, and to some extent was, reassertion of the primacy of the traditional Democratic New Dealers. Carter's victory came at a time when economic issues were more important than they had been for some time in the past. He was able to draw a number of key constituencies—the South, the Catholics, and the white working class—back into the Democratic fold, making every attempt to use his conservative image as a naval officer, a nuclear engineer, a businessman, a farmer, and a twice-born Christian in his campaign.

But while Carter won, his victory didn't dissipate the conservative core that began to emerge as early as 1968. By 1980 the "silent" and growing majority of the American electorate could no longer remain silent. Fed up with the economic situation, with high taxes, crime, pornography, divorce, drugs, defeatism, and poor public education—to name only a few of the more prominent issues—they rose up and "threw the rascals out." Ronald Reagan expanded that conservative core and united the disparate movements into a triumphant electoral coalition.

The growing conservatism of the United States electorate, confirmed by Reagan's 1980 landslide, was, therefore, not an overnight develop-

---

* Kevin Phillips, *The Emerging Republican Majority* (New Rochelle, N.Y.: Arlington House, 1969).
† Ibid., p. 465.

ment. The New Deal coalition, fragile from the outset, was eroding steadily because of changing attitudes among different blocs (especially blue-collar workers, small farmers, and big-city ethnics) as they grew more affluent or discontent with increasingly liberal economic and social policies. The growth in the influence of Western and Southwestern states was also a factor in its decline. Given the likely development of American politics in the years ahead—based on demographics, social attitudes, and levels of affluence—we are unlikely to see the New Deal coalition return as the dominant force in American politics. There will be many attempts to revive it, and while most of these attempts will be largely abortive, there will still be much political agitation and rhetoric to come out of even the failures.

But this does not mean that the Democrats might not take large elements of the Reagan coalition back either by outpromising Republican promises or as part of a backlash against policies which to some are "hard," "unjust," and/or "unworkable." Whether or not Republicans remain dominant is not as important as whether the kinds of policies they are following remain dominant, at least for the next decade or two. It seems unlikely that such policies will have much staying power if the various blocs of the current "Reagan coalition" cannot be kept together.

One weakness of the Reagan administration, the fact that its ideological intensity seems to make it somewhat uninterested in relatively technical issues, may also affect the success of new initiatives. For example, one of the most important single issues is the consumer price index (CPI). As discussed in Chapter 5, it should be fixed so that it can be used as an index to correct for inflation, or else a new index should be created to accomplish this. While the Reagan administration understands the problem, no one seemed willing at first to take the political risk of antagonizing beneficiaries of the existing CPI (e.g., labor unions and Social Security recipients), or to put in the effort and intensity required to make the needed change. One explanation is that some Republicans hope to gain as much by underindexing as the inflation goes down as was lost by overindexing on the way up. As explained in Chapter 5, this is causing current problems and could be both dangerous and unfair in the future.

My own guess as to why members of the administration have not shown the same interest in relatively technical and nonideological issues as they do in ideological ones is that these matters just don't "turn them on." They would rather invest their limited resources (time and political capital) into fighting for the success of Reagan's ideological program. We are not criticizing the ideology but simply pointing out that it can distort perspectives.

Nevertheless, ideology is probably more important in America now than it has been in many years. And the particular skill of President Reagan is that he has corralled the current ideological trends, brought them into the presidential arena where they can have practical—i.e., political—consequences, and joined defense, social, and economic conservatives together to form a new coalition of major significance.

The "strong America" bloc of the new coalition is composed of people whose overriding concern is with national security issues and the need to rebuild America's military capabilities. Public support for increased defense spending has grown rapidly in recent years, but President Carter refused to use this trend to support much of a military buildup. Moreover, Carter was president during one of the most humiliating periods in the history of American foreign policy, the Iranian hostage crisis, which clearly pointed out many of our national security and foreign-policy weaknesses. Thus many people, including traditional Democrats who probably would not have been drawn to Ronald Reagan on the basis of economic or social issues, became a part of the new coalition because of concern about defense and national security.

Numerically, the largest component of the coalition consists of the social conservatives, those broadly characterized as supporting traditional American middle-class values. Social conservatism is essentially a movement of the middle and lower-middle class. Its members have seen their economic position, as well as their social values, increasingly eroded. They turned away from the New Deal coalition because they were no longer beneficiaries of the current version of that "deal"; they became resentful of minorities for the apparent "free ride" given to them by welfare and affirmative-action programs; they believe that government now intervenes in their lives only to make them more difficult. Most of all, they deplore what they regard as a catastrophic disintegration of moral and societal values.

The "Moral Majority" and other religiously oriented groups have attracted a great deal of attention, but they do not adequately represent most social conservatives. Included also are big-city "ethnics," small-townspeople, farmers, blue-collar workers, and residents (both new and longtime) of the rapidly growing Sun Belt states. These people are horrified by the "decadence" in America today as evidenced by legal rulings and government policies on abortion, pornography, welfare, drug use, crime, busing, and so on. They seek a return to traditional American values such as hard work, deferred (rather than instant) gratification, sobriety (within limits), sexual self-discipline, and a public morality clearly and overtly linked to religion. They want lip service paid to these values, and think that the government should actively encourage both the appearance and the reality of these morals and mores.

The growing number of social conservatives is not surprising, given the nation's recent sociocultural history. During the mid-1960s, when the United States entered a period of deep malaise, almost every major social indicator—from crime statistics to youth unemployment to the number of abortions to Scholastic Aptitude Test (SAT) scores to productivity and inflation—went to hell, often despite widely publicized government programs (and large amounts of government money) to prevent or halt such trends. Many Americans feared that their families were being exposed to dangerous or immoral ideas which were tolerated—or even encouraged—by our nation's leaders. They saw pornography displayed blatantly on newstands and brought into their own homes through cable television, and even through network programming. They saw minority heads of households receive large welfare payments for not working while their own take-home pay barely kept up with inflation. They saw their children forced to ride buses to inferior schools many miles from home—a system of educational reform that was never supported by a majority of blacks, has always been of dubious efficiency, violates some of the most elementary rights of parents and children, and would have been unthinkable as a widespread practice until it was actually instituted by the courts. A referendum on the issue could never have won an election.

Many social conservatives are amazed that some state governments permit abortions as late as twenty-six weeks (just over six months, when the fetus is clearly viable) and that state and federal monies are available to finance these procedures. Indeed, they have a legitimate right to object to their tax dollars being spent on something they consider to be murder, and a legitimate right to believe that the other side is totally callous.

These kinds of social issues, issues in which the "traditional value" people felt their beliefs and attitudes were most vehemently being trampled upon, ultimately united "Archie Bunker" conservatives and the president.

Critics of social conservatives often seek to portray them as narrow-minded intolerant bigots whose desire to impose their own values on others is undemocratic or, at the extreme, fascistic. At its most combative, social conservatism probably does exhibit some such characteristics. But most adherents are not extremists and do not seek to bludgeon others into accepting their views. They mainly just want to do away with the *public* flaunting and support of those practices and values which they find most troubling and oppose most strongly. They are not much concerned with such behavior if it is private, but they make an enormous distinction between what is public and private, open and discreet, professed and unprofessed.

This is nothing new. American society has long made such distinctions. Ostensibly "immoral" (but nonviolent) behavior is tolerable as long as it is done quietly and discreetly. Pornography is a good example. It is highly popular in the United States, even among groups that publicly deplore it. But what the critics are actually decrying is not the existence of pornography itself (which, even if objectionable, is understandable), but rather its flagrant, blatant exposure and availability—and the implicit corollary that this is socially acceptable. Such hypocrisy might be considered vital to the healthy functioning of American society—it permits questionable or objectionable behavior to occur without giving it society's stamp of approval. Appearances are kept up, and appearances are essential if society is to avoid excessive permissiveness and the breakdown of authority. Appearances allow families to raise their children in a way which reinforces behavior that many liberals consider to be "uptight," but that many "squares" think (and we agree) to be essential to *their* values and family structure (as opposed to quite different values and methods of socialization in most upper-middle-class families).

The economically conservative members of the new coalition are fundamentally concerned with taxes, regulation, and other government intervention in the economy. They do not necessarily oppose government regulation of business. They are against only what they consider to be unreasonable and excessive regulation—"health and safety fascism" (or more accurately but less colorfully, "health and safety authoritarianism"), i.e., rules that do not meet reasonable cost/benefit standards or infringe too much on personal freedom. They do not oppose reasonable aid to what they consider the deserving poor but are against the scale (and sometimes even the principle) of many federal welfare programs which they believe provide disincentives to work, create nonproductive employment, and give too much aid and support to the undeserving poor. Economic conservatives believe the private sector can provide the only long-term solution to minority unemployment. They support sharp reductions in government spending to "balance the federal budget" and to reduce taxes. The so-called "supply-side" economists among them support large-scale tax cuts to stimulate growth through more savings and capital investment; the "monetarists" usually oppose the use of government spending and/or tax programs to stimulate or deflate the economy.

Economic conservatives are usually pro-business, pro-free-enterprise (not necessarily the same thing), and pro-growth. They include corporate executives, Wall Street analysts, many professionals (lawyers and doctors), and most "neo-conservative" intellectuals and commentators. Economic conservatives are generally well off, well educated, and connected to the (largely East and increasingly West Coast) "establishment." Mainly, they are white Protestants who live in the nation's large cosmopolitan cities, though a good deal of the recent intellectual and ideological support has come from Jewish and Catholic scholars.

The growing strength of economic and social conservatism would seem to have provided a solid base for forming a new political coalition before 1980, but the conservatives couldn't get their act together. This was very much in evidence in 1968 when the split in conservative voting between Richard Nixon and George Wallace almost gave the election to Hubert Humphrey.

The biggest problem in creating the coalition has been the traditional hostility between social and economic conservatives, rooted largely in class differences. The traditional lower-middle-class antipathy toward impractical "professionals," big business, and the wealthy, combined with the near contempt of the upper-middle class for "Archie Bunkers," has prevented the two groups from working together for a single candidate. Economic conservatives tend to look with disdain on the parochial, narrow-minded social conservatives of the West and Southwest, especially the doctrinaire Baptists, Mormons, and Evangelicals who make up their ranks. The social conservatives see the economic conservatives of the establishment as being irreligious and arrogant, and indistinguishable from the rest of the "elite" which they believe mismanage the country and attack traditional values and culture.

The social conservative often sees himself as the little guy pushed around by big business and big government. Yet as a group, social conservatives are not necessarily supportive of free enterprise: many support protectionist trade policies to safeguard American jobs and support wage and price controls as a means of controlling inflation.* The anti-big-business views of social conservatives reflect the opinion of a majority of Americans. The Opinion Research Company asked people in 1965 whether "business as a whole is making too much profit, a reasonable profit or not enough profit"; 14 percent said "too much." By 1979, 51 percent thought so. Hostility toward profits and business (and other establishment institutions) therefore has increased even as the nation has become more conservative, while support of free enterprise has also increased somewhat, but not by as much as a casual observer of the legislative success of Reaganomics would believe.

Ronald Reagan's long-standing conservative credentials, as well as his personal political skills, enabled him to unite the economic, social, and defense conservatives, and to gain support among all three blocs. Let us hope that these same credentials and skills will help to give the coalition staying power. Although another candidate might have defeated Jimmy Carter (who was vulnerable to almost any reasonable alternative by the end of the campaign), probably no other Republican could have succeeded in forging the coalition.

In order to expedite America's resurgence and create opportunities for a revitalization, this growing conservatism had to be translated into a political call to action—a workable program for an incumbent administration. The translation required the cooperation of all elements of the conservative movement, most of whose views had not been effectively represented at the level of national government in fifty years. Many social conservatives still feel that they are not getting enough representation; others are satisfied by the changes in symbolism and rhetoric.

The question remains whether President Reagan—and ultimately his successors—can maintain and build on the opportunities of the present. Intra-coalition strains will be exacerbated as the different factions struggle for priority for their particular causes. As is already apparent, Reagan will not support any group all the way down the line. The nomination of Sandra Day O'Connor to be the first woman on the Supreme Court was a victory for the women's movement; Mrs. O'Connor's less than definitive opposition to abortion was a great disappointment to Reagan's pro-life supporters.

Anyone who voted for the president on a "one-issue" basis is going to

---

* In February 1981, the ABC News/*Washington Post* poll found that the public favored "having the government bring back wage and price controls" by 53 to 38 percent.

have to accept the trade-offs necessitated by political realities. Some social conservatives feel betrayed and are opting out; some economic conservatives are doing the same. Other early Reagan supporters are simply no longer actively endorsing administration efforts. But most are sticking with it, partly because they are still getting a better deal than they could find elsewhere, and partly because of their strong personal ties to the president.

It is not yet clear if the Reagan administration is going to be as much a watershed in American history as the Roosevelt administration was, but this is clearly the goal. Americans are now in a particularly good position to benefit from the opportunities being forged. The direction, scope, and focus of government is changing. The better one understands these changes, the more directly one can benefit from the coming boom and understand that it is more than just economic. It is a genuine revitalization of America.

AN IDEOLOGY OF PROGRESS

One of the most important causes (as well as effects) of the recent malaise was the widespread pessimism about the present and the future. Two out of three Americans polled in recent years believe that their grandchildren will not live as well as they do—i.e., they tend to believe the vision of the future that is taught in our school system. Almost every child is told that we are running out of resources; that we are robbing future generations when we use these scarce, irreplaceable, or nonrenewable sources in silly, frivolous and wasteful ways; that we are callously polluting the environment beyond control; that we are recklessly destroying the ecology beyond repair; that we are knowingly distributing foods which give people cancer and other ailments but continue to do so in order to make a profit.

It would be hard to describe a more unhealthy, immoral, and disastrous educational context, every element of which is either largely incorrect, misleading, overstated, or just plain wrong. What the school system describes, and what so many Americans believe, is a prescription for low morale, higher prices, and greater (and unnecessary) regulations.

Even the Club of Rome has officially repudiated its position that the world is running out of resources. It still believes that pollution is likely to have catastrophic consequences worldwide, and while we disagree and argue that it exaggerates existing trends, we cannot prove it is wrong. But right or wrong, these beliefs will survive for a long time in the school system and among the media, even though they have already been discredited by most experts and much of the literature.

It is therefore important to the coming boom to reestablish an ideology of progress. Ideologies are important in themselves. They emphasize values and attitudes; they contain a theory of the past, a theory that both legitimizes the present and inspires a dream for the future. Ideologies extol, justify, and often indicate paths to honor, glory, meaning, and purpose—even to material success and riches. They help shape responses to current issues, often providing the energy and motivation needed to make those responses effective.

It seems to us almost certain that there will emerge a much brighter and more reasonable picture of the world than that presented during the past decade. But it makes a difference how rapidly and convincingly this new picture is propagated. With the help of the U.S. government (see Chapter 10), a more optimistic "Weltanschauung" can and will be created; it will probably do as much to hasten the coming boom and give it staying power as any single policy maneuver can.

CHAPTER 4

THE NEW DYNAMISM OF HIGH TECH

One of the reasons we expect relatively high and sustained growth rates through the 1980s and 1990s is that a whole host of new technologies and technological improvements are now (or soon will be) ripe for large-scale exploitation. There is normally a fairly long lag between the invention of a technology and its commercial application; there is also often a relatively long period between the time it is first marketed and the point at which it has a significant impact. Both of these lead times have been getting shorter in most areas of high technology, but if questions of environment or health are raised, the lead time may be increased substantially—even with the reforms introduced by the Reagan administration. Many of the technologies we are interested in are already achieving great and growing impact; others will achieve their impact in the late 1980s and 1990s. Collectively, they are very likely to make an appreciable difference in the growth of productivity and the GNP—as well as in the "quality of life"—to the end of the century and beyond. Indeed, unlike many earlier technologies, few of the newer high technologies have any direct adverse impact on environment and ecology—though they may help generate problems associated with the emerging super-industrial world economy.

I am much indebted in the last two thirds of this chapter to my collaborator Charles Lecht. Some of his ideas have appeared in an essay written for Nikkei–McGraw-Hill, Inc., entitled *The Massive Service Centers of the 1980s,* by Charles P. Lecht, President, Advanced Computer Techniques Corporation.

THE COMING BOOM

The coming boom in technology—particularly high technology—will be considerably more than just an economic phenomenon. It will also help foster:

- a constructive synthesis of old and new values;
- a resumption of the U.S. role as the leading source of technological innovation (a role it never really lost but the perception that it did was detrimental enough); and
- a new sense of excitement about technology and science and of being proud to be American.

In the area of technology, the United States has the potential of being a lot more than first among equals. Part of this involves the use of technology and affluence to live well and to achieve a desirable "quality" of life, as well as a high standard of living. In addition to providing us with more goods and ensuring an increased life expectancy, technological advancement also promises to help us feel healthier, enjoy ourselves more, and get more out of life. Many opportunities are open to an affluent and technological society, opportunities which will continue to expand not only because of innovations and advances, but also because of the elimination of many recent restrictive conditions to innovation and application such as stagflation, adverse government regulation, and the "new emphases" of the New Class—all of which made it difficult to exploit much of the available technological potential in the late 1960s and the 1970s.

Low morale and anti-growth ideologies affected technology as much as they did other areas. The counterculture movement seems now to have peaked, however, resulting in a noticeable return to math and science (as well as an apparent increase in SAT scores) in the high schools. Many people are even beginning to recognize that technology can be "caring." For instance, there are automatic elevator sensors to prevent passengers from getting caught in the doors; supersensitive smoke detectors; burglar alarms, air-conditioning systems; new advances in medicine and health care. All are designed for our comfort, security, enjoyment, and improvement. But most important is that the emergence of high technology promises to bring back a sense of excitement, achievement, and progress which even astronauts and outer space can no longer elicit.

Karl Marx said that one can make a number of small quantitative changes and the effect is normally just more of the same. But at a certain point the small changes result in a transition to a completely new state.

He used the example of water. If one cools water slowly it just becomes colder. But at a certain point—zero degrees centigrade—the water freezes and becomes ice, i.e., a dramatic change to a new state of solid mass. We believe changes of this magnitude are on the way. While the S-shaped curve may begin to be effective in the United States as far as population and economic growth is concerned, technological invention, innovation, and application will continue to accelerate.

What are the technologies that will make the '80s and '90s so exciting to the advanced nations?* We list and discuss ten of the most dynamic:

1. *Energy.* There will be a great expansion of non-OPEC sources of gaseous and liquid fuels from both conventional and unconventional sources. These will result in part from extraordinary improvements in the technology of exploring for and developing oil and gas as well as other mineral resources. Recent advances in the technology of seismic detection (particularly in the use of computers which are similar to the CAT scanners used in hospitals) have made possible the development of such areas as the Tuscaloosa incline and both the Eastern and Western Overthrust belts of the United States. (There are also new techniques for drilling, tertiary recovery, etc., but their real potential is still in the future.) There will very likely be a synthetic-fuel industry which may or may not take off, but which should benefit from new technologies in the 1990s. Many other energy sources are also being developed. The following list indicates the various possibilities that seem likely to be available in the 1990s or early in the twenty-first century. In reverse order of their likely importance (but mostly in the order of their romantic appeal), they are:

Fusion
Geothermal:
   Hydrothermal
   Hot dry rock
Solar:
   Heating and cooling of buildings
   Process heat for industry
   Solar thermal electric power
   Photovoltaics (solar cells)—now $10/watt; needed, 40¢ watt
   Solar satellite power systems (SSPS)

---

* The Third World will also be greatly affected by technological advancement, but often by different (and usually older and less advanced) technologies. But equally often the new technologies allow the Third World to leapfrog over traditional developments.

Windpower
Ocean thermal electric power
Bioconversion
Photolytic decomposition of water
Fission:
  Conventional
  Near-breeders
  Breeders
Coal
Oil from conventional sources and/or liquid synfuels
Natural gas from conventional and unconventional sources

2. *Protection of the environment.* While the Japanese have already developed a sizable export trade in the technology of protecting the environment, much work is also being done in the United States. One focus is on the reduction of pollution caused by industry and transportation (current models of American cars produce less than one tenth of the pollutants they produced ten years ago). Another is the treatment of sewage and the protection and recuperation of water resources. The very production of this environmental technology will be an important part of the GNP (and therefore of the boom). Equally important will be the reduction in the cost of providing very high-quality (but not usually 100 percent) protection.

3. *Food and agriculture.* One concern is that the era of significant annual improvements in the agricultural productivity of the best farms may have come to an end. We doubt it. There is some evidence of a slight topping out of many of the traditional methods of increasing agricultural productivity (at least in the highly advanced countries), but new methods are now being used. In any case, great improvements in the rest of the world are still possible and will occur. There will also be genuine innovations and breakthroughs, e.g., unconventional production of unconventional foods such as cheap proteins for humans and animals or edible plants that thrive in salty water. There are many other dramatic possibilities, in part because of the developments discussed next.

4. *Biotechnologies* (*bioengineering, biochemistry, biophysics, bioindustry, and genetic engineering, etc.*). At the moment, the possibilities for these technologies seem to be unlimited. While limits will eventually emerge, we don't yet know where. In addition to new genetic strains for conventional agriculture, there is the use of biological processes and organisms to replace mechanical and electrical methods in areas as diverse as clean-

ing up oil spills, refining various kinds of ores, and producing new manufactured products and pharmaceuticals. There are already a thousand companies engaged in this kind of activity in the United States.

The payoffs (in agriculture, medicine, phamaceuticals, and industry) of the extraordinary developments in genetic engineering are only beginning to take place. Their massive impact is not likely to come until the later 1980s (though individual venture-capital companies may well make a lot of money before then).

5. *Space.* While we doubt that the 1990s will see genuine space colonies, we do believe there will be a major expansion in satellite activities and possibly some small settlements or "hotels" for the personnel who operate and maintain the systems. While it is clearly possible to get enough solar power from space to satisfy all of man's needs, it is unlikely that this source will soon be exploited because of the huge initial investments that would be needed. But the use of space for communications, observation, and manufacturing is on the way. There will also be some exciting innovations for use by home and office; it will soon be possible to buy a satellite antenna for about $500, enabling individual homes and businesses to receive TV signals and other communications directly from space satellites.

The really big "space-induced" changes should occur in the late 1980s or the early 1990s, in part as a result of improved shuttle and satellite technology. Instead of putting relatively small objects into space and large installations on the ground, the objects in space can be of great size and the corresponding ground installations relatively small. At some point in the 1990s the antenna in space may be as big as 5 square kilometers and the receiver on the ground will be as small as the proverbial Dick Tracy wristwatch. When this happens, an incredible range of applications is possible.* Another especially exciting set of applications exploit the low temperatures available in space to enable the use of super electronic devices such as super-sensitive detectors and super-fast computers.

6. *Medicine and health care.* This is one area in which the costs have been burgeoning in all developed countries. New technologies and new organizational techniques should have a very big impact in bringing those costs down, as well as in improving the accuracy of medical diagnoses. Computers read electrocardiograms better than many doctors; they

---

* See William M. Brown and Herman Kahn, *Long-Term Prospects for Developments in Space (A Scenario Approach)*, Hudson Report No. H1-2638-RR.

often pick up symptoms earlier than physicians do; for some doctors they are an excellent "first opinion," for others they serve as a "second opinion" (in this case doctors check themselves against a later computer diagnosis which is usually not as good as theirs; but the computer never gets tired or careless). There will be dramatic advances in pharmaceuticals, many of them produced by the new techniques of biotechnology. A host of diseases including many cardiovascular and cancerous diseases should become susceptible to treatment. The CAT scan will be complemented by the PET (positron emission tomography) scan, enabling bodily functions to be studied in much the same way that the CAT scan permits internal observation of structure. Prostheses will also be greatly improved. In general, the real payoff offered by this area as a major industry rivaling electronics in its dynamic, innovative character will be less in terms of economics than in better health and living.

7. *Mass transportation.* One important innovation may be the pervasive use of the new commuter aircraft, such as VTOL, STOL, and/or helicopters, which are now being redesigned to be quieter, safer, and more adaptable for use in small neighborhood airports. In areas where adequate bodies of water exist, it seems likely there will be floating or land-based runways for seaplanes. The current movement from cities to suburbia and exurbia could be made more efficient (and greatly accelerated) if a mass transportation system going from point to point and working in relatively low-density population areas becomes available. (Standard mass transportation systems now depend on a linear array of very high density.) Conversely, this movement creates a demand for such a transportation system. There will probably also be innovations on our highway and railroad systems, especially in the use of very high-speed trains. Buses and cabs run electrically or perhaps fueled by hydrogen or other clean-burning fuels should help limit pollution in cities.

8. *Developments in materials.* While this is usually regarded as a relatively pedestrian field, extraordinary progress is now expected in almost every area—fibers, foams, ceramics, crystals, fixatives (glues and adhesives), molecular coatings, metallic compounds, plastics, and so on. In fact, there are so many advances being made that instead of being the age of computers, genetics, or medicine, the late 1980s and '90s may turn out to be the age of materials. The improvements generated by better, longer-lasting, and more easily maintained structures, higher-performing and more rugged and reliable equipment, and various other applications of wonder materials are going to be vast.

9. *Silicon chips.* The silicon chip was the marvel of the 1970s; by 1980 it had a $2.5 billion market, but this number hugely underestimates its importance and impact on the economy. The most complex chips, which now hold about 65,000 bits of data, will hold about fifteen times as much (a million) by 1990, at which time the market is expected to be about $15 billion a year. Competition for the silicon chips is also expected from technologies based on new uses of such materials as gallium, arsenic, and even antimony. Finally, it seems likely that the new biotechnologies will be used to develop "organic" computer elements with very high and/or new kinds of performance. The speed at which these components operate will increase enormously, probably by a factor of as much as 10 to 100 in the 1990s. (Several totally new concepts should also be available by the end of the decade.) In twenty years, a "black box" the size of a cigar box should be able to store the equivalent of ten Libraries of Congress.

10. *Automation of home, office and factory.* The factory use of robots will increase by about 35 percent per year in the 1980s. Roger B. Smith, the chairman of General Motors, was recently quoted as saying that "every time the cost of labor goes up $1 an hour, one thousand more robots become economical." But the office use of automation—while not necessarily via robots—will probably increase almost as rapidly. So far, the application of new technology to the office is represented mainly by word processors, computers, and copiers—all of which usually operate independently; by the 1990s, most pieces of equipment will be able to communicate routinely with one another and with the outside world, and many will be multi-functional. At the same time, the files of most large corporations (and many small ones) will be stored collectively in mass storage devices and available to any authorized person (or device) from almost anywhere in the world. All this filing will be easy to do, since most of the material will originate in a digital form and not require conversion from a printed page to storable digital data, but in any case, by the 1990s optical readers will be so practical that it will be easy to convert most documents into digital data. In addition, voice-operated typewriters and other voice-sensitive equipment will be able to adapt to specific dictation, and once adapted to a particular speaker, will be able to recognize even slurred, mispronounced, and badly accented words. The extensive use of electronic technology to improve production in the service industries will have a major impact in increasing overall productivity. Indeed, the use of computers and microprocessors to introduce some level of intelligence to

almost every kind of operation or piece of equipment seems likely to contribute as much as or more than any other technology to the coming boom.

COMPUTER NETWORKS

Automation of home, office, and factory directly leads to one of the most important high-technology areas of all: computer networks, i.e., the intimate marriage of computers, communications, and various sensors and input devices to form a hierarchical and/or distributed processing system. With appropriate sensors and other input-output devices these computer/communication systems can tie diverse and remote operations together and greatly decrease the problem of distance as a cost or complication. In any case they will have enormous capability and flexibility in application.

We will discuss several applications in the rest of the chapter. We will also touch on the dangers of these computer networks, dangers which are less widely discussed and much more subtle than those of pollution, nuclear accidents, or physical damage normally raised by new technologies. Yet even seemingly benign systems like computers and communications can be misused or misapplied, can decrease productivity as well as increase it, and can harm humans as well as benefit them.

Some of the most imaginative applications of computer technologies are likely to come as part of "big systems" which will take advantage of developments in related peripherals (terminals, cathode-ray tubes, advanced copiers, mass storage, and so on). Similar systems are already operative in business and government (especially in the military). We expect "big systems" eventually to come in all sizes and shapes. An example would be a series of related technologies which we group together under the heading C^4I^2—command, control, communications, computing/information and intelligence. They are usually called C^3I, with computing and intelligence left out, but we feel these concepts are so important they should be explicitly included.

The distinction between "information" and "intelligence" is an artificial but an important one. Information tends to be relatively formal, systematic, official, and routinely obtained. Intelligence is here used more in the sense of "military intelligence" than of "human intelligence" (which is more or less included in "computing") and is both broader and more specific, and very much less official and formal than what we call information. Intelligence involves knowledge about events and people that may be conjectural, intuitive, private, and/or obtained at random, unofficially, or clandestinely. Intelligence data is normally not found in standard files, while information usually includes the routine data that the system is expected to know. It is difficult to make the distinction between information and intelligence very much more precise than this, but when intelligence is put into the system it is generally due less to mechanical or electronic programming than to the good fortune (or planning) of having the right people in the right place at the right time. The advent of the C^4I^2 systems can add a new dimension to the procurement, processing, and use of intelligence. While these systems usually cannot guarantee the quality and availability of the raw data, they can help to extract the maximum information out of whatever data is on hand.

TWO EXAMPLES OF C^4I^2 SYSTEMS

The present technology is ripe for the development of massive C^4I^2 services. Some especially spectacular examples will come about from a merger of the communications and computing industries. We note two examples: product codes combined with cable TV and massive data bases maintained in real time, i.e., kept up to date.

Most readers are familiar with the "product code" lines that are now printed on almost all goods in supermarkets. These codes can be read at the checkout counter by a scanner device which not only tells the clerk what the price is but automatically informs the computer that a particular item was sold on a particular day. The device enables supermarkets to keep their inventory current, to have better control of their overall operations, and to monitor in-store theft more carefully.

Most readers are also familiar with cable TV and know that some cable systems can vary the programs shown to groups of listeners or even specific listeners. These two systems—product code lines and cable TV—have now been put together to conduct experiments on marketing. Families which sign up to participate are exposed to different kinds of ads on TV. Records of their shopping are kept through the scanner device; the system processes the data so that information becomes available on the effect of specific ads on specific consumers. To the extent that the advertising is useful, there will be enormous increases in the productivity of the advertising process. To the extent that the whole system is tied into various MISs (management information systems) for real-time feedback and reaction, we would have a genuine C^4I^2 system.

Many people are concerned about potential abuses of this kind of system. In particular they fear an Orwellian social-engineering world. While there is this possibility, it probably will not come directly or rapidly out of the system itself. A much more ominous possibility comes from the use of massive data bases. One such data base was in fact the subject of a proposal seriously considered during the Kennedy and Johnson administrations, wherein all federal and other governmental records on each inhabitant in the United States (including visitors) would be amalgamated into a single huge computer system operated as closely as possible in real time. The records would be coded and controlled in such a way that only aggregated information and very limited amounts of personal information would be available to other agencies of the government.

The objections, of course, are clear. A massive data base would make "1984" much more possible, and in any case Americans have ambivalent attitudes toward this kind of "efficiency." For example, New York State once installed a computer on one of the bridges going into Manhattan. The computer automatically recorded the license number of every car that drove past, so that by the time the car crossed the bridge the police had data feedback on whether or not there were any outstanding summonses against the vehicle. If there were, they arrested the driver. There was great public uproar. Drivers protested that it was unfair (like shooting quail on the ground), and the experiment was stopped. Nonetheless, state troopers can still use their two-way radios to get a complete record, within seconds, on any motorist they stop.

A massive data base for use by the government is a proposal which is sometimes advanced on the grounds that it would save taxpayer money, which it would. But its main virtue is the comprehensive data it would provide on the economy, the health and education of individuals, and many other important aspects of society, thereby enormously improving governmental policy-making and the research base of socioeconomic theorists. While the whole scheme was rejected by Congress when it was first suggested, we would argue that on balance such a comprehensive data system is probably worth having, a conclusion based primarily on our desires to understand societal issues better.

TIME-SHARING DATA NETWORKS

Another interesting example of a computer network is demonstrated by the General Electric Information Services Co. (GEISCO) system of computers and its associated communications system (which often uses existing telephone networks in a way which does not interfere with their normal use). The system enables instantaneous, inexpensive communication with major cities around the world, making it possible to connect from almost any part of the developed free world, and some other places as well, with files stored in a single location. Except for artificial charges and limitations set by various national governments, the system can be used for only slightly more than the cost of a local telephone call (plus GE charges). The result of having a large number of data bases stored in the same location is that it is possible to operate a worldwide business as though it were all in one building—in fact, sometimes with less difficulty.

Such a network is already commonplace, and it will soon be more so as nationwide public telephone and telegraph companies are permitted or encouraged to enter this kind of business. Communications and computer companies are discovering that their products and services, once very different, have suddenly become strikingly similar. For example, the microprocessor logic chip tied into a time-sharing system and a nationwide communications network with computers at various modes are essentially the same device: a collection of communication busses, signal processors, message switchers, etc. It is now apparent that IBM and AT&T have always been, at least potentially, in the same business. That we did not recognize this for the first thirty years of the computer industry was quite natural—AT&T built only one computer, a nationwide network covering the North American continental shelf; IBM built thousands of computers, each of which occupied a small space in a small office somewhere.

By 1980, however, capabilities in the distributed processing technology gave us the ability to link discrete processors located in different places. As this linking occurred, discrete computer systems became nodes in a network which began to resemble AT&T's network. At the same time, it was no surprise to discover that AT&T's network contained nodes which were virtually identical to the processors found in computer rooms. Conclusion: companies which appear quite different but which are mainly in the business of both producing and using these processors are essentially in the same business.

From single chips (whose elements vanish into the microscopic world), to collections of chips, to mammoth networks of processors, computer and communication systems resemble each other more closely every day. With computer companies entering the communications business and vice versa (e.g., IBM with Satellite Business Systems; AT&T with Advanced Computing Services), it is inevitable that both will compete for the same clientele. (AT&T has recently entered the computer business in a significant way—it has become a software house.) As these and other computing and communications companies add complementary resources to gain market share, each will produce its own massive service centers—quarters from which immense data-processing and communications power will be derived in the later 1980s and beyond. Whether they will process more data and generate a greater communications capability than smaller centers working by themselves or linked together via switching centers is an open and much-discussed issue. But the main point is that both will be growing by leaps and bounds and working.

Operating under the banners of mammoth corporations and governments, these combined information-processing centers can either be highly localized or else globalized to serve entire continents. But they will be quite unlike massive electrical utilities. Information used by a client is not used up; it can still be sold to other clients. Further, the computer and communications systems often share common ground with their competition.

Imagine linking users and facilities in a massive network which feeds and transmits information across all forms of input/output (1/0) links, coaxial cable with fiber optics, including VHF and UHF radio transmissions and even laser beams.

Imagine information systems having an extraordinary range of memories (very slow to very fast) and in all forms and supporting all data structures.

Picture a sea of terminals of all types and shapes, a sea of receptacles and connectors to provide a more harmonious input of human thought into the artificial world of computers and networks and input of artificial power into the human world.

Finally, imagine a library of programs constituting vast repositories of human experience in methods and results, to be made available on demand from any location anywhere in the world, including planes, cars, ships, hotel rooms, camps, and, of course, offices and homes.

Such massive service centers have long been a staple of fantasy and science fiction. By now they are very close to reality. By 1985–86, AT&T will be operating a digital data network capable of great speeds (5,600 kilobits per second) and linking all major U.S. cities. Satellite carriers, private microwave networks, and resale carriers will upgrade services to provide new high-speed data services. Radio and television bus carriers, two-way coaxial cable, and point-to-multipoint microwave (already available) will be used to connect users to nationwide and worldwide open-data networks.

There is one important issue which will make a lot of difference in how rapidly worldwide simple time-sharing data systems and complex C^4I^2 systems develop: the impact of restrictions that are being enacted by various countries on the transmission of information across boundaries and on the easy interchange of data between systems. These restrictions or arbitrary changes are already a problem. Some governments claim they want to keep sovereignty over these capabilities or argue for the need to preserve the privacy of files on their citizens. Often they have other reasons for controlling the flow of information—the classical arguments over "free trade," the same as those often used on material goods. The same principle of "protectionism" by which a country discourages trade is put forth against any technological transfers it believes will hinder the development of its own capabilities.

The issue of protectionism is important because the full development of time-sharing and C^4I^2 systems will come only if users can fully exploit the technology and create area-wide and even worldwide systems in which the transfer of information from one part of the globe to another is less difficult than walking over to a file cabinet or a copying machine. Many systems exist which already have this capability but are precluded from using it by various national restrictions.

Technological advancement over the past twenty-five years has caused the cost of computing hardware and storage technology to plummet. Multi-use business computers which incorporate data processing, word processing, data storage and retrieval, and typesetting and communications switching are becoming progressively less expensive. Many believe they will eventually replace much of the need for most specialized computers. But these too are becoming very cheap. Whatever happens, the user will be well served.

Moreover, with the ability to transmit and store vast quantities of data at remote sites, the nature of many traditional data-base services is undergoing rapid change. The services are beginning to function like radio stations, broadcasting data at high speeds to many terminals which then record the transmission within their own memories.

Eventually these developments will enable people everywhere, endowed by nature with small and short memories, poor calculation capabilities, and faulty logic, to augment their own abilities. Equally, or more important, will be improvement in operations due to the better integration of disparate or separate activities (see list below). Both the improvement in capabilities and the synthesis and integration should be very helpful in overcoming many natural, human, and regional deficiencies. The question of how far this technological revolution can go is open. Not only are there bureaucratic restrictions that must be dealt with, but there are technical issues as well—issues that require answers to the question of how complex and flexible we can make programs and how far we can go toward artificial intelligence or similar capabilities.

Some Possible Applications of Network Information Services

BUSINESS APPLICATIONS
  Remote computing and analysis
  Mass mail; selective advertising
  Management systems
  Interfirm transactions
  Analysis and simulation
  Personnel data base maintenance and inquiry
  Scientific and engineering analysis
  Remote graphics
  Computer conferencing
  Message routing and recording
  Electronic message systems
GOVERNMENT APPLICATIONS
  Remote computing and analysis
  Vocational counseling and placement
  On-line polling
  Remote testimony in court trials
  Emergency vehicle scheduling and control
  Remote lookup of city directory
  Management systems
  Traffic control systems
  Pollution monitoring
EDUCATIONAL APPLICATIONS
  Remote library access
  Adult courses via terminals
  Computer-aided school instruction
  Pre-school language instruction
  Drill and practice exercises
  Current events programs for children
  Educational management systems
  Gaming and simulation
MEDICAL APPLICATIONS
  Remote diagnosis
  Emergency medical information
  Medical management systems
  Patient information systems
  Remote computing and analysis
  Access to public health data bases
  Computer conferencing of physicians
CONSUMER APPLICATIONS
  On-line catalog shopping
  Work at home or local work centers
  Consumer advisory services

Some Possible Applications of Network Information Services

CONSUMER APPLICATIONS (Cont.)
Water, electric, and gas meter reading
Hotel, theater, and travel ticketing
Plays and movies from stored libraries
Tailored news reports (dedicated newspaper)
Home protection services
Personal data management
Personal tax preparation services

Chess, bridge, and other interactive games

OTHER
Electronic funds transfer
Cashless transactions
Point of sale recording
Architectural analysis and design
Legal information and counseling
Weather reporting networks

SOURCE: Herbert S. Dordick, Helen G. Bradley, and Burt Nanus, *The Emerging Network Marketplace* (Norwood, N.J.: Ablex Publishing Corp., 1981), Table 1.

THE IMPACT OF C^4I^2 TECHNOLOGIES

It has long been held, and until recently, correctly held, that it is much easier to increase the productivity of the goods-oriented sector of the economy than the service sector. One characteristic of modern electronics in general, and of C^4I^2 technologies in particular, is that great as their impact on the goods-oriented sectors will be, their greatest impact will be on the service sectors and the service component of the industrial sectors—e.g., the white-collar jobs in industrial enterprises.

The service sector of the U.S. economy is growing faster than ever. While only 5 percent of the new jobs in the 1970s were created in manufacturing (only 11 percent in the production of goods as a whole), 80 percent were in the service sector. The most rapid growth occurred in firms less than four years old with fewer than fifty employees. Many of these companies were labor-intensive "thoughtware" organizations providing information-based services.

But even the most advanced information systems—for example, an MIS (management information system)—can miss the "heart of the matter" in some crucial aspects of improving productivity. In many cases, improvements require changes in judgment, ideology, intuition, taste, leadership, personal choices, motivation, and training—intangibles for which even the most elaborate and capable MIS may not be very helpful and may even turn out to be harmful. For example, the productivity of teachers is affected by how many facts they can find by manipulating a CRT terminal, by their ability to grade more true-false tests than ever before, and by their proficiency in manipulating audiovisual aids. But the main issues today are likely to be: Can teachers keep their students disciplined, interested, and inspired? Do they teach things that are relevant? Are they good role models of what the students can reasonably aspire to? Do they motivate students to learn?

A modern MIS may be incredibly good at collecting and processing huge amounts of data and breaking out the results in a variety of ways. It gives management the feeling that it knows what is happening and is therefore in control. But decisions made by management that are "wrong" are more often than not due to the lack of sufficient data in the system rather than to managerial ignorance or misuse of information which does get into the official information channels. The errors stem from what is called "faulty information."

An elaborate system will not necessarily tell management who is stealing, or that quality control is very low because no one is monitoring products accurately, or that marijuana is being used on the production floor. Though it may note that there is a drop in productivity, the causes of that drop are more likely to be picked up by the "intelligence" part of the management information systems. Normally, if they are detected at all, they are found out only by direct observation, either through immediate contact or via somebody who knows what's happening. While causes can sometimes be detected by properly processing data from the information system and then drawing conclusions, or at least speculations, more often they are not found and perhaps cannot be found in this way.

Ultimately, then, the quality of the management itself is still the critical variable. How good is its judgment, trained intuition, and real knowledge? How much relevant hands-on experience has it had? How many in the management team have dealt only with preprocessed and aggregated information? How many know little or nothing about the objective world of individuals and components which they are eventually trying to manage?

Many vendors are now concerned with MIS and C^4I^2 systems and are attempting to provide tools and aids to help management better control its organization and information systems. Such giants as Exxon, Citibank, American Express, Xerox, Dun and Bradstreet, American Satellite Corporation, Reader's Digest, and others are planning to become "complete" information-systems companies which provide highly specialized services designed to maximize the usefulness of these systems. But such services could make genuine "hands-on experience" and direct contact with reality even more scarce and more difficult to obtain. As a result, managers could become victims of what we call "educated incapacity" (see Chapter 9)—i.e., they could acquire so much specialized training, as well as aggregated and processed information, as to be rendered incapable of relating to (or even understanding) important basics. This problem is becoming more important, not less. And it's likely to get even worse, unless carefully devised control functions and procedures are put into place that supplement the C^4I^2 and MIS systems with "hands-on" experience. In short, the systems will be of great assistance in aiding management only if managers know how to use them.

As information-systems technology continues to advance, many corporate or governmental data-processing facilities will become less important. On the one hand, the massive service centers will provide, in a very competitive way, the capability now located in individual facilities. On the other hand, much will be done by the individual with his personal micro- or minicomputer. Additionally, the shortage of trained computer staff (an increasing problem) will be abated by a *de facto* distribution of skills to the service centers. Indeed, one of the forces behind the growth of the centers will be the shortage of highly trained professionals for use in individual companies. This shortage has always been a limit on the computer industry's growth, but it has also brought about the development of highly skilled (intelligent) devices to reduce the need for highly skilled (and intelligent) professionals at the user level.

To what extent, then, will so-called "artificial intelligence" be achieved and used in the next decade or two? There is no question that many activities which are traditionally associated with human intelligence can now be done as well or better by computers and C^4I^2 systems. It may turn out that human intelligence will eventually be defined as that which cannot be done by machines. Some people argue that computers will one day be able to simulate everything that humans can do, including learning from experience and having their own version of intuition, emotion, aesthetics, creativity, and judgment. If and when computers can do everything that humans can, and do it better, a catastrophic backlash effect on man's self-image may occur.

This erosion in the "status" of what it means to be a human being has, of course, been under way for much of the last five hundred years. It more or less started with Copernicus, who pointed out that the earth was not the center of the universe. Darwin demonstrated (quite plausibly) that man was not made in God's image, but evolved from some missing link. Marx argued that there isn't very much free will and that all of history is the "history of class warfare." Freud asserted that people are not really making their own conscious choices, but are dominated by unconscious motivations, most of them not particularly worthy or admirable. Pavlov and Skinner argued that man was basically a programmed animal who should be consciously and explicitly programmed.

From our point of view, however, and considering the projected economic and technological advances over the next *two decades,* it is not likely that any new developments will have a catastrophic impact on our self-image. Whether or not super computers, complex microprocessors, and/or advanced C^4I^2 systems (not to mention gene-splicing and the "creation" of test-tube species) will in the *long run* have that type of impact—ranging from "big brother" to computer "takeover" to other deleterious effects on social institutions and mores—is an open issue, the effects of which will probably not be felt until we are well into the twenty-first century.

There has also been much discussion over whether elaborate time-sharing and C^4I^2 systems will encourage the growth of a new kind of "cottage industry" in which most people work at home. It is clear that there will be much more of this in the future. There will be great possibilities for being location-independent for more or less extended periods, e.g., one can carry computers and communications devices on a trip and remain in close contact with the office at all times (not only from hotels, but from planes as well). But most people are still likely to work in an office, shop, factory, or other situation under direct supervision and in direct contact with co-workers—at least much of the time. Most people simply do not work well without a fair amount of supervision and contact; even most managerial and creative functions cannot be done well if there is a physical separation of people who have to interact with each other. It takes a very atypical kind of person to do free-lance or solitary work well; most people don't like it. (A friend of mine, I. P. Sharp, who runs the I. P.

Sharp time-sharing company, once gave computers to his staff and told them they could work at home. After two years, almost all of them decided they preferred coming to the office, and yet by both personality and function I would judge programming most lends itself to becoming a cottage industry.)

As noted, the computer is very effective when communicating well-understood official information and theories, but not so good for furnishing serendipities and synergisms. (Serendipities are good things that result from more or less accidental and unexpected events or discoveries; synergisms occur when the whole is greater than the sum of its parts.) Both depend on "being there." For example, one accidentally meets somebody in the hall and finds out some new information or accidentally observes something one isn't normally expected to see. This can't happen unless one is in a position to have it happen (i.e., works in an office instead of at home).

Properly designed systems can still be an important source of different kinds of synergisms and serendipities. But organizations which rely totally on processed information or distant observation will probably not have the competitive advantage of those which, in addition to having a computer, include (and even emphasize) direct contact, hands-on experience, and personal observations to perform well the various functions of business.

The Japanese tell us that if a manufacturer wants to get good quality control, senior members must personally spend time on the factory floor. It used to be well understood in the U.S. that top people must go onto the production floor to see what is actually happening and to have direct contact with blue-collar and other workers. Supervisors cannot do the job through intermediaries—whether the "go-betweens" are human beings or electronic systems. This once well-known fact seems to have been largely forgotten or deemphasized in the United States in recent years, in part because of fascination with high-tech systems.

It is interesting to note that while the Japanese and Europeans (particularly the former) are technologically catching up with Americans, Americans are still solidly in the forefront with C^4I^2 capabilities (components as well as systems). There are some areas where the Japanese have already caught up, e.g., robots for industry, manufacture of microprocessor chips and very large and fast computers, and preparation of government agencies for the future information society, but there are many more areas where they have not even reached, much less surpassed, current American expertise. This specifically applies to the imaginative and pervasive use of computers and microprocessors either by themselves or in C^4I^2 systems. American society combines easily the activities of thousands of tinkerers and small entrepreneurs with gigantic corporations and elaborate national and private laboratories. This ability enables it to make extraordinarily rapid progress in advanced information and other technologies.

There will be endless variations in 1/0 devices fulfilling every conceivable need. The creation of equipment designed for access to and from those networks will challenge the creativity of people everywhere. The requirement to support various scenarios that mix local as well as massive service-center processing facilities will define a virtually unending stream of new products and new technologies. Such accessing requirements are factors which should cause American electronics-industry companies to forecast continually bright futures.

Information-systems power will be available to almost all people in developed countries, providing them with facilities that will make life much easier. Many devices, some of which contain their own local intelligence, will be controlled via broadcast signal on the sidebands or local radio and TV stations. Professional people—doctors, lawyers, certified public accountants, professors, etc.—will use data-base facilities to relieve themselves of tedious clerical activities. More people will be able to do more jobs than ever before; some of what we lack in personal experience will be made up by artificial experience delivered across communications networks. More and more aspects of our private lives will be a breeze.

From optimization of transportation flow through food production, applications of technology will revolutionize all aspects of our public and private lives, and soon. Corporations, governments, educational facilities, and other institutions are already becoming more effective and less wasteful. Various departments of government and private industry should be able to reduce their competition for resources and personnel to carry out their missions. Financial systems and production systems should realize a better correlation of their efforts. Heretofore rough means of balancing supply and demand will inevitably be improved through better gathering, processing, and analyses of data.

Clearly, all of these new technologies will be used to increase the U.S. gross national product and to revive a long-dormant economic dynamism. But they will also revive the fun and pride that Americans associate with electronic and computerized gadgetry. The poet may feel dehumanized by the computer, but the man who uses it feels his own power is intensified. His feeling may exaggerate reality, but only partly. In any case, he feels good. The opportunities for both fun and gain, self-fulfillment and self-advancement, are great and growing. All of these positive trends are part of what we mean by the revitalization of America.

CHAPTER 5

CONTROLLING AND ALLEVIATING INFLATION AND ITS EFFECTS

BREAKING THE GRIP OF SUPER-INFLATION

Inflation is more likely than any other single problem to prevent or diminish the impact of the coming boom. No other problem seems as complicated or as resistant to policy solutions. There is now extensive if controversial literature on its causes, its costs, and the various means to control, reduce, or correct for these costs. Without systematically reviewing the controversies we would like to make a few points relevant to understanding the "what, how, and why" of the inflation and some of the pitfalls which could hinder or delay the boom.

Our outline of the Kondratieff theory (Chapter 2) noted that before World War II, prices went up and down in long cycles, but unlike after other wars, there was no fully compensating deflation after World War II. The OECD countries became accustomed to a low inflation in the 1950s, but during the '60s, when inflation rates began to rise and the excessive number of dollars overseas started to become embarrassing, everybody (slowly) came to understand that something very threatening was happening. These fears were more than borne out, in part because the U.S.

Much of this chapter is the product of close collaboration with my colleague Dr. Irving Leveson, Director of Economic Studies at the Hudson Institute, but he would not agree with everything in it.

government and most of its advisers, including economists, did not take them seriously enough. The current stagflation and structural problems were by no means inevitable; they could have been prevented had constructive action been taken at least a decade ago.

The current inflation is costly, disruptive, and dangerous. It undermines both morals and morale, inflicts the greatest harm on people who are least able to cope with it mentally or financially, distorts many economic processes, and threatens the stability of the U.S. economic and political system. These dangers are so clear and present that for the moment a consensus has emerged which holds that strong, even painful, measures are urgently needed to assure that the current inflationary spiral is curbed, and that a new surge in inflation does not quickly arise.

But few expect the inflation will be brought to zero. Indeed, the consensus in early 1980 (at least among corporate planners) was that an inflation in the region of 10 percent would continue for five or ten years and that we would have to learn to live with it. At present many people feel it might be less than 10 percent, but few believe it will be less than 5, and almost no one believes the inflation will disappear before the end of the decade. In fact, the financial and business community as well as the general public all seem to accept the idea of some degree of ongoing inflation. They would be pleased just to have the administration keep it in single digits for the rest of the decade. I, on the other hand, believe the government has made a good start in bringing inflation down to zero, particularly if it uses some ingenuity (as suggested in this and the next chapter).

Many Americans think the administration complicated its current economic problems by enacting excessive tax cuts, some of which may turn out larger than anticipated (e.g., the all-savers certificates; the new depreciation allowances). We agree that several of the cuts were inadvisable or too generous. However, we would also argue that most of the cuts were important and that while good arguments could be made for deferring some until the inflation had been brought under control, at that point the sense of crisis and urgency would have passed, making it almost impossible to put in anything as drastic as the Reagan tax program. Further, at a later date there would have been little or no pressure to cut the budget, particularly if the inflation had begun to erode. In fact, many still feel that the Reagan legislation achievements were close to miraculous and depended on exploiting every bit of momentum the administration had as a result of its election and its accumulative legislative success. From both a political and practical point of view, therefore, the administration was justified in complicating its own fight against inflation, though clearly the final bill complicates the immediate fight against inflation more than is desirable.

Most members of the administration probably did not think in terms of long-term vs. short-term chances for passage of the tax cuts, but simply argued that the cuts would lead almost immediately to a burst of energy for the economy by encouraging savings and investment, spur increased productivity, and generally foster greater incentives for higher economic performance. In the long run these will happen. But it was naive to expect a very rapid change in the attitudes and actions of businessmen and the general public, particularly when many have been so traumatized in recent years by the inability of the government to change its course or to control its own failures. Most Americans didn't expect the inflation they have; now they expect it to be around for some time.

The effects of an inflation depend on the degree to which various groups anticipate it. If it is unanticipated and the "money illusion" (the belief that money has a relatively fixed value even when it doesn't) is widely held, then there may not be immediate insistence on increased compensation to offset the effects of higher prices. Such a "moderate" response allows an enormous transfer of wealth from creditors to debtors and from the private economy to the government. If the inflation is expected but there is uncertainty about the rate, then the transfer could go either way. The question of who gains and who loses also depends on such other factors as the impact of taxes. Finally, if the inflation is overanticipated, it makes the system more vulnerable to an inflationary explosion but it also tends to reverse the income transfer that accompanies underanticipation.

But inflation does more than just transfer income: it increases risks; it creates distortions; it decreases the efficiency of the system; it erodes morale, integrity, and discipline; and it destroys investor faith and consumer confidence. The manner in which inflationary expectations and corrections are built into the system determines the type and magnitude of losses, the specific pattern of transfers of wealth, and the distortion of values and attitudes. The common remark is that no one gains from inflation. Unfortunately that isn't true.

It is true that eventually almost everyone is harmed by the overall deterioration of the economy and society, but many people gain in specific areas, at least for a while. Businessmen gain as long as the inflation is *un-*

anticipated and the public doesn't become militant. Government gains from unanticipated inflation by underpaying its employees, by increased taxes due to bracket creep, by the erosion in the real value of its debts, by creating money and credit, and so on. Homeowners with an overpriced house or a fixed-interest mortgage have benefited enormously in the last twenty years at the expense of the depositors in lending institutions. But recently, with inflation thoroughly anticipated and about out of control, we can argue that for most people, losses are mounting, and gains are lessening and in many cases being reversed. The most important order of business is now clearly to eliminate inflation—not just contain it—even if such a drastic goal will cause painful, difficult, and risky readjustments. The second important priority is to cope better with the inflation—and fear of inflation—that remains.

A SIMPLIFIED MODEL OF THE ECONOMY

It is useful to consider the economy as having two parts or aspects. One is real and tangible, the other is symbolic and abstract. The first includes factories, workers, managers, plants, vehicles, equipment, skill, training, and so on. Anyone can observe, photograph, describe, and pretty well understand what is going on in the real economy. There isn't even much difference between the real economies of a socialist and a capitalist society at the same stage of development.

The symbolic economy is the world of accounting, stocks and bonds, budgets and fiscal issues, and, above all, money and credit. The symbolic economy is important in all societies, but much more so in a politically free, market-oriented capitalist system than in a centralized, command-operated socialist economy. Indeed, in an advanced capitalist country, which is driven mostly by market forces and which has a high degree of personal and political freedom, the symbolic economy may, as in the case of the United States today, dominate the real economy, or at least until recently be the main concern of the political decision-makers and economic analysts.

Looking at the real and symbolic economies from the point of view of historical development, the crucial impetus for a primitive economy's "takeoff" into industrialization could have come from either sector, but most of the critical issues were in the tangible economy. They included capital accumulation and investment, productivity, training, organization, entrepreneurship, and so on. Hence at this stage of development (early in the Great Transition) economists tended to be supply-oriented and "micro" rather than demand-oriented and "macro." Somewhat later during the early twentieth century and heyday of the quantity theory of money put forth by the noted Yale economist Irving Fisher (the concepts of the so-called monetarists that the level of economic activity is largely determined by the quantity of money) and even more during the Keynesian revolution, as well as during the initial popularity of Friedman concepts, there was much less interest in the real economy, and much more in symbolic economic aggregates (the GNP, money supply, total debt, etc.) and in the study and control of these aggregates. When Keynes was questioned about his lack of interest in supply-side issues, he argued that if the demand-oriented policies were appropriate, then supply issues would handle themselves. He was basically right at the time.

In an advanced, efficient, and dynamic economy in which there are few restraints (social limits to growth) on the supply side, the objective is to make the symbolic economy work well, to see to it that the structure of credit, interest, money, and so on is operating appropriately. Adam Smith pointed out the extraordinary capability of the "invisible hand of the market," the system of prices created by the interaction of the symbolic and real economies. In a healthy capitalist economy this "invisible hand" automatically coordinates the whole economic system: it allocates resources, provides information, structures the system of incentives and disincentives, and determines the level of economic activity.

The need for this kind of decentralized, "invisible" adjustment mechanism is obviously not as great in a command economy as in a capitalist one. Whereas an army or village economy can be operated by centralized coordination, it is almost impossible to manage a modern complex economic system by centralized direction. Thus almost all centralized economies soon develop gray and black markets to supplement the official market—often in very important ways. They also have to have extraordinarily large inventories to make up for the rigidity of centralized planning, and they still don't do too well. And contrary to much current discussion, computers and economic models don't yet make much difference. Modern dynamic economies are still too complex—and change too rapidly—to be closely guided by a centralized computer model or a group of experts in offices in the capital city.

But the formerly superb system of coordination in the United States of giving incentives, signals, and information by prices and profits is no longer working properly. The most obvious reason stems from overdoing Keynes' lack of concern for supply issues. This is both a characteristic and a danger of an emerging post-industrial economy (such as ours) and perhaps of a mature post-industrial economy as well. One can almost define a post-industrial economy as one in which productivity and capital accumulation are so large and effective that they are taken for granted; the society has largely turned its attention to other matters. But disregard—or benign neglect—of the real economy, whether it occurs because a society is post-industrial or, as in our case, because the symbolic, demand-oriented economy worked so well, can lead to a combination of indifference and hostility. In the last twenty years we have seen the result of taking entrepreneurships, productivity, capital accumulation, and investment for granted. The result is a crisis caused by an emphasis on societal goals which are worthwhile, but which have brought about greater taxes and regulations and a reordering of traditional values. Many of these new goals interfered gravely with economic growth. The correction is to turn specifically to "supply-oriented" policies which focus on entrepreneurship, productivity, capital accumulation, investment, and ultimately on the proper operation of the "invisible hand of the market"—all things which an inflation interferes with.

One important way in which the symbolic economy conveys detailed information about the current state of the economy, as well as information about past and likely future conditions, is through its system of prices. Since price variations are meaningful only if the currency is stable, it is crucial to have a stable currency—at least in the long run. The United States had this for almost a century and a half. For most of the period from 1800 to 1950, Americans were willing to lend their money to the government or to private companies for periods as long as thirty years for a 2 to 3 percent (nominal) interest rate. The only time this changed was during or immediately after wars, and then only briefly. The ability to borrow money for thirty years at low interest rates made possible thirty-year plans and thirty-year write-offs. The confidence that a dollar today would be worth a dollar in thirty years also meant that one could arbitrage across time. But all this has almost totally disappeared.

Today, even if a bond is nominally thirty years, the interest rate contains at least a 10 percent allowance for inflation. This implies that in seven years the real value of the bond is only 50¢ on the dollar; in thirty years, it is worth only 5¢ on the dollar. We would argue that as much as anything, the absence of genuine thirty-year bonds, upon which the United States was built (roads, bridges, railroads, canals, utilities, buildings) is the cause of many economic problems in the United States today. For example, an American businessman making an investment wants to earn 15–20 percent discounted cash flow after taxes. Before recent changes in tax laws this meant he had to earn 25–35 percent before taxes. He was, in effect, expecting to get his money back in three or four years. But very few projects pay off in three or four years; many pay off in thirty years (e.g., synthetic-fuels plants; see Chapter 6). One can argue that among the most urgent tasks of government is to help restore the thirty-year perspective, to allow once again for a long-term view and a long-term write-off; indeed, to encourage it. (We discuss this later, and in Chapter 6.)

The reason why contemporary American businessmen have such short-term perspectives is partly the result of the training given in American business schools, partly due to the system of executive bonuses tied to short-run results, and partly due to the fluidity of U.S. personnel which limits the interest in long-term results. But the main reason is simply that present accounting systems, financial modes of thought, and high interest rates literally force the average company into a high discount rate in its calculations of discounted cash flow. This automatically (perhaps too automatically) forces a very short-term perspective. But a long-term perspective is essential to the adequate economic development of this, or any, country.

TROUBLE WITH ACCOUNTING METHODS

One important problem in current accounting methods becomes apparent by looking at the annual report of any large American corporation today. The companies are required by SEC rules to keep books calculated according to three different principles: historical-cost accounting, inflation-indexed accounting, and replacement-value accounting.

Historical-cost calculation is the basic accounting system used for centuries and the one which most people are familiar with; the reports are supposed to set forth "fully and fairly" the condition of the company, and when there is no inflation it probably does an adequate if not totally satisfactory job. At the moment, most corporate managements still calculate and make decisions according to this accounting system. But it is often very, and sometimes totally, misleading.

Corporate managers and stockholders used to believe that the market price of their stock was determined by investors analyzing the results of the historic accounting. This is clearly not true, however, and it has not been true for almost all of the 1970s, during which the market focused on what was called the "quality of earnings," meaning that one must look past the accounting to see what is really happening. Thus the market has been very much concerned with the inventory evaluation method (LIFO or FIFO) or with the evaluation of assets on the books. Property purchased many years ago is often carried at a fraction of its real value (e.g., lumber companies carry land at a few cents per acre even when it's worth thousands of dollars). This is also true of capital-intensive assets whose book value does not reflect the effects of inflation, so that depreciation allowances are inadequate to cover eventual replacement costs.

For many companies, then, the bottom line as reported by historical-cost accounting is either incorrect or irrelevant. Depending on details, this method of accounting can overestimate or underestimate grossly the value of the company and its recent performance. Nevertheless, its results are used to guide most corporate decisions (and executive bonuses), though top managements are increasingly beginning to recognize its inadequacy. (General Electric has a program in which almost all of its senior personnel and many of its middle-level managers are put through lengthy courses in order to acquaint them fully with the principles of inflation accounting.)

In the second method of reporting, inflation-indexed accounting, the money figures are adjusted to be in constant dollars—an enormous improvement over historical-cost accounting. But probably even better, although more difficult and controversial, is the third system, replacement-value accounting, which tries to estimate the real value of various assets or index them by specific indices. In replacement-value accounting a genuine effort is made to represent "fully and fairly" the condition of the company by correcting for actual changes in real-world prices and costs.

The three different systems produce three very different sets of numbers; the second is an enormous improvement over the first, the third can be a significant improvement over the second. Unfortunately, they are utilized in reverse order of their quality.

To the extent that the invisible hand of the market is guided by historical-cost accounting, the capitalist system in the United States has both a bad compass and a bad rudder; it means that huge misallocations and inefficiencies are encouraged and ratified by a standard accounting system. The system may work better than a centralized one would, but the lack of better accounting methods is an extraordinary failure; the lack of institutional and instrumental fixes is a disaster. We suggest some short-term and ad hoc remedies in the next chapter; the basic remedy is to eliminate the inflation and deal better with the remaining expectation of it.

THEORIES OF INFLATION

One basic theory of inflation is provided by the monetarists; in simplified terms, it begins with the following equation:

$$\text{GNP} = MV$$
$$= (\text{quantity of money}) \times (\text{velocity})$$

This equation is really more conceptual or symbolic than real. M is the total quantity of money available and V is its velocity, the average number of times per year the money is turned over—i.e., spent. The product is the total value of all transactions involving the sale of goods or services. This is proportional to the GNP. Since V is normally defined by dividing the gross national product by M, we can take the proportionality constant as equal to 1. We can then say: "The value of the GNP is determined by the product of total quantity of money, multiplied by the number of times it is spent per year."

Let us assume for the moment that the spending of money (velocity) is constant or firmly predictable so that the value of the GNP varies solely by the quantity of money available. Let us assume also that the total amount of goods and services being produced is below the country's theoretical capacity. If one then increases the amount of money available, the GNP goes up (mostly because some of the surplus capacity is used to produce more goods and services), but the value of the money remains relatively constant. This process continues until production capacity is strained, at which point it is likely that the price, more than the quantity, of goods and services will go up (i.e., the value of money will go down and inflation will result). The process can also be reversed. Either way, it becomes very complicated in the real world. In particular, there are important lags from the time the quantity of money is changed to the time the GNP is changed.

Thus, the value of money (or the price level) is related to the availability of GNP (goods and services) and the supply of money, the price of money (i.e., the interest rate is related to the supply and demand for credit), and the likelihood of changes in the value of money. While the price of money thus is related to the supply of money, the relationship is not simple, since it is determined by the supply and demand of credit, which is not at all the same as the supply and demand of money. The most common definitions are known as M_1B and M_2. M_1B is the sum of the cash in the hands of the public plus the total of demand deposits (checking accounts in commercial banks) plus NOW accounts. M_2 includes all of the above plus savings deposits and money funds.

A simple graph (Figure 5-1) suggests that the average rate of monetary growth for the past three years provides a good rule of thumb for estimating the current trend rate of inflation. Almost everybody (Monetarists and Keynesians) now believe that wringing inflation out of the system will require steady and persistent declines in the growth rate of the money supply.

This concept is not as simple as it looks. Indeed, it is in some ways counter-intuitive (as opposed to various cost-push theories of inflation). For example, assume there is an increase in the cost of imported oil. Does that automatically cause inflation—i.e., push up such indices as the CPI or GNP deflator? The monetarist would say no, that if the government kept the money supply fixed, buyers would be forced to allocate the cash available among imported oil and all other goods and services. Since the price of oil has gone up, there would be a decrease in oil consumption as well as a decrease in the purchase of other goods and services,* leading eventually to reduced production. The ultimate effect would be a readjustment (sometimes painful, since it may involve bankruptcies and un-

---

* If the oil is imported, this represents a real rise in costs to the country, a decrease in the standard of living, in savings, or in more importation of capital. If the oil is domestic, it may just be a transfer of income to the owners of the oil, and the average standard of living or savings is not necessarily affected. If as a result of increased prices there is increased oil production in the country and this oil costs more than the oil used to cost, then there is still a loss in the performance of the economy. We therefore think of both the imported higher-priced oil and the use of domestic higher-cost oil as "impoverishing events." We will discuss later that when one indexes certain kinds of income, it is probably wrong to include these effects; we should include only that part of the inflation which can be thought of as a pure monetary issue. Impoverishing events which occur quite suddenly are called "supply-side shocks."

Figure 5-1

Money and GNP Growth

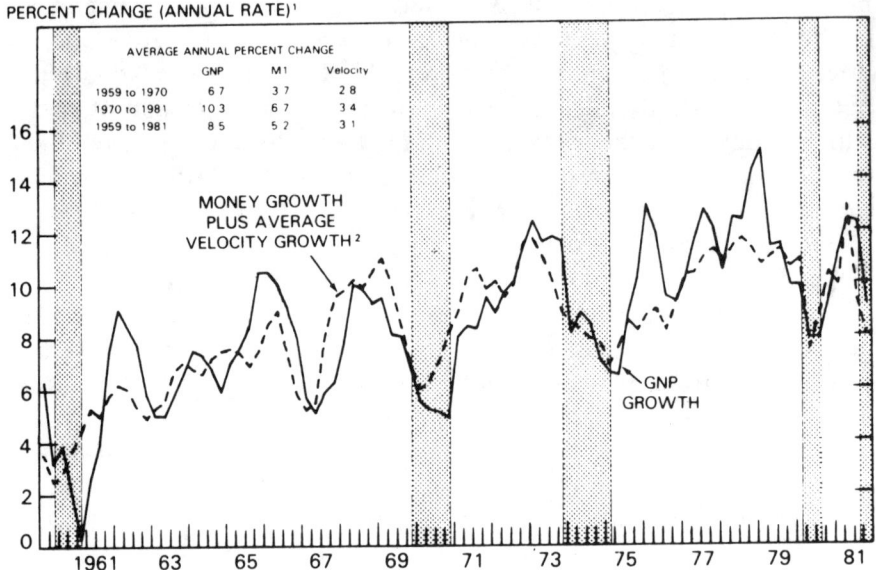

[1] PERCENT CHANGE IN 4-QUARTER MOVING AVERAGES OF SEASONALLY ADJUSTED MONEY STOCK (M1) AND GNP.

[2] AVERAGE VELOCITY GROWTH IS AVERAGE ANNUAL PERCENT CHANGE OVER THE PERIOD 1959 TO 1981.

NOTE.—SHADED AREAS INDICATE RECESSIONS AS DEFINED BY THE NATIONAL BUREAU OF ECONOMIC RESEARCH.

SOURCES: DEPARTMENT OF COMMERCE AND BOARD OF GOVERNORS OF THE FEDERAL RESERVE SYSTEM.

employment) of the price level of other commodities so that average prices remain about the same.

There is great pressure on the government not to force that readjustment. Usually the government prefers some inflation—which diffuses the pain over a larger number of people and over a longer time. Furthermore, if there is a widely held money illusion most people won't even know they are hurt. Therefore the government, rather than accept a painful readjustment, will expand the money supply to maintain purchasing power.

An increase in the price of oil does cause immediate inflationary pressure, since other prices tend to have downward inflexibility, but to what degree this pressure materializes as price increases depends on whether or not monetary policy accommodates it (i.e., is "permissive"). This position is now widely accepted, even by so-called Keynesians who tend to emphasize the effects of fiscal policy and downplay the importance of monetary choices, in part because they believe that as a practical matter these choices are determined more by the political realities than by the economic conditions.

Strongly influencing the analysis of inflation and anti-inflation policies are a number of typical differences between people who think of themselves as "mainly monetarist" and those who consider themselves "mainly Keynesian." Many of the arguments between the two groups result from their basic perspectives: Keynesians tend to be relatively liberal, monetarists tend to be relatively conservative. There are good historical and practical reasons why each group takes the approach it does, but they are not necessarily based on logic and rational economic analysis.

The basic difference between the monetarists and Keynesians is on the importance of quantity of money vs. interest rates. Keynesians, unlike the monetarists, tend to believe that the cost of credit, i.e., interest, is much more likely to affect total demand for goods and services than the actual quantity of money available. In addition, for ideological more than strictly logical reasons, the two groups usually differ on the size of the gap between actual and potential GNP and employment. Keynesians tend both to estimate potential GNP and potential employment on the high side and to think of the economy as being less than fully employed. Monetarists tend to feel that the gap is smaller and the inflationary pressures greater or closer. There is also a difference in their beliefs about the practicality and importance of trying to avoid and alleviate even mild recessions and the importance of business profitability and of a positive business environment (i.e., positive in political, legal, and social terms).

The two schools also differ on the relative importance of reducing inflation vs. reducing unemployment. Keynesians argue that prices and wages are very sticky and the country would be unwilling (and shouldn't be willing) to endure the hardships connected with maintaining deflationary pressures over a long period of time. They believe such measures are relatively ineffective and the consequences severe and unfairly distributed. Monetarists argue that the country is (or could be) made much more willing to accept these hardships, which in any case they do not believe would be as great as the Keynesians estimate. Any unfairness which may result is either inevitable, unfortunate, or exaggerated. Inflation, according to monetarists, is even more unfair. It should be noted that at the moment there is an unprecedented downward flexibility in U.S. wages. This is one reason why the tight money policy may work out better than is usually expected.

Although monetarists feel that prices are relatively flexible downward, they usually don't support jaw-boning or other income policies (attempts to control wages and prices). They regard the tendency of many Keynesians to encourage jaw-boning to be a mark of a basically illusionary approach to economic issues. We tend to agree. For example, at a time when there was very little jaw-boning by either Nixon or Ford, American labor unions were quite responsible about enacting wage increases, which barely kept pace with inflation. They would not have been so responsible, however, if they had been jaw-boned. Union leaders would rather have been criticized for irresponsible behavior by outsiders than risk the suspicion of union members that they were either currying favor with the administration or showing a lack of courage in representing the interests of their members. (It is even more unwise to threaten impersonal auction markets such as the major exchanges, as happened briefly in September 1981 when the markets refused to respond favorably to a legislative victory by the Reagan administration.)

In addition to Keynesians and monetarists are the supply-siders, a "new" group which now plays a significant role in shaping economic policies. Emphasizing the importance of incentives in stimulating savings and investment, supply-siders believe that ideally the incentives should be given directly to the consumer or the investor, not to business. They tend to accept several monetarist concepts, but many are very hostile to current monetary policy, which they feel is eroding or even destroying the beneficial impact of the Reagan tax cuts. Many monetarists are equally hostile to the size of these tax cuts and their early impact in fueling inflationary expectations and making monetary policy unnecessarily difficult. Many supply-siders are now recommending a return to a gold standard instead of using tight money policies, as a method of stabilizing the currency. We will argue (later in this chapter and the next) that whatever the merits of using gold—and there are several—it is not going to be an automatic or quick fix; it is likely to have many of the same problems as the current tight money policy, and in any case has almost no chance of being accepted in the immediate future.

INFLATION CORRECTION BY APPROPRIATE INDEXING

In the OECD world (except in France, and to a lesser extent among the opposition in England), inflation is now almost universally considered a problem of major importance, even more so than the problem of unemployment. This has been true for most of the last five years but has been difficult for many people to accept. In fact, many still believe that the idea of accepting unemployment to reduce inflation is immoral. Nevertheless, at various points during the recent recession even the unemployed felt that inflation was the more serious problem. As one congressman said, "Ten percent of the people in my district suffer from unemployment but one hundred percent suffer from inflation." As a result, most Western governments have now come to recognize inflation as a political and moral problem as much as an economic one.

Further, almost no one's perspective is now obscured by the monetary illusion, and in any case, whatever illusion still exists cannot last forever. While many individuals may not react immediately to a 1 to 2 percent inflation, they prefer not to suffer even this loss if they can avoid it. Reaction to a 2 to 3 percent inflation is much quicker and may destabilize the system. Eventually, both government and private employees will insist on higher salary increases, savers and investors will want higher returns, and so on. An appropriate index for correcting inflation, especially in a system in which indexing is a major element in private and public contracts, is therefore very much needed.

There are two very different ways of indexing and, by extension, of correcting for inflation. One is "preset"; it tries to estimate future inflation from present trends and then factors an estimated correction into long-term contracts. The other is "ad hoc"; it follows the actual inflation and adjusts contracts accordingly (based upon either the consumer price index, the wholesale price index, the GNP deflator, or some other economic indicator).

Ad hoc indexing has many pros and cons but is usually a much better idea than preset indexing, which, given that the rate of inflation is uncertain, can be expensive or risky. Consider, for example, a twenty-year raw-material contract. If mine owners wish to protect themselves against future inflation by a preset escalating contract, they would presumably today insist on something like 8 to 10 percent. Buyers probably would not be willing to allow more than 5 percent, because they cannot lock themselves into a contract by which they would stand to lose a great deal if inflation fell much below 5 percent. It would be very difficult for the two sides to get together without resort to ad hoc indexed contracts. In fact, the raw-materials industry would probably collapse. Economic theorists would offer a great many explanations for the collapse, but the only correct explanation would be the inability to index contracts in a mutually acceptable manner.* The same obviously holds for labor or any other long-term contracts.

One serious defect of preset indexing is that under current conditions, it creates a vested interest in continuing inflation. Consider, for example, a government bond that has a fixed interest rate of 14 percent for thirty years and is not recallable before twenty-five. If the inflation goes to zero, the interest rate on the bond is about 12 percent more than it should be and represents a very high debt-service cost. If a government had a large stock of such bonds outstanding there would be heavy pressure to maintain inflation at least as high as the average inflation premium built into the debt.

On the other hand, sometimes the appropriate index for ad hoc indexing does not exist. It is now generally recognized that the so-called cost-of-living index has exaggerated inflation in most countries where it has been used because it has focused too much attention on urban prices (in the United States this index has had much more serious troubles, as discussed later). In the United States, the old wholesale price index was even more distorting because it double- and triple-counted energy and usually registered list prices, not transaction costs (which are often lower than list prices).

Almost as crucial as the need and use of an appropriate index is the manner in which the indexing is carried out. Consider, for example, a home mortgage. One can index either the principal or the interest rate, with quite different results in terms of the cash flow, and perhaps the taxes, of the lender and the borrowers. The same is true of government bonds.

In the future, people who issue and buy bonds or who make and give mortgages are going to be deeply concerned about inflation. Unless the

---

* We prefer multiple explanations for most phenomena and are suspicious of single-cause explanations, but sometimes a single cause is correct. The general bias against the seeming simplicity and narrowmindedness of those who argue for single causes of complex phenomena militates against even experts' recognizing the single cause when it actually occurs.

lender is protected from the risk of inflation, he will want to have a premium, and this premium could be quite large. The borrower has to be protected from a deflation that burdens him with excessive interest payments. In order to make risk premiums unnecessary it will be useful to index ad hoc, which in many cases is best done if the principal, instead of the interest, is indexed. This should be clear from the following example. Assume that one issues a standard $1,000, thirty-year bond at 3 percent (standard during the period from 1800 to 1950). Such a bond clearly would be much too risky for a lender today. Assume therefore it is indexed (using, say, the GNP deflator or reformed CPI). If there is no inflation, the interest will be $30 a year. If inflation is 10 percent, the interest will go to $133. This is an increase by more than a factor of 4 in terms of cash flow—and is unacceptably high. If instead the principal is indexed and there is a 10 percent inflation, then the principal will go from $1,000 to $1,100 (in terms of constant dollars, it in effect stays at $1,000). The interest now goes to $33 (3 percent of $1,100) and there has been only a 10 percent increase in cash flow (actually unchanged in constant dollars).

It should be noted that by 1974, savings and loan associations and others were aware that it was dangerous to write a straight-interest mortgage. They tried various methods of having variable interest. One technique was to have the mortgage renegotiated every five years or so. If the two parties couldn't agree on the new interest, they simply applied some index to the interest. This has caused a lot of troubles, however. Many such mortgages were made in 1975 and 1976 when the interest rate was about 8 percent. But in the next five or six years, interest rates on mortgages rose to as much as 20 percent, and many people who could afford the 8 percent mortgage simply could not afford the 20 percent. When it came time to renegotiate mortgages, the homeowners found they couldn't carry the house any more and there were many foreclosures.

Some of the banks have suggested the following scheme: that instead of increasing the interest by 10 percent, they would take the increased interest and add it to the mortgage principal. This is called a "reverse amortization" mortgage and is a bad name because actually the principal is going up only in nominal terms; in real terms it is going down. It should be noted that this concept of adding the increased interest to the principal can, by changing the payment to correspond to the (nominally) increased value of the principal, be made the exact equivalent of indexing the principal by the increase in the inflation rate. The "reverse amortization" is then only a simple way of applying the concept of indexing the principal; this does not mean that the terms of the mortgage would have to be extended, only that the payments would be increased proportionately.

We think that it is most important that the concept of indexing the principal be applied generally in the future. If it is, then many of the current problems we are having with inflation, particularly the extreme front-end loading of the payments, would be eliminated or decreased to the point where they would no longer make difficult or impossible much current financing.

It is also important for the government to extend the maturities of its debt and to do so in a way which does not create a vested interest in continuing the inflation or which, to put it differently, does not bring about huge losses if inflation stops. The best way would be to index the principal of future bonds with either the GNP deflator or MCI (monetary correction indicator, discussed later).

It is true that the government, by *not* indexing, has made huge gains from inflation. It has in effect penalized the bondholders, who trusted the government and the stability of its currency, by billions of dollars. Today, however, it seems certain that if the government carries through its anti-inflation programs (even more certain if they improve them), then inflation will go down fairly rapidly and the government will penalize itself by selling long-term bonds at fixed rates. If it indexes the principal, then these bonds would in effect be written in constant dollars (or if the MCI were used, somewhat less than constant dollars) and the government would be able to come down from the inflation to a soft landing. The bonds would not double, triple, or even quadruple in value as rates went down to the normal 2 percent or so.

Furthermore, by indexing the principal the government reduces its cash-flow requirements and in so doing greatly helps the anti-inflation program (see Chapter 6). It might also find some new markets for long-term bonds that it couldn't attract without indexing (bond buyers who want a hedge against inflation). But it is important in every case that the principal and not the interest rate be indexed, because the latter does not immediately decrease cash-flow requirements and could increase them at a most inappropriate time. Such a system would restore the principal of the long-term 2–3 percent bond which, as noted, has always been so important for the United States.

Finally, if the government wanted to limit its paper losses, it could set an upper limit on the amount of indexing it will actually allow—e.g., no more than 20 percent a year.

One question immediately arises: Should the increase in the indexed principal be taxable? We would argue it should not be. After all, it is only a correction; it is not real income. This would begin to establish an important principle (see Chapter 10): eliminating as an income or expense that part of the interest that corrects for the inflation. The fact that it is allowed as a deduction is one of the reasons the tight money policy isn't working well. Even a 20 percent interest that is half inflation and half real is effectively zero after taxes in real terms to a taxpayer in the 50 percent bracket.

We can think of no "simple" change that would be more important in both fixing the current inflation and to some degree guarding against a renewed vicious circle (as described in Chapter 1) than this reform in the tax treatment of interest. The government would no longer be subsidizing the borrower by allowing payments on the principal (the inflationary component of the interest) to be deducted as a genuine expense.

APPROPRIATE INDEXING TO DISTINGUISH BETWEEN PURE MONETARY INFLATION AND IMPOVERISHING EVENTS

In recent years there has existed the classic condition for worldwide inflation, that is, "too much money chasing too few goods," whereby most of the "too much money" was created by the United States. Many hundreds of billions of dollars went abroad because the United States ran a larger negative balance of payments than was needed in order to satisfy world needs for liquidity—i.e., for enough dollars to support a growing world trade. These dollars were later devalued to the short-term profit of the United States. (For example, when the Smithsonian reevaluation of 1971 occurred, overseas holders of U.S. dollar-denominated assets lost about $50 billion in purchasing power overnight. This was called the "biggest single ripoff in world history" by the *Financial Times* of London.)

The "too few goods" part of the inflationary syndrome was also partly caused by U.S. policies. The United States actually benefited from excessively large deficits in its balance of payments. For one thing, it obtained, in effect, interest-free (or very low-interest) loans. For another, by being able to import goods in exchange for pieces of paper, the U.S. could better cope with its own inflation, making available imported goods without having to send exports abroad. While reducing the "too few goods" pressures at home it increased them around the world.

Pure monetary inflation is similar to the classical debasement of currency indulged in by governments since the invention of coinage. In principle, however, a government can fairly easily correct for a pure monetary inflation. Assume that a country has no inflation. The government decides to double the currency in circulation, but makes sure that everything is carefully indexed or adjusted so the system (including tax brackets) can make the appropriate corrections. As a result, every price doubles. Nothing is changed except that what was once $1 is now $2. Apart from the "monetary illusion," everybody is just as well or badly off as before. Further, the government no longer profits from the inflation and thus is unlikely to be tempted to follow inflationary policies.

Imagine now that 20 percent of the gross national product is physically destroyed. There is no method of making corrections (such as indexing) to restore the status quo. But the government does not reduce the amount of money in circulation. There will now also be an inflation, but the difference between it and a pure monetary inflation is dramatic: the latter is more or less correctable; the former is a basically uncorrectable "impoverishing event."

If 20 percent of the gross national product is destroyed and half the country is protected from this "too few goods" inflation through some indexing scheme, then instead of everybody's income going down by roughly 20 percent, the indexed half of the country would find its real income preserved. The other 50 percent would have to take the full loss, so their real income would go down by 40 percent rather than by 20 percent. This is most unfair. If one wishes (as we do) to index long-term debt instruments, then it is important to index them in a way that makes a distinction between impoverishment and pure monetary inflation.

Two important areas in which indexing is needed to make such a distinction are Social Security and wages. There are two theories why Social Security pensions (and in many cases wages) should be indexed. One is that there is no reason why the recipients should lose at all if there is a general inflation. This theory is acceptable if the inflation is purely monetary. But if there is a serious impoverishing event, then Social Security recipients and wage earners should not lose more than their fair share. (Poll data indicates that the general public accepts this second concept.) Further, it has been suggested that Social Security be indexed either to the CPI or to the average increase in wages during the previous six months, whichever is smaller. Since the average increase in wages is likely to reflect the effects of impoverishing events, this suggestion would probably solve some of the problems that have occurred in the last two or three years.

For example, Social Security payments rose by 14 percent in July 1980—the increase in the CPI from the first quarter of 1979 to the first quarter of 1980. Of this 14 percent, only 10 percent was really appropriate. About 2 percent was due to the increased price of imported oil (an impoverishing event) and another 2 percent or so resulted from the way the CPI measures (incorrectly) the impact of increased interest rates on mortgages and the increased cost of homes. The latter are being misinterpreted as current costs rather than as investments which occur over many years, and the index also assumes that everyone who has a mortgage is paying current interest. (It also ignores that the inflationary component of the interest is really a payment of principal.) The case against including overstated housing and mortgage-interest costs in adjusting Social Security payments is especially persuasive. Very few Social Security recipients have found that their cost of living went up in 1979 because they negotiated a mortgage or bought a house.

An even better idea is to have a special monetary correction indicator (MCI) which could be used for most indexing purposes. The indicator could be a reformed CPI, but one which is also adjusted for changes caused by impoverishing events. In other words, the MCI would reflect only that part of the inflation which was a pure monetary inflation. And while an MCI correction is difficult to calculate, the problems that can arise as a result are usually manageable. In fact, they are more manageable than those caused by an index that includes impoverishing events, in which case the index itself can help touch off an explosive inflation (such as happened during the 1973 and 1979 oil shocks). The government should in any case continue to publish the CPI or equivalent index to let people know what is happening to the purchasing power of their money. There should be no attempt to fool people that their purchasing power is unchanged.

A SUMMARY PERSPECTIVE ON INDEXING

To summarize our position on indexing: if used appropriately, and if done gradually or selectively, official and private ad hoc indexing can:

- —increase downward flexibility of prices, wages, interest rates, and otherwise facilitate a soft landing from an ongoing inflation;
- —reduce the need to guess the inflation rate (and therefore the premium to be paid for uncertainty), reduce other costs of adjustment to inflation, and restore faith and credibility in contracts. If applied to the principal rather than the interest, indexing will revive the validity of long-term bonds and mortgages;
- —prevent inflationary gains to government and others;
- —serve ends of relative social justice, business stability, and equity (at least the inequities are chosen by the government);
- —prevent excessive "inflation protection reactions" by a population that has already been "sensitized to," or at least alerted to the possibility of, an inflation and tries excessively to protect itself;
- —encourage savings and investment (particularly long-term); and
- —make accounting, decision-making, and discussion more realistic and less distorted.

Indexing is not a panacea. Indeed, it can be very dangerous and, if used inappropriately, can:

- —try to compensate for the uncompensable, e.g., hide a real increase in the price of oil or a change in international terms of trade;
- —destroy certain automatic compensatory measures that mitigate an inflationary shock and add automatic compensatory measures that increase the effect of the shock;
- —eliminate important lags, austerities, and political pressures which slow down or create pressure against inflation;
- —destroy important utilities associated with having a reliable and constant monetary frame of reference;
- —cause the degree of inflation to be even more politically motivated and in effect create a new area for "bungling government interference" and for making the simple complex; and
- —shift a magnified burden to the unindexed or less indexed groups, i.e., shield some groups from impoverishing events or supply-side shocks and thus make other groups bear even greater costs.

SOCIAL AND GOVERNMENTAL FORCES OF INFLATION

In all OECD countries the government has, more than ever before, assumed a larger role of consumer, employer, income redistributor, and regulator. Of course, there are good reasons for the expansion of these roles, but each generates inflationary pressures, especially if done badly or to an excess.

Excessive governmental expenditures (even if part of a balanced budget) can help create pressures for inflation by being a general drag on efficiency and productivity. This is not only a question of high taxes. When the government spends money, it tends to be a bureaucratic ally and politically motivated, and has a very low level of resistance to price increases; indeed, it responds poorly to the market mechanism in general. It is much less efficient from an economic and growth point of view than if the private sector makes the same expenditures.

Aspects of what we call "regulatory income transfers" (or "mandated transfers") are an example of the government's inefficient—indeed, harmful—policies when it forces public or private groups to spend their money to benefit other groups.

The National Transportation Act, which concerns transportation for the handicapped, prohibits any special measures which remove the handicapped people from "the mainstream of American society." In a sense, this comes directly out of civil-rights legislation when the country was convinced that "separate but equal" is not in fact equal. It was therefore mandated that people in wheelchairs must have full access to subways. The Washington, D.C., transit authority spent about $2 billion to make this access possible. On average, less than fifty people in wheelchairs use the facilities each day, resulting in an extraordinary capital investment for fifty people—$40 million per chair. Moreover, most of the potential users confined to wheelchairs don't like the subway—they have a better system, a system of vans. Any handicapped person can call the dispatcher and ask to be picked up and driven anywhere. This service is available twenty-four hours a day, free, and is relatively inexpensive for the city to maintain. However, since it is separate from the "mainstream" subway, Washington bureaucrats argued it was not equal.

The Department of Transportation subsequently ordered New York City to "mainstream" its own subway system—at a cost of about $2 billion and a reduction of about 25 percent in the number of trains available during rush hour. The city instead offered to put in the same van system as Washington. The Department of Transportation said New York would lose $400 million a year in government subsidies if it did not comply, even though the city, as well as its subway system, was already in severe financial trouble. Fortunately, the Reagan administration reversed the ultimatum.

One can associate the large deficits of the mid-1960s with improper financing of the joint Vietnam War/Great Society package. (It should be noted that contrary to most popular and expert belief, the increases in the civilian budget caused by expenditures for Great Society programs were much larger than the increases in the military budget. The two together basically broke the system.)

The evaluation of social attitudes and government response that brought about the National Transportation Act and other regulatory mandates is perhaps the central factor behind the upward drift of inflation rates over the past several years. However, most of the traumatizing effects of that inflation have passed through the system, although inflation rates in most countries remain high (but now show signs of fading away). Most governments have not significantly changed the ways in which they go about their business. There are still many politically powerful (conflicting) claims on output, and governments still tend to be excessively involved in issues of equity, income distribution, and social welfare. Since all of these issues have an inflationary bias, one cannot expect inflation rates to fall significantly unless there is a fundamental change in our approach to solving social and ethical questions. The Reagan administration is making that change by reorganizing national priorities: economic efficiency over social programs; long-range benefits over short-range gains; and most important, a concentration on making the United States a great global power rather than just a great society, though since this last costs money, in the short run it probably increases inflationary pressures. It should be noted that Reagan's "reorganization of priorities" is not being done at the expense of programs put in by Roosevelt or even Kennedy. They represent a political rollback or reform of programs initiated or increased by Johnson or by subsequent administrations.

THE GOLD STANDARD*

There has recently been much discussion about how gold might be helpful in solving some of our monetary problems. The recently established Gold Commission may suggest that the United States return to some kind of gold standard. But there are other possibilities in the flexible use of gold, not all of which are dependent on a return to a full gold standard (some of which are discussed in the next chapter).

First, however, it might be useful to note that different attitudes toward gold are more likely to be determined by social and cultural background than by rational analysis. Over the years we have held many seminars in Europe and have often asked our audiences how they feel about gold. Until the rise to $800 per ounce (an event which compelled respect for gold from almost everybody), people who were raised in an Atlantic Protestant culture almost invariably considered gold to be "a barbaric remnant of a prerational past" (the Keynesian position and phrase). Those raised in Catholic or other non-Atlantic-Protestant cultures thought of gold as a method of social coordination among countries and individuals with many different backgrounds. The first group also often thought of gold as something "dug up at great expense, moved at great expense, and reburied in a vault at great expense." The non-Atlantic-Protestant cultures thought of gold as "dug up at reasonable expense, moved at moderate expense, and stored in a vault at trivial expense."

In response to the query "Why do so many French families have thousands of dollars in gold stored (or hidden) where they can get their hands on it relatively easily?" the immediate answer was "As a hedge against inflation." The real reason is that many Frenchmen (and most others not raised in an Atlantic-Protestant culture) don't really believe in their government and its basic integrity. They fear that events of man-made or natural violence could break down the social order and make paper money and credit worthless. Under such circumstances even a little gold

* Gold, platinum, and silver are precious metals in part because of their intrinsic physical qualities, but also because they are accepted worldwide as a store of value, a medium of exchange, and a standard of value. If one had to invent a more or less universally acceptable substance or commodity, it would be almost impossible to get agreement on what this should be. While the "precious metals" would clearly be candidates, some would want an energy standard, others diamonds, and so on. The problem could probably not be solved by voluntary social coordination. Fortunately, history has already solved it, and it is probably important not to destroy the historical solution.

would help buy essentials or bribe officials (think of trying to bribe a border guard with an SDR*). With regard to a gold standard, therefore, most judgments (including those of experts) are culturally determined.

One of the major arguments in favor of returning to gold is that it would help provide a means of insuring (relative) price stability over the long term. This, in turn, would help bring back the thirty-year bond, again making it possible to engage in the long-term contracts which we believe are so useful to economic development. But the primary pro-gold position holds that the operation of the standard is more or less automatic, greatly decreasing the extent of human intervention required for its efficient operation.

Even enthusiasts for the gold standard will admit that in practice no mechanism is completely automatic; that even with a gold standard, adjustment would have to be supervised and judiciously carried out by mere mortals. And it makes a difference how this is done. Nonetheless, a properly designed gold standard has some elements of relative automaticity, and the perception of automaticity could go a long way toward restoring public faith in an "objective" monetary system.

Those against the gold standard offer a number of reasons why the United States would be foolish to return to what they consider to be an outdated system. Gold is expensive; many instabilities may be created if there are fluctuations in either the price or production of the standard. Most important, a rigid gold standard, by forcing rapid adjustments, is also likely to lead to relatively high short-term price instability and unemployment (even if it helps make long-term stability more likely—in fact, this may be the basic trade-off of having or not having a gold standard, that is, the trade between long-term and short-term stability).

We think there are valid arguments on both sides, and that in any case the outcome of this issue is going to come too late to affect the coming of "the coming boom," though it could affect its staying power. If we had to take a position it would probably coincide most closely with that of Joseph Schumpeter, who defended the gold standard (assuming it would be adopted worldwide) as follows:

> It links every nation's money rates and price levels with the money rates and price levels of all the other nations that are "on gold." It is

---

* An SDR (special drawing right) does not even have an independent paper existence; it is a mark on a magnetic tape or an entry in a ledger—the quintessential symbol of a symbolic concept.

Controlling and Alleviating Inflation and Its Effects

extremely sensitive to government expenditure and even to attitudes or policies that do not involve expenditure directly, for example, to foreign policy, to certain policies of taxation and, in general, to precisely all those policies that violate the principles of economic liberalism. This is the reason why gold is so unpopular now and also why it was so popular in a bourgeois era.

It imposes restrictions upon governments or bureaucracies that are much more powerful than is parliamentary criticism.

It is both the badge and the guarantee of bourgeois freedom—of freedom not simply of the bourgeois interest, but of freedom in the bourgeois sense. From this standpoint a man may quite rationally fight for it, even if fully convinced of the validity of all that has ever been urged against it on economic grounds. From the standpoint of *etatisme* and planning, a man may not less rationally condemn it, even if fully convinced of the validity of all that has ever been urged for it on economic grounds.*

Whether or not it makes sense to return to any version of a gold standard, it is almost certain that the United States could not do so in the near future by itself. Such a unilateral action would create especially great problems. Most nations would probably not follow a U.S. lead until they saw how well it worked. Of course, if it worked well, people would want to write contracts in the now-stable dollar and this would put pressure on other countries to tie their currency to the U.S. dollar—i.e., also go on the gold standard. But until this happened there could be great pressures on the U.S. currency, as well as great resentment of the United States for forcing a new kind of economic order.

In addition, there would be great difficulties in picking the initial value of gold, difficulties which would be much greater if the value is determined by negotiations. But wherever the value is fixed, it must remain for an appreciable period. Any attempt to be flexible early in the experiment would be likely to be disastrous for the effectiveness of the standard; it would lose both its credibility and its ability reliably to exert monetary discipline. For all these reasons it is unlikely that much will happen in terms of returning to a gold standard in the next year or two.

But inflation, and especially the fear of inflation, can be dealt with in other ways. Specifically, some methods of unconventional financing, as

---

* Joseph Schumpeter, *History of Economic Analysis* (New York: Oxford, 1954).

discussed in the next chapter, can turn inflation-ridden investment choices into attractive options—and without taking such a controversial and difficult step as going on the gold standard. In reducing the pressures on a gold standard, however, these methods also make it easier to return to one should the government decide to do so. But basically the methods of unconventional financing are neutral with regard to an eventual move to a gold standard; they are simply worth pursuing by themselves.

CHAPTER 6

UNCONVENTIONAL FINANCING

The unavailability of conventional financing—i.e., the low-fixed-rate mortgage or bond—has made the use of unconventional financing extremely important. If properly used, it can help control, soften, or alleviate many of the problems caused by inflation or by the expectation or fear of inflation. Appropriate unconventional financing could also gradually reduce the system's downward rigidity (and correspondingly increase the effectiveness of a tight money policy).

Some concepts have already been applied and have had an important positive impact, e.g., variable-rate mortgages, without which the housing industry would have collapsed even more than it did. Other methods, such as those involving commodity bonds, are likely to be widely used in the next few years, while still others are more uncertain or controversial but could nevertheless prove very useful in putting excessive inflation behind us (e.g., separation of interest payments into a true income or expense component which compensates for inflation and which is neither a tax reduction for the borrower nor taxable income to the lender).

I first got interested in the subject of unconventional financing in 1974 when giving a series of talks to audiences drawn largely from savings and loan associations (S&Ls). I started each talk by mentioning that most S&Ls had made many low-interest loans—say, 6 percent—and that interest rates were now 12 percent. Most of the old mortgages lost about a third or more of their market value. As a result, 95 percent of the people I talked to probably worked for organizations which were technically insolvent in the sense that if the market value of their assets were compared with the sum of their liabilities, the latter would exceed the former by a very substantial amount. Their current net (market) value was therefore negative. I expected to be told that my remarks were irresponsible; I also expected some in the audience to say that *their* institutions were in the solvent 5 percent. Nobody protested. Rather, they assured me that everyone was in the same boat and knew it. I had said nothing new or controversial, though many would have felt better had I not said anything at all. The idea of liquidation—the danger and damages that would ensue if this theoretical collapse of financial values actually occurred—was one of the subjects that many believed would have been better left undiscussed.

In fact, in 1974, almost all the big banks in New York City were in the same boat. If one had added up the market value of their tanker loans, real estate investment trusts, and New York City bonds, then factored in the results of the Franklin Bank bankruptcy, the decline in value of various types of interest-bearing securities, and so on, one would have found the market value of the banks' assets, too, to be well below the market value of their liabilities.

The theoretical earning power of assets written down to their market value would be very high. In other words, if one holds a 6 percent mortgage and writes it down to 60¢ on the dollar because current interest rates are 12 percent, then the earning power of the asset is also 12 percent. That would mean a rapid recovery of financial health, making banks, S&Ls, etc., very, very profitable in terms of the percent return on the market value of their assets and in terms of the possibility for capital appreciation. Nevertheless, it is too risky for financial institutions to be even technically insolvent; the danger of liquidation, even if the absolute probability remained low, would be greatly increased, and there would be great losses if in fact liquidation did occur. I suggested in 1974 that it might be advisable to reform the system and that this could be done quite simply and expeditiously.

At the moment the situation is even worse. Even the nominal net worth (as opposed to that determined by current market values) of the savings and loan associations is rapidly eroding or turning negative. In 1980 many S&Ls were earning an average of about 14 percent on their loans, but paying about 14 percent on their deposits (including CDs). They were therefore not able to meet their overhead and operating expenses, which often were about 2 percent of their assets. These expenses had to come out of the S&Ls' nominal net worth, i.e., book capital and surplus, but they could be met in this way for only three or four years, since most S&Ls normally have about 6 or 8 percent equity. The result: a slight feeling of desperation.

The recent legislation allowing the S&Ls to issue tax-free all-savers certificates has made the outlook considerably brighter, but possibly at great expense to the government in terms of lessened federal tax receipts. (While the government estimated a tax loss of almost $5 billion, some plausible estimates run as high as $10 to $20 billion.) This loss of revenue comes at a time when there is a desperate need to reassure financial markets that the federal deficit is under control. If interest rates come down relatively soon, however, S&Ls will benefit even more and the cost to the government will be less. In turn, some reassurance will be reestablished.

INDEXING BOTH SIDES OF THE LEDGER

In 1974 we suggested that it was irresponsible to run a huge financial system in such a way that any sharp change in the inflation rate would cause a large number of institutions to become technically insolvent, especially if this solvency could be fixed rather easily. Our favorite "fix" called for the indexing of the principal of the deposit by some appropriate index such as a reformed CPI (or the GNP deflator or the MCI discussed in Chapter 5). Similarly, the principal of mortgages (or other loans) should be indexed by the same number. Both sides of the ledger would go up and down together—and without causing excessive cash-flow problems to either the lender or borrower. Had this been enacted a decade or two ago, it would, of course, have denied many homeowners the high profits they earned because they had fixed-rate mortgages, because the inflation was so great and because they could deduct the high interest from their income taxes. But the gain by the homeowners would mostly represent a loss by the depositors; and it is this kind of transfer of wealth which our society should not encourage or even tolerate.

If the principal of the mortgage were indexed, the initial cash flow (or rate at which the mortgage interest and principal is paid off) could be much lower than if the mortgage were made at a fixed interest rate. Indexing allows for both the anticipated inflation and the possibility that the estimate will be wrong. As noted, the cash-flow requirements for the borrower are about ¼ to ½ less if the principal, rather than the interest, is indexed. Any risk not covered by indexing the principal could be corrected by a premium on the interest.

If a reformed CPI or the GNP deflator is used as an index, then both the deposits and principal amounts of the mortgage are in more or less constant dollars, cancelling out the effects of inflation on the value of the money. If a monetary correction indicator (MCI) is used, then the indexing is usually less than would be required to keep everything in constant dollars. If the inflation is greater than the MCI, the depositor does not gain quite as much, while the mortgagee (homeowner) appears to gain a little more but in fact comes out even if his income is also indexed to the MCI.

This concept of using the same index on both sides of the transaction (and the ledgers) could also be used for pensions, insurance situations, and many bonds. The indexing organization could invest the fees it received into manufacturing some product or furnishing a service which would also be indexed. Again, the same index would be used on both sides of the transaction even if not always on the same ledger. The recipient of the pension or insurance or the buyer of the bond would be protected from inflation, while the mortgage holder would benefit from the low cash flow and low initial rates (which might well go up over the life of the mortgage, but then presumably so would the holder's income).

COMMODITY BONDS

An idea which has recently appeared, and which looks as if it may be widely exploited in the near future, is to borrow money on the basis of an instrument which is denoted in—or indexed to—some commodity. The commodity normally chosen is of a sufficient quantity that it is either held by the company issuing the bonds or can be produced by investing the proceeds of the loan. In either case the ability of the company to repay the bonds is not critically dependent on the future value of the commodity market, but only on its ability to produce that commodity. In other words, the borrowed money is invested in productive facilities that make more likely the reliable repayment of the bond.

An obvious application is the use of oil bonds to finance synthetic-fuel plants. Even problems such as the uncertainty over the costs of building and operating the plants would be reduced. If the project is financed by oil bonds the cost of the final product becomes less sensitive to these uncertainties. But the primary purpose of using the bonds is to make practical and acceptable the extension of the write-off period to twenty or thirty years and to eliminate the front-end loading of finance charges—indeed, sometimes to reverse it to a back-end loading.

Assume for the moment that there is neither inflation nor fear of inflation, and that we could totally finance a synthetic-fuel plant with guaranteed government loans at about 2 percent interest. The average cost of the capital, therefore, would be about 2 percent both before and after taxes (interest is not taxed). But if instead of writing the bonds, say, in terms of $1,000 payable in the year 2012 (i.e., in thirty years), we made it 40 barrels of oil payable in 2012 (assuming a $1,000 bond and $25/bbl as the price of oil), and if instead of paying $20 (2 percent) a year interest, we offer the bondholder the equivalent of .8 of a barrel of oil annually, then as long as there is no inflation and no expectation of inflation and the price of oil remains constant, the result is exactly the same as denominating the bonds and interest in dollars of a constant value.

Now let us assume that there is a fear of high inflation but that oil is a good index for constant dollars. Under these circumstances, since the contracts are written in terms of oil, the actual fact of inflation makes no difference; the terms are in objective quantities and all financing goes through as if inflation didn't exist. The institutional arrangements for borrowing the money have simply been changed so that inflationary expectations do not manifest themselves in front-end loading of contracts or in premium payments. The choice of an appropriate index is solved fairly easily because the price of oil is a natural index from the viewpoint of the borrower who is going to produce oil. In effect, the borrower is sharing the risk/opportunity of the future price of oil with the bondholder. He is also reducing his initial cash-flow requirements by a factor of 2 or 3 and can therefore set the initial price of his produce much lower. The fact is that the capital charges for producing a barrel of oil can vary from $5 to $50, depending on how the financing is accomplished.

While it is true that selling oil bonds is the equivalent of selling a futures contract, the bond seller is not going short on oil. He is using the proceeds of the sale to invest in a plant which will produce even more oil. His total gain is greater if the price of oil goes up, smaller if the price of oil goes down. His gain is not as great as it would have been if the bonds were in dollars, or if he held all the bonds himself (because he has to share his gains with other bondholders). But he also does not lose as much if the price goes down. The point is that he is (net) long, not short, on oil.

We emphasize this because at one time in a number of conferences on unconventional financing most people, even financial experts, thought there was a psychological contradiction between being willing to build a plant to produce oil and at the same time selling an oil bond for future delivery. But when people who build a plant opt for this kind of financing, they do so in order to share the price risk. In effect, it enables them to invest a much greater total more safely and inexpensively than would otherwise be possible.

The fact that the price of oil does not necessarily track the CPI or the GNP deflator or even our monetary correction indicator (MCI) can be a plus or minus depending on the assumptions and objectives of the various investors. If, for example, investors are speculating (as opposed to hedging or just investing), then they are betting that oil prices will go up more than the index.

It would have been very advantageous for borrowers to finance synthetic-fuel plants with oil bonds in 1979 and 1980, when the price of oil was high and, most people thought, sure to go up even more. But the oil companies, which were even more convinced than the general public that the price of oil would rise, were not interested in oil bonds (we suggested it to several of them). Many are now dubious that the world price of oil will necessarily continue to rise; rather, they believe as we do that the long-term outlook is more likely to trend downward. But many experts and investors disagree, and they are the ones who might be interested in buying oil bonds. Investors may also buy the bonds simply to hedge against an oil price increase, either because they want to hedge against inflation in general or because they think oil prices are likely to be more sensitive on the up side than other prices.

Of course, the bonds are not foolproof. If, for example, the price of oil collapsed completely, then the oil company might not be able both to cover its operating expenses and to pay off the bondholder, though it would have less trouble with oil bonds than dollar-denominated bonds. Another caveat is that most people in business feel that pioneering does not pay, and that it is better to be a fast second. The pioneer is, after all, the one who has to face all of the uncertainties.

The idea of a commodity bond recently came into prominence in the United States about three years ago because of a deal that was put together for Sunshine Mining Corporation by Chris Anderson of the brokerage firm of Drexel Burnham Lambert. Sunshine, a company which had had its economic troubles, was nonetheless able to borrow about $30 million to buy new reserves of silver that would be worth about $300 million when they were mined. Only about 10 percent of that silver was needed to guarantee repayment to the bondholders, a clear example of how selling futures enabled the company to go long on silver. Except for the commodity bond, investors would not have been willing to loan Sunshine Mining $30 million on acceptable terms.

We can summarize the value of commodity bonds as follows. Most important, under current conditions it is a very advantageous way to finance certain productive facilities—in effect to establish a long position (net) in a commodity at the cost, or virtue, of sharing the future-price risk/opportunity of that commodity with the bondholders. If the proceeds of a loan are actually used to establish a long position, by either financing a plant that manufactures the commodity or by financing reserves or stockpiles, then repayment is made credible. Since the lender does not have to risk unanticipated inflation, a very much lower interest rate (both nominal and real) may result.

Commodity bonds create a "non-zero-sum" long-term futures market and establish an appropriate form of interest-bearing futures contract. This futures market can perform all of the functions that futures markets perform everywhere—for buyers and sellers, for hedging, and for speculative purposes.

There are also a number of special situations in which indexing of commodities can be very useful. For example, many business or government operations involve holding semipermanent stockpiles of some material. The classic example is the platinum used in refineries as a catalyst. Typical refineries can hold several million dollars' worth of the catalyst which is not used up in the process but it is tied up in the operation of the plant. When the plant becomes obsolete and is retired or torn down, the catalyst is either used for another plant or sold. In principle the owner of the plant has no particular interest in speculating on the price of platinum and does not want to tie up his money in holding it. An alternative is simply to finance the platinum by issuing platinum bonds. Presumably the plant owner will pay interest in dollars because he doesn't want to buy any more platinum than he needs, or he will use the equivalent of a high-discount bond which is written in terms of platinum.

The concept of a high-discount or a "deep-discount commodity bond" is that instead of paying out interest every year, the owner of the platinum (or other commodity) offers to deliver some fixed amount in a particular year. Since it pays no interest, the bond is sold at a discount. However, under current IRS rules an equivalent annual interest can be calculated and taxed as annual income, even though the bondholder is not receiving any cash flow. But the seller of the bond is not allowed to deduct this imputed interest as an expense. If the deep-discount bond were issued as a "commodity bond" without interest, then it would be a simple futures contract not subject to taxation on imputed interest. Speculators, investors hedging against inflation, and users of the commodity who want to hedge against a future price rise might all be potential buyers.

COMMODITY BONDS IN THE GOVERNMENT

The use of commodity bonds to market U.S. strategic stockpiles is potentially also very interesting. The bonds could be used by the government either to finance all or part of the initial purchase, or to later divest itself of the commodity in a predictable, nondisruptive fashion. If the bonds were scheduled to become due over, say, a twenty-year period, no commodity-related economic or political upsets should occur; yet the government could recoup most of its investment immediately. Alternatively, if the government itself wanted to repurchase the outstanding bonds it could negotiate an equitable settlement.

The U.S. petroleum stockpile seems a particularly good candidate for such bonds, an option the government has considered and rejected. The decision not to go ahead was probably partly based on the belief that there would be difficulties in marketing them. And, indeed, a market would have to be built up very gradually via a well-designed marketing plan. In addition, if and when it decides to sell the bonds, the U.S. Treasury would probably prefer to distance itself from the transaction by setting up a separate government corporation to carry it out.

Gold bonds are another commodity option the government might consider, especially before making a final determination on a return to a gold standard. (The long-term futures market which would be created seems as good a way as any to gather information about the likely future price of gold.) Subject to the same marketing instruments as any other commodity bond (deep discount, dual denominations, various tax treatments, and short- to long-term maturities), the bonds would raise current government income without creating any immediate cash-flow problems or tying the government to high-priced interest rates.

The fact, of course, is that because the nominal deficit is creating havoc with government policies, the government must find ways to reduce its need to borrow large sums of money at high interest rates at inconvenient times. Therefore, the issuance of a variety of long-term bonds, tapping as many new markets as possible, would (1) enable the government to finance its current expenses; (2) retire its outstanding long-term bonds, thereby removing much of its vested interest in inflation, and enable it to cancel some long-standing debts by buying U.S. bonds below par (a debt which is then turned into a profit for the Treasury); and (3) prevent crowding out of private borrowers.

If the government could issue, say, $200 billion worth of long-term commodity and indexed bonds over, say, two or three years, then just announcing the program, starting it, and showing that it works would make credible any plans to initiate a major commodity-bond program in the future. The creation of some self-fulfilling expectations alone might decrease significantly most of the government's current cash-flow and crowding-out problems.

The bonds should be recallable within a five-year period (as is true of many current U.S. bonds) so that the government can choose the time to refinance them. This convenience is necessary, as there may well be future crises similar to those of today, when the government may desperately wish to minimize its refinancing operations in some years and go to the market very strongly in others. The biggest problem the government has today is the short-term maturity of the debt, partly because of the high interest rates that represent rapid repayment of principal and partly because of the nominal short maturities. The result is that it has almost no flexibility in its refinancing operations.

We would suggest the government eventually issue a variety of bonds—say, $20 billion in commodity bonds, $30 billion in various kinds of oil bonds (both for the strategic stockpile reserve and just for current consumption), about $20 or $30 billion worth of gold bonds (or about a quarter of its gold reserves), and about $50 billion worth of bonds indexed to the GNP deflator and another $50 billion to some kind of MCI.

It might even index a number of these bonds to a revised CPI and/or the PPI (producers price index). Presumably the market itself, once it was active enough, would calculate reasonable prices for all these commodities. The basic objective is to raise long-term money from new sources to avoid crowding out. The government could then simply stop issuing those bonds for which there was no great demand.

THE TWO-FOR-ONE BOND

Many oil-producing nations claim a wish to limit or even cut back current oil production in order to ensure their "national heritage" and their ability to produce into the long-term future. Some of the British and Norwegians have argued for this, as have all the other oil producers at one time or another. To the extent that the British and the Norwegians want to be able to have oil in the future, the United States might offer to borrow oil from them today and pay them back in twenty-five to thirty-five years at a rate of two barrels for one. (The oil would presumably be obtained by the United States from unconventional sources, new reserves, synthetic fuel plants, etc.—or it might be readily available at reasonable prices because of the efforts of conservation. See Chapter 7.)

Two barrels for one in twenty-five years is equivalent to almost a 3 percent compounded interest rate, while a payback in thirty-five years would correspond to a compound interest rate of 2 percent. The oil-producing country is presumably better off if it gets two barrels returned for every barrel it lends than if it had deferred production and produced just one barrel. While the producer country still needs to pay for the operating costs of producing oil, in most cases this is only a small fraction of the selling price (though not in all cases—the British and Norwegians have some relatively high-cost fields). The United States could either use the oil or put it in its strategic stockpile. It could pay for it later out of the money saved by using the oil to back up a commodity bond, thus reducing the borrowing costs dramatically. It could also use the capital obtained to finance synthetic-fuel plants. Even more important, the United States would cut down its nominal deficit and official borrowing requirements by reducing its cash-flow requirements. And most important of all, it gets the oil when needed, without disrupting markets, and repays it when it is relatively convenient to do so.

Again, this was an idea that would have had a much greater impact if it had been put into effect in the late '70s. Just the existence of such contracts would have made it clear that a barrel of oil in the ground was not the best bank in the world; a better bank would have been to produce and sell the oil and invest the proceeds in some appropriate way. It is usually a mistake to hoard even a "national treasure" or "national inheritance"; it's better to make it productive and invest the proceeds. Further, the early promulgation of this concept could have had many useful political and economic effects; for example, it could have forced OPEC to clarify the value of its oil reserves.

It should be noted that an approximation of the two-for-one bonds could be offered to the private market. Assume that the price of oil is about $33 a barrel (which is about what it is at the moment). The United States government might issue a simple future delivery contract for, say, 60 barrels of oil to be delivered twenty-three years later. If the government sells the contract for $1,000 today and with that money buys 30 barrels of oil, delivering 60 barrels to the holder twenty-three years later, this would be exactly the equivalent of paying the buyer 3 percent in terms of oil and as such is just another example of a "deep-discount commodity bond." When issued in dollars as well as commodities, such bonds are often bought by pension funds, which don't pay taxes; funds like the automatic reinvestment feature. But the oil bonds, being a simple futures contract and not paying any income taxes until either sold or redeemed, might have a much larger market than the deep-discount commodity bond.

That market would, however, exclude pension funds, which under current rules cannot purchase bonds solely denominated in units of a commodity. On the other hand, if the government really wants to sell oil bonds to pension funds it would have to denote the bonds in two ways, i.e., in cash (say $2,000) or in oil (say 60 barrels), and give the buyer the option. The government could also protect itself against too great an increase in the price of oil; it could stipulate that payment be either in oil or in a minimum cash payment, at the bondholder's option, or else stipulate a maximum payment at the government's option. Either or both payment options might be indexed. Alternatively, the government could specify an annual redemption price (in either dollars or oil or both) and then retain the right to pay early if it wished—i.e., the commodity bonds could be recallable with a penalty. (The penalty presumably should be reasonably large to prevent the government from resorting to this option.) But if the government specifically sets aside oil to repay bondholders, then—at least for accounting purposes—the price of oil at the time of redemption is unimportant.

INDEXING OF U.S. GOVERNMENT BONDS

It would be most useful for the U.S. Treasury to issue long-term indexed bonds, particularly those in which the principal was indexed to the MCI. First and foremost, this could reduce the cash flow of the Treasury enormously (which now includes the rapid "rollover" of debt because of the fact that the inflation component of the interest is really repayment of principal, and in any case the nominal average maturity is about three years—down by a factor of 3 from ten years ago). Indexing in this way might also be "fairer" (more valuable) to the buyer, given that the nominal interest the government paid for most of the period from 1965 to 1980 was equal to or barely above the inflation rate, in part because the general public underestimated the inflation rate and/or was too influenced by the monetary illusion. If the bonds had been indexed to the inflation rate, the government would probably have had to pay 2 percent real interest on them. If, on the other hand, the bonds had been indexed with the MCI, which in turn would not have corrected for the "impoverishing event" of the oil price increase, the government would actually have saved money. Furthermore, it would not have had a large nominal deficit, because instead of having to borrow money to compensate the bondholder for the declining value of his bonds, the indexing would automatically have corrected for the inflation and deferred the need to finance the increase to the date when the bond became due. The bonds, in effect, have their principal designated in terms of constant dollars, or at least dollars corrected by the MCI.

There are three significant gains that will accrue to the government if it turns to appropriate methods of indexing bonds. One, it will pay a much smaller premium, if any at all, for the risk of inflation. Two, it would decrease the need to "roll over" debt in the short term, a practice which is probably one of the most important destabilizing influences on the bond market today, particularly if the rollover is accompanied by a tight money policy. (In addition, tight money policies would be much more effective without being as tight, because the government deficit to be financed would be much less.) Three, and perhaps most important of all, if inflation decreases dramatically the government is not locked into paying high interest rates. It no longer has a vested interest in continuing the inflation. It is this aspect of indexing which ultimately might be the most significant—the ability to create a soft landing from an ongoing inflation. (It should be noted that when the government sells a thirty-year 14 percent bond it is betting against itself. If the inflation should be greatly reduced such a bond could easily sell at double or triple its nominal value.)

THE ALASKAN GAS PIPELINE

This project is not only important in its own right, it is a good example of how useful unconventional financing can be. And yet at present it looks as if the financing of the Alaskan Gas Pipeline will be judged infeasible. The main reason for this is that in accordance with normal utility practice, the pipeline has to set a fixed price for servicing the capital costs. Since this price will be the same, at least in nominal terms, over the entire life of the project, its real value will fluctuate with inflation. The fact that the economy is in an inflationary period, and that the value of the imbedded capital will increase, is simply ignored. Thus, at the moment the thinking is in terms of about $10 per 1,000 cubic feet, a figure which represents about three-quarters carrying charges and profit, and one-quarter for the gas producers. However, since many retail distributors or other customers of the pipeline gas can now buy gas for less than $5 per 1,000 cubic feet. it would be foolish for them to tie themselves up in a $10 gas contract (even if they can "roll in" the high-priced gas with less expensive gas from other sources). Over a long period of time, such a contract might make sense: if one assumes a 10 percent inflation rate, then within seven years the value of the $10 payment drops by a factor of 2 in real terms, and in thirty years by a factor of 20. In thirty years, the $10 becomes equal to about 50¢ in purchasing power.

But this is exactly the point. An investor doesn't want the real rate for a service to drop over time as a result of inflation. Rather, one wants the price more or less constant in real terms and therefore to increase in nominal terms.

Now consider what would happen if the gas pipeline were financed with indexed bonds. Again assuming a 10 percent inflation, one could afford to charge *less* than $5 per 1,000 cubic feet, as long as the selling price of the gas were indexed to keep up with inflation or at least were indexed with the monetary correction indicator. The principal of the pipeline bonds would be indexed, not the nominal interest rate. The bonds could then be amortized over time, using the cash flow from the sales. Since both sides are indexed with the same index, it is a basically safe method of financing.

Applying this concept when the idea of a pipeline first came up would have made the project both competitive and profitable. In fact, even with an allowance for a substantial cost overrun, the project would have been financially acceptable. But many of the concerns the oil companies had about being innovative with oil bonds apply to some degree for the gas pipeline. First, the pipeline owners have to be sure that the gas will be available over the life of the project. Second, they have to believe that the chance for a catastrophic drop in the price of gas is low, because even though they have "firm contracts" for the output of the pipeline, many people might conveniently forget that this now expensive gas once looked quite inexpensive. There could as a result be some reneging on contracts, and some government intervention by the regulatory authorities, or there could be lawsuits filed by customers. In fact, it is conceivable (though unlikely) that the regulatory authorities might decide that the index price rise is not allowable if the price of gas in general has dropped.

As always, then, there are many ways in which this kind of innovation can go wrong. The element of pioneering is probably the primary deterrent to its application. But it's also the best argument for government encouragement and support. The benefits of a successful example are great indeed, but since few of the benefits will accrue to the entrepreneur, the government has to provide all the incentives it can—or at least help remove the roadblocks. A creative and serious government could make all the difference in facilitating the rapid application of this idea, both because it ought to be done this way and because it would be a most useful example.

In sum, commodity bonds seem to be a reasonable way to alleviate the government's current cash-flow problem while at the same time greatly improving its debt structure. Since those are two of the major problems today, any possible remedies—and especially the imaginative use of unconventional financing—are worth a try. This is a most opportune moment for new initiatives, but unfortunately many influential individuals, particularly investment bankers and government officials, are (properly) very conservative and believe that if the U.S. government tried these concepts it would risk its credit rating. We would argue that issuing long-term bonds at a fixed rate of 13 percent or so is an admission of defeat in the anti-inflation battle or a kind of stupidity or irresponsibility. It may well be necessary for even the most conservative to use new techniques under new conditions. The theoretical argument for trying some of these ideas is almost overwhelming.

CHAPTER 7

ENERGY: WE MAY WELL LUCK OUT, BUT SHOULD HEDGE

U.S. ENERGY "PREPAREDNESS"

The coming U.S. economic boom will be "fueled" by growing supplies of energy which are likely to be available at lower real prices as the decade progresses. The supply disruptions and huge price increases that characterized the 1970s should be replaced by a vastly more stable energy environment in which oil is basically viewed as just another commodity whose price is "managed" but is still responsive to the interaction of supply and demand. The influence of the Organization of Petroleum Exporting Countries (OPEC), already greatly overrated by most observers in the 1970s, should decline still further as increasing amounts of oil and gas are found in non-OPEC nations and as reliable, cost-effective alternatives are developed. This position, which we have held for a long time,* is now common—by the time this book appears it may even be the conventional wisdom. But, as we explain later, such widespread acceptance could become a self-defeating prophecy.

This chapter draws on work done in collaboration with William M. Brown, Director of Energy Studies at Hudson Institute, for *Fortune* magazine articles.

*See Herman Kahn, *World Economic Development* (Boulder, Colo.: Westview Press, 1979); or Herman Kahn and William M. Brown, "Why OPEC Is Vulnerable," *Fortune,* July 14, 1980 and "Can OPEC Survive the Glut?" *Fortune,* November 30, 1981.

Energy: We May Well Luck Out, But Should Hedge

For much of the world, the energy crisis of the 1970s created a revolution in international financial and political affairs. In constant 1980 dollars the oil shocks of 1973 and 1979 sent the average world price of oil from around $5 per barrel to almost $40 (at the peak in late 1980), shifting enormous sums of money and political influence away from the world's industrialized nations to the OPEC countries. Those shocks contributed substantially to the worldwide malaise of the decade; they were partly responsible for the recession of 1975 and the recent high rates of inflation, though both of these latter impacts have been greatly exaggerated. The high price of oil also made a lot of energy-consuming equipment and buildings virtually obsolete and contributed to the slowdown in productivity.

The impact of the oil shocks was felt particularly strongly in the United States, which had built its high-growth postwar economy on the availability of "cheap" energy.* In addition, Americans suddenly had to face unaccustomed frustration and vulnerability—the reality of not being able to crush the OPEC oil cartel or even weaken its apparent influence. The fate of the United States seemed to be in the hands of a few sheiks. This erosion of self-confidence contributed to the appearance (and existence) of American impotence which dominated the decade.

The government of the United States obviously did not "cause" the energy crisis. But it can certainly be faulted for its failure to respond effectively. For the past ten years, U.S. energy policies have been misguided, inappropriate, and counterproductive. Presidents Nixon, Ford, and Carter all agreed that the energy crisis threatened the basic security of the United States, yet all of them pursued policies which increased dependency on foreign oil. In 1970, the United States imported 24 percent of its oil; in 1979 it imported 45 percent. (But by 1981, various adjust-

---

* We have found it useful to think about energy prices on a three-point scale: cheap, inexpensive, and expensive. Energy is cheap when it can almost be ignored as an important economic factor. This was largely true prior to the 1970s, at least in the United States. Energy is inexpensive when its prices become bothersome to the consumer, but not to the extent of forcing any basic changes in life-styles. That is, energy is still inexpensive when a typical family can still live in a suburban house—though it may have more insulation and smaller double-glazed windows and be so located as to take advantage of the sun. The family car may also be smaller than formerly; at least it will be more efficient. Energy becomes expensive, however, when it exerts a major impact on the economy, consumers, and their life-styles—for example, when many persons bicycle to work instead of motoring, or many families must move to a small urban apartment or condominium from a house in the suburbs. For the average U.S. citizen, we have always found it difficult to visualize energy becoming and remaining expensive in this sense for very long.

ments resulting from high prices, new policies, and the passage of time brought imports to 30 percent, a figure which seems to be going down rapidly.)

Throughout the decade the government kept the price of domestic oil and gas artificially low (i.e., below world market prices), thereby greatly reducing incentives both to conserve and to explore and develop new domestic sources and alternatives. For example, at a time when the world price of oil was about $14 a barrel, the United States kept the average domestic price to about $9. This represented, in effect, a subsidy to consumers of $5 a barrel. Since oil consumption averaged about 6 billion barrels a year, this meant an annual subsidy of $30 billion, or enough to allow consumers to use much more oil than they would have if domestic prices had been the same as world prices. Further, the production of new sources of energy, such as natural gas, was discouraged by an even more maniacal policy of repressive price controls. When we contrast the past scenario with the current situation in which world prices (now around $30 a barrel in 1980 dollars) have been allowed to prevail, we can get a sense of the power of prices to force conservation: in the two years, 1979 and 1980, U.S. consumption dropped by about 20 percent, and in the first eight months of 1981 it dropped another 20 percent.

Early in the energy crisis the United States announced a national policy to increase the production of coal but then proceeded to attach so many regulations that digging for coal and especially transporting or burning it became expensive and risky (in part for fear of changes in government regulations). And when Three Mile Island happened—despite the limited damage and the success of the nuclear reactor's multiple safety systems—the government found it politically advisable to delay the licensing of additional reactors that were otherwise ready to go, a decision which would have been most difficult to justify to any but an antinuclear audience. Three Mile Island did demonstrate that there were problems in the system, particularly with the training and competence of personnel. But these are problems of the reactors presently in service, not of ones under construction, and the changes needed to fix current reactors automatically apply to those under construction as well.

Despite various federal attempts to formulate energy programs, there is still no coherent or effective U.S. energy policy. At the time the Reagan administration came into office, more than seven years after the Arab oil embargo precipitated the oil crisis:

- —there was no rationalization of the red tape which so increased lead time for construction that in a period of high interest rates the building of nuclear reactors became completely uneconomical (U.S. reactors took two or three times as long to build as Japanese and European reactors, with no increase in safety);
- —there was no clear policy on radioactive waste disposal—a key roadblock to the increased use of nuclear power (this problem has been around since the end of World War II); if one is not familiar with governmental bungling one could conclude (incorrectly) that the problem is overwhelming;
- —there was little practical (as opposed to rhetorical) urgency to encourage the increased use of coal as an oil alternative;
- —"strip mining," the most economical and safest form of obtaining coal (and which was also relatively clean), was excessively restricted by inappropriate land-use and pollution regulations, many of which were based on political attempts to protect producers of existing (relatively dirty) coal in Kentucky, West Virginia, and Illinois;
- —there were excessive delays in leasing areas in Alaska and off the continental shelves for oil exploration;
- —prices for "old" oil and gas prices were held well below those of imports;
- —price controls were still maintained on most new oil and gas;
- —there were no large-scale commercial synthetic-fuel plants under construction, and the few demonstration plant projects were being terminated; and
- —there was still no widespread understanding of the effects of inflation on various discounted cash-flow analyses—and almost no understanding of the possible use of oil bonds.

The government is now taking the best possible remedial action—it is drastically reducing its involvement in energy matters, allowing the industries involved greater freedom of operation. Oil and gas decontrol has brought or will bring domestic energy prices up to or close to the world level; decontrol has already produced a substantial increase in domestic exploration. The likely relaxation of overly restrictive environmental regulations, if done wisely, will not destroy the nation's ecology or cause any significant increase in damage by pollution. It will allow U.S. industry to use coal on an effective, meaningful scale, and should encourage the development of other previously unavailable energy resources such as oil from shale. The U.S. government is finally becoming part of the energy solution instead of the problem, which is one reason why there has been such a dramatic improvement in the last two years and why we are now basically optimistic about the energy outlook in the near-term as well as long-term future. However, we are concerned about the possibility of a "failure of success"—of the optimism growing so great that certain potentially useful, even if not clearly essential, programs are neglected or ignored and then later turn out to have been desperately needed.

OPEC

However guarded, our optimism is also based on our assessment of the relative strength of OPEC and its role in determining both the level and price of the world's oil supplies. Until quite recently OPEC was regarded as one of the most effective cartels in world history, capable of manipulating oil prices at will. This view was reinforced every time the news media reported another OPEC meeting and subsequent oil price hike. Indeed, the view seemed logical, given the vast quantities of oil both produced and held in reserve by OPEC's member nations and the upward course of oil prices.

But despite the extraordinary rise in real oil prices since mid-1973 and the resulting benefits to OPEC countries, we are convinced that the image of OPEC as a hugely successful cartel setting oil prices at will is mostly misleading. For one thing, official OPEC oil prices, when measured in fixed dollars, *declined* about 25 percent between January 1974 and December 1978. (In fixed marks and fixed yen, the declines were still larger—40 and 50 percent respectively.) It was one of the great unreported stories of the middle 1970s that every time OPEC raised the price of oil it raised it by *less* than the inflation rate raised other prices. The actual decline in the purchasing power of the dollars received by OPEC was even greater. Yet the impression given by the media was that OPEC was able to raise prices freely and easily, but that's not what happened. What did happen was massive misreporting, which was neither sinister nor conspiratorial, but was nevertheless stupid, ignorant, and fashionable.

Further, there was a good deal of under-the-table discounting of OPEC oil and all kinds of special deals made by most OPEC members—e.g., excessive credit at favorable terms or trades of oil for overpriced goods or services. Even more important, the price of the products that most OPEC countries bought, such as military products, heavy construction, engineering goods, luxury goods, etc., had strong tendencies to increase much more rapidly than the average inflation rate. It is estimated that the actual purchasing power of OPEC oil, in terms of the cost of the "market basket" the OPEC governments actually bought, declined by significantly more than 50 percent, perhaps by as much as two-thirds. These two factors limited OPEC's real income until the autumn of 1978, when year-end buying (to avoid a possible modest price increase) combined with the outbreak of riots in Iran to eliminate most of the discounting. The Iranian revolution and the Iraq-Iran war subsequently eliminated the production of about 6 million barrels a day and set the stage for the price rises of 1979 and 1980.

But these price increases were not a triumph of OPEC planning—or even of the OPEC nations' concerted action—but the results of an unanticipated bonanza that fell OPEC's way, and which OPEC was in fact relatively slow to grasp or fully exploit. Oil buyers increased petroleum stockpiles in 1979 by an estimated 500 million barrels because of fears of further interruptions and price hikes. As a result, increased market demand, and not a fall in supply, pulled up OPEC prices.

Our contention is that OPEC's behavior might be characterized as that of a very loose association for restraint of trade in which Saudi Arabia, with occasional assistance from other countries, attempts to furnish price leadership and in which there is a low and uncertain level of cooperation by the other members. Under these circumstances, price leaders try to cut their production rather than give discounts when the market is soft; when the market is tight, they attempt to raise production in order to restrain "excessive" increases. Consequently the leader or leaders are nearly always trying to correct for changing economic forces; other member nations are somewhat less stability-oriented. The situation is very far from what we usually think of as a cartel, i.e., an organization which sets quotas and often makes side payments to compensate less efficient producers for not producing. Up to now, OPEC has done neither of these.

The Saudis' ultimate "dream" is to use their price leadership position to establish unified OPEC prices at a reasonable level that provides stable long-term markets. By varying its flexible oil-production capability the Saudis would prevent oil prices from rising too high or sinking too low. However, despite the Saudis' enormous oil reserves, it is still unclear whether they can make this dream come true. The OPEC meeting in August 1981 again showed the "looseness" of the cartel; in particular, the members were not yet ready to have the Saudis call the shots for them. In any case, the price of oil has become so high that there are enormous incentives for the world's energy importers to reduce consumption and to seek alternatives to OPEC oil.

ENERGY PROSPECTS: SCENARIOS AND CURRENT TRENDS

A combination of reduced consumption and increased non-OPEC production is bringing about a substantial reduction (perhaps eventually an effective elimination) of any critical dependence by the United States and others on OPEC. Until recently this "guarded optimist" projection contradicted most forecasts that insisted the "glut is temporary" and there would be continued critical world reliance on OPEC. While we concede that with sufficient bad luck or bad management such reliance could go on, it shouldn't and is in any case relatively unlikely in the near and medium-term future.

We'd like to present two scenarios, either of which seems plausible in the next decade or so. In the first, let us assume that world demand for oil increases only 1 percent a year, but there is about a 7 percent growth rate in the production of oil by non-OPEC countries (or about 1.5 million barrels per day—MBPD—average annual increase). Assume also that oil production of communist nations grows by about 2 percent and that there is a 5 percent increase in worldwide use of natural gas. (All of these numbers are compatible with a reasonable extrapolation of recent and likely future trends in each area.) Under these circumstances a relatively simple analysis of the consequences of these assumptions shows that the exports of OPEC oil to the rest of the world would decrease steadily until by the end of the decade there would be zero external demand for OPEC oil.*

Obviously this could not happen: there would be a sharp break in the price of OPEC oil long before external demand ever reached zero. But until recently most people would have found such an extrapolation, even with the concession that the drop in demand could not continue indefinitely, totally implausible.

---

* Kahn and Brown, "Why OPEC Is Vulnerable."

A slightly different scenario is also possible. Assume that there is a 2 percent growth in world demand, that non-OPEC oil increases only by about 5 percent a year (or only by 1 MBPD), that the use of gas goes up only by 4 percent a year, and that communist oil production does not grow at all. In that case a simple analysis shows that the demand for OPEC oil will rise to about 25 MBPD by the end of the decade and there is likely to be upward rather than downward pressure on oil prices.

Can we choose between the two scenarios? Not reliably. But we believe a better case can be made for the first than the second, although the range of uncertainty is quite large.

Our positive outlook for the next five or ten years is becoming increasingly accepted and is in fact shared by some oil experts. It is persuasive since it rests on little more than a continuation of the current vigorous responses of most nations to the severe economic shocks caused by energy prices in the 1970s. The one crucial caveat to any optimistic short-term projection is that such optimism assumes no new severe interruptions in oil supplies will occur as a result of political troubles in the major oil-exporting countries, particularly Saudi Arabia.

Several key trends are shaping the more stable energy environment of the 1980s. Perhaps the most important is the steady increase in oil exploration and discovery which is taking place outside the OPEC nations. Almost every country which believes there is even a remote chance of discovering oil within its boundaries has become more willing to cooperate with major Western oil companies which have the necessary capital, exploration technology, and skills. Extensive arrangements have now been concluded in Argentina, Australia, Brazil, Chile, China, India, Malaysia, New Zealand, Peru, and several African states. And it seems likely that the pressure on these states to be economically reasonable and politically rational will continue. Canada (with its current nationalistic oil policies) is an obvious exception to this trend, but it is the exception and even there the government is likely either to work out or reform its current policies (which now seem likely to hold back greatly increased production of oil and gas and help worsen that country's current shortage of investment capital).

A prolonged boom in exploration and development could last at least through the 1980s. Discoveries during the first half of the decade, not expenditures, will determine the potential for the second half. The petroleum industry's prospects for success will be dependent upon improving the technological sophistication of the exploration process. Recent advances have been encouraging, mainly as a result of the application of high-speed computers to the processing of seismic data. This technology has been given credit for enabling the successful exploration of several exciting prospects for oil such as those recently found in the Overthrust Belt in the United States and in the West Pembina bay in Canada. Many other advances, including improvement in drilling, safety procedures, environmental protection, and so on, are also in the cards.

Improvement foreseen during the next five years may make it possible for seismic systems to detect many hydrocarbon accumulations with high confidence and to provide reliable data on the dimensions of reservoirs. Exploration will be further aided by such new advances as self-contained seismic instruments which can be dropped by helicopter into relatively inaccessible areas and can return the required data by telemetry.

In addition to oil exploration, oil production has also increased rapidly in non-OPEC nations. Table 7-1 offers both "low" and "high" projections for increased production in fields *already* discovered. Even the "low" estimates will add an additional 1 million barrels per day to world oil supplies.

Oil production is also increasing in the Soviet Union, despite highly publicized and then retracted predictions by the Central Intelligence Agency that Soviet output would peak by 1980. In the most recent analysis (September 1981) by the Defense Intelligence Agency, it was finally recognized that the U.S.S.R.'s energy prospects for the rest of this century appear "highly favorable" and that Moscow will be able to increase its oil production and exports. At that point Soviet oil production was already 3 percent higher than the peak forecast earlier by the CIA. In addition, the Soviets have natural gas reserves estimated at 1,000 trillion cubic feet— the energy equivalent of 170 billion barrels of oil, roughly equal to known Saudi Arabian oil reserves. This makes most implausible any medium-term decrease in the export of Soviet oil even if there is a decrease in domestic production. These oil exports earn vitally important foreign exchange, and the Soviets can if they wish increase the production of gas and substitute it for domestic use. Though most Soviet gas reserves are located in the farther reaches of eastern Siberia, many of them are still accessible enough to supply all current and future Soviet needs for a long time to come. The CIA once rejected this argument on the basis that the Soviets would have trouble building pipelines, and indeed they do, but they are surmounting these problems, as can be seen from figures on the increased gas use in the Soviet Union. Furthermore, it seems likely that

Table 7-1
A Guarded Optimist's Projected Growth in Non-OPEC Oil Production, 1980–1985

	LOW		HIGH	
MEXICO	.40	–	.50	MBPD
UNITED KINGDOM	.30	–	.40	MBPD
NORWAY	.10	–	.15	MBPD
UNITED STATES	.00	–	.20	MBPD
CANADA	.00	–	.10	MBPD
AFRICA[1]	.05	–	.15	MBPD
SOUTH AMERICA	.05	–	.10	MBPD
ASIA[2]	.15	–	.20	MBPD
TOTAL[3]	1.05		1.80	MBPD

[1] Includes Egypt.
[2] Includes Malaysia and Philippine Islands.
[3] The range 1.05–1.80 MBPD is equivalent to 5-year growth rates of 5 percent to 8 percent.

Japan and the West, particularly West Germany and France, will help the Soviets in their pipeline effort.

Non-OPEC production estimates, therefore, seem to offer substantial justification for a guardedly optimistic view of future world oil supplies. Contrary to the assertion of many analysts (including, surprisingly, most oil company executives), world oil production has not yet come close to peaking, nor are there signs that the world has reached the limit of discoverable petroleum reserves. In fact, most of the world is only now being explored seriously and vigorously.

Natural gas exploration and production have also been increasing rapidly worldwide as a result of rising oil prices and the fear of renewed shortages. The recent U.S. decision to decontrol gas prices, as well as the newly awakened interest in gas as an alternative to oil in developing nations, will encourage even further exploration and production in the decade ahead. Increases in domestic supplies of natural gas can effectively reduce the need for an equivalent amount of imported oil. And where gas can be substituted for oil, there are usually only minimal retrofitting costs.

Natural gas has great potential to become *the* fuel choice of the twenty-first century. It is clean and easy to use, and should be available in ever increasing quantities, mainly from three major sources: conventional, unconventional, and manufactured.

The consensus of informed estimates is that the United States should ultimately find conventional gas reserves sufficient to produce about another 1,000 trillion cubic feet (TCF), or enough to last about fifty years at current rates of consumption. Some projections expect two or three times that amount to be discovered. Differences in estimates of long-term supplies cannot now be resolved, but if our "guarded optimist" position turns out to be correct, a smooth transition from oil to alternative energy sources will be relatively easy to make. If the more optimistic projections prove valid, then natural gas production could increase in the decades ahead, and gas would indeed become the fuel of choice by early next century.

Unconventional sources include areas where extraction of natural gas after discovery is relatively difficult. For example, gas can be found at low pressures, widely dispersed through shale or coal deposits; it is contained in very low-permeability sandstones; it is dissolved in hot brines at great depths; it can be found "frozen" in a loose association with ice in a crystalline form (clathrates) at moderate depths, usually below the ocean floor in the colder regions of the world. Gas might also be found in places where exploration normally would not take place—for example, in reservoirs far from petroliferous basins.*

All these unconventional sources are now being studied; they show varying degrees of commercial promise. Current estimates indicate that the potential from these sources varies from a few hundred TCF (gas from coal deposits) to millions of TCF (from clathrates). Over time, some of them are likely to become competitive, at least in some parts of the world.

The third source of gas to be used commercially on a large scale is manufactured from organic materials. Almost anything will do—wood, coal, shale, peat, trash, manure, etc. Many of these materials are available in enormous quantities; the amount of gas which can be obtained from them depends on their economic feasibility, which is partly an issue of the

---

* According to a recent theory advanced by Professor Thomas Gold, most natural gas may not be a fossil fuel, but is escaping from lower levels of the earth where it was trapped when the earth solidified. The theory has attracted much discussion and attention. If it turns out to be true, then there may be more gas available than is usually estimated.

technology available, but even more (as discussed in Chapter 6) it depends on the institutional and financial arrangements that can be made through what we call unconventional financing. To date, no large-scale conversion facility has been built, but if current energy prices persist, or if some of the unconventional financing techniques are accepted, gas manufacturing should become a rapidly expanding industry.

The other key trend which is fundamentally—and unexpectedly strongly—changing the international energy environment is the decline in oil consumption (demand). Energy experts and analysts predicted energy demand would increase steadily throughout the 1970s and 80s, especially in the United States and other industrialized nations. (Figure 7-1 is a graph of the Exxon Corporation's projections of world energy demand between 1973 and 1980. It was revised four times during those years because each previous projection was too high.) Oil demand has proved to be far more elastic than many economists and most governments and oil companies estimated; demand does fluctuate in relation to price.

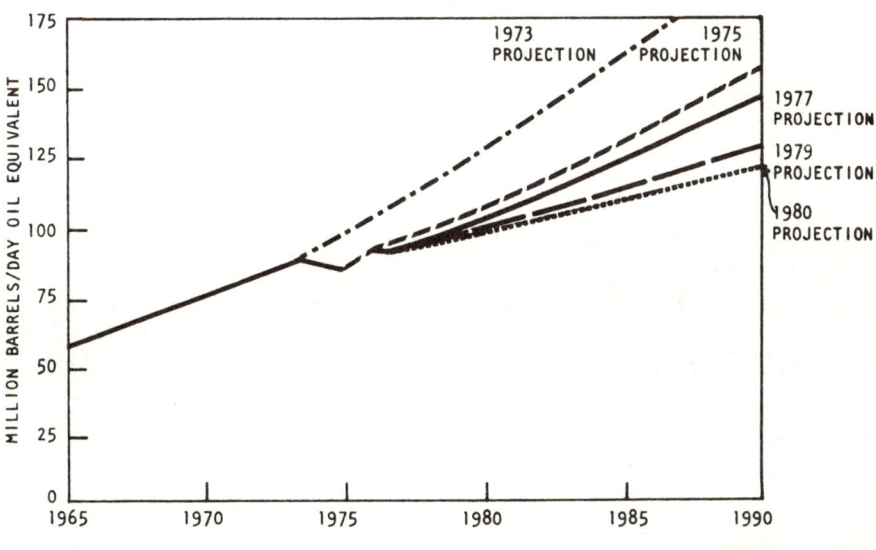

*EXCLUDING COMMUNIST AREAS.

(Data from Exxon's *World Energy Outlook*, April 1978, December 1979 and December 1980.)

Figure 7-1

Indeed, conservation efforts throughout the world have been spectacularly successful. U.S. imports of OPEC oil declined more than 1 million barrels a day from 1979 to 1980; total U.S. petroleum consumption fell more than 1.5 MBPD during the same period. At this writing both numbers seem likely to fall even more from 1980 to 1981 before leveling off. This trend has been consistent among the major industrialized nations. Although some of the decline has been due to the slower economic growth experienced during the 1970s, more efficient energy usage and planning should keep demand from rising sharply, even with the increased growth expected during the coming boom. At current and foreseeable future prices, the incentives to reduce oil demand will remain in effect. We believe that our "guarded optimism" is especially justified in the long run, barring some "not implausible" combination of political problems, a relatively sustained collapse in oil prices which discourages production and conservation, and a rapid increase in world economic growth. It is unlikely that the world will ever be energy-poor (i.e., energy becoming "expensive") for any long period of time, though temporary shortages can clearly occur again.

This optimism is justified not only by the large number of technological/geological opportunities which are being pursued and by estimates of the even greater number of such opportunities becoming available in the future, but also by the possibility that the financial aspects of many of these projects might improve enormously. Unconventional financing and/or a sharp reduction in the inflation rate which results in real long-term financing and write-offs could make a world of difference. Usually projects which increase production, and many which decrease energy demand, are capital-intensive. Anything which makes more capital generally available and/or on better terms will help improve both sides—i.e., production and conservation—of the energy equation dramatically.

ENERGY PROSPECTS: SELF-DEFEATING PROPHECIES VS. SYNFUELS

The United States and other oil-importing nations will, however, continue to remain vulnerable to cutoffs of OPEC and even non-OPEC oil supplies, though less vulnerable than before. Any cutoff or drastic reduction in Saudi Arabian exports, for example, could still have a disastrous impact if it occurred within the next decade. And the future is even more uncertain. For example, some analyses indicate that if the price of oil went down much below $20/bbl (in 1980 dollars) and looked as if it were going to stay there, the developing world would eventually use so much of it that crises could occur again. In that event, the result might be a self-defeating prophecy.

In some ways it is the possibility of a self-defeating prophecy that troubles us the most. If the energy picture looks too rosy, there may, for example, be a slowdown in U.S. efforts to become less dependent upon foreign oil. While reliance on oil imports has been built into the U.S. economy and cannot, despite great success with conservation, be eliminated overnight, failure to diminish that reliance over time would be both unfortunate and dangerous. Given the situation in the Middle East (which is too volatile to be taken either lightly or complacently), continued U.S. energy dependence could be severely affected by an eruption of political troubles in that area.

Further, an overly optimistic picture may trigger excessive cancellation of many potentially necessary, yet relatively expensive domestic energy projects (e.g., a synfuels program). There could also be an erosion in the momentum for conservation; in fact, recent data indicate that this may already be happening with respect to gasoline usage in the United States.

We believe, then, that it is very important for the United States to hedge against a potentially disastrous medium-term energy shortage or price explosion by creating a large industry to convert coal and oil shales into synthetic liquid and gaseous fuels (synfuels). An industry with a capacity of more than 1 million barrels per day of oil equivalent could be operative within a decade. The United States is unusually well endowed with the necessary natural resources, as well as with the capital, technology, and research and development capability. And as noted, with proper use of unconventional financing (e.g., oil bonds) the net economic cost could be quite low, possibly even negative. This is an important point. If appropriate financing could not bring the price down as much as we think, then we wouldn't be in favor of investing about $40 billion to build about twenty 50,000-barrel-a-day plants for a total of about 1 million barrels a day. Our optimism about costs is based mostly on the possibility of improved financing. But we also believe that the history of the last twenty years, with its excessive increases in construction costs and with what could be called "reverse learning curves" (costs that have gone up instead of down with further experience), was a temporary phenomenon of the general malaise and of mismanagement and should be less true in the future.

The reader may feel that 1 million barrels a day is not a lot, and he is basically correct. World production in the 1990s will presumably be about 60–70 million barrels a day; 1 million barrels a day would represent less than 2 percent of this. Nevertheless it is not insignificant. Much more important, by the early 1990s the principle should have been established—the principle that the cost of synthetic fuels does set, in the long run, an upper limit to the price of oil. Since the limit would be less than $35 a barrel (in 1980 dollars), perhaps much less, it would put any long-term planners on notice that it would be wrong to put too much pressure on the market.

If the synfuels program were initiated, the possibility of the establishment of an oppressive oil cartel or of some other oil crisis would be lessened. If it occurred anyway, one response of the United States could be to launch a program of building about ten 50,000-bbl/day plants a year at an annual cost of about $20 billion. The United States could then announce that it would continue doing so—or more—until the cartel was broken or the crisis resolved. Accelerated programs for the building of plants which are urgently needed and which could proceed if all details had been ironed out in advance could be completed in two to three years. They would then represent a significant threat to any cartel and, like the pre-attack mobilization base discussed in the next chapter, could provide the ability to cope with a genuine emergency. Plants could be built in Canada and Venezuela (if that area seemed safe) and so on, as well as in the United States.

Numerous problems are connected with building and operating the huge installations which are required for the efficient conversion of coal or oil shale into desirable fluid hydrocarbons. Serious environmental, land-use, water-rights, health, and safety problems must be resolved through a horrendously complex regulatory process. As a result, the economics of pioneering in synfuels production seems forbidding. Further, there is the accepted current belief that the cost of producing useful synthetic fuels, using conventional financing, ranges from $35 to $60 per barrel (in 1980 dollars), depending on size, location, coal costs, interest rates, and returns on equity. Processes which might price synfuels below $35 now look competitive, but only barely so—hence the need for government encouragement. Without it, the projects appear so risky that the industry is unlikely to be launched on a significant commercial basis.

Until recently, however, there was economic justification for investing in synfuels based on the forecast that oil and gas prices would continue to rise and therefore make such projects competitive in the near future. But even then the risks of new price controls and uncertainties associated with government regulations tended to deter entrepreneurs and investors. The ability of private industry to produce synfuels at competitive prices without special subsidies and/or guarantees must, therefore, be established before a large-scale industry becomes viable.

But as we have pointed out, if the costs of producing synfuels according to standard engineering estimates are remotely accurate, then their high cost (as conventionally calculated) could be substantially reduced by financing such projects in any of several nonconventional ways. Such imaginative financing of synfuels projects could have six important benefits: (1) it would hasten the development of domestic supplies to reduce U.S. dependence on OPEC; (2) it would help restrain further price increases by reducing demand for OPEC oil; (3) it would reduce the U.S. balance-of-payments deficit; (4) it would encourage similar projects in other countries; (5) it should eventually (within twenty years) make synfuels plants the marginal producers that determine the world price, since other fuel sources, domestic or foreign, would need to compete with them; and (6) it would make current U.S. resources of coal, oil shale, and tar sands much more valuable.

GOVERNMENT INTERVENTION TO PREVENT A SELF-DEFEATING PROPHECY

If it turns out that the average world price of oil has peaked at less than $40 per barrel (in 1980 dollars), which we believe to be the case, then there is a good chance that the more expensive and uncertain energy-producing (and even some conservation) projects will be deferred or canceled. If this cancellation turns out to be a mistake, the individual investors who put their money elsewhere will not lose much; their new project will probably have as much chance to be successful as the one they canceled. The loss will be to society as a whole. If, on the other hand, the projects are carried through and result in a permanent decrease in oil prices (or in a mobilization base for a crash program should a new oil crisis occur), the individual investor will make his profit, but this time the major gains will go to the entire society.

This is a typical example of a "welfare economics" argument. It has long been recognized that there are four or five good reasons for governments to intervene in the market. One is for protection of infant industries. That argument holds in this case, particularly for any industry that makes coal or oil shale more useful. Since the United States is among the largest owners of coal and oil shale in the world, anything that makes either of these more valuable substantially increases the national wealth.

Another justification for government intervention may arise when external (i.e., societal) costs or gains should be internalized (i.e., charged to the entrepreneur). As these external costs and gains sometimes cannot be internalized successfully, it could then make sense for the government not to depend solely on market forces, especially if, as in this case, the economic and financial costs of intervention are really quite small. If intervention costs as much as is generally believed, we would probably be opposed to it. But properly designed programs properly financed can operate remarkably inexpensively. Hence our suggestion that this is a situation in which the welfare economics argument may be correct.

Nonetheless, we believe, for reasons already discussed, that even without any government intervention we will more likely than not luck out. But we also believe, in the language of Chapter 8, that bad luck is "not implausible"—the possibility that it could occur is high enough to warrant serious governmental consideration. Furthermore, appropriate intervention increases the likelihood even more that we will luck out and can do so relatively inexpensively.

The argument for government intervention is therefore almost overwhelming, but the Reagan administration, despite its possible acceptance of the argument, might ultimately conclude that such intervention would set a very bad precedent. In fact, the more successful the program, the worse the precedent and the greater the pressure later to intervene in areas where it would not be as justified. There is little one can say in answer to this except to weigh the costs against the gains and to note that the government intervention can be designed to minimize its impact as a precedent—e.g., there could be great emphasis on how special in nature the energy projects are and on how extraordinarily justifiable the intervention is.

Nevertheless, such intervention goes directly against the ideology of the Reagan administration and against its current high-priority programs. This is a typical situation where a general ideological position which may well hold in most cases should not be held to a fanatical degree or to the extent that appearance of ideological consistency is maintained at any cost.

Samuel Johnson once said that the last refuge of a scoundrel is patriotism, by which he meant that scoundrels would turn to patriotic arguments in pursuing their nefarious schemes. Many in the Reagan administration tend to think (and with some legitimacy) that almost all appeals to economic welfare arguments are made by scoundrels, fools, ideological liberals, or special-interest groups. We like to think we are none of the above, but still would like to make a welfare argument for suitable energy projects.

In sum, our position on energy is as follows: economic forces are gradually forcing a solution to the long-term threat of ever-rising petroleum prices. Their impact is already pronounced and could become overwhelming well before 1990. The major caveat is the possibility of a self-defeating prophecy.

The principal forces over the next twenty years that will bring about a brighter energy picture will be conservation; substitution of coal, nuclear power, and natural gas for oil; and increases in worldwide exploration and development of oil and gas. Unconventional financing of energy projects may also play a big role.

The emerging energy sources which are likely to become increasingly important during the 1990s and potentially large in the twenty-first century are enhanced recovery of conventional oil and gas; other unconventional (speculative) sources of oil and gas; the synthetic-fuels industry; the inexhaustibles (solar, geothermal, fusion); and breeder reactors.

Finally, with a vigorous energy policy the United States should be able to fulfill the worldwide leadership role which its resources and position both justify and require. This leadership calls for more than a simple optimal policy designed for the most probable future environment—the price system will do that as well as or better than government guidance and intervention are likely to do. What are also required are some specific hedging strategies that the price system will not normally encourage.

CHAPTER 8

U.S. DEFENSE POLICY: THINKING CONSTRUCTIVELY ABOUT THE UNTHINKABLE

AN OVERVIEW OF THE STRATEGIC ISSUES

Whatever it accomplishes in the way of rearmament, the United States has entered a period during the early 1980s when, for the first time, the Soviet Union has achieved a useful—and perhaps usable—strategic nuclear superiority over this country. Part of this nuclear advantage is the well-known "window of vulnerability"—a period in which, at least, theoretically, American land-based missiles are extraordinarily vulnerable to a Soviet first strike. (The U.S.S.R. will also enjoy, in many important areas, superiority in both conventional and tactical nuclear warfare.)* The degree to which our vulnerability really is a window of danger for the United States (and others) or a window of opportunity for the Soviets is an open issue, which we will return to later.

Primarily, this chapter discusses how and why such a remarkable shift in the balance of strategic nuclear power developed and why it was largely ignored as it was happening. In addition, we will look at what it may mean, both for this country and for the world in the decade ahead,

---

* The focus of this chapter is on U.S.–U.S.S.R. strategic issues, but this is not to suggest that other defense issues are unimportant. They are not, but we believe the U.S.–U.S.S.R. strategic defense relationship is most central. The other issues must also be dealt with if there is to be sufficient insurance against military and political disasters and a revitalization of U.S. world status and influence.

and suggest some possible remedies. While the "shift" is now essentially a "given," its duration, degree, character, and consequences will very much depend on U.S. and, to a lesser extent, allied efforts to redress it. The Reagan administration properly regards correcting the U.S.-U.S.S.R. military imbalance to have as high a priority as any it has, though here as everywhere trade-offs have to be made with other high-priority issues such as European political issues, arms control, and the control of inflation.

The main reason the Soviets were able to achieve such a dramatic reversal of the military balance was that the American military budget, under various political, budgetary, and arms-control pressures, was, except for the operational expenses of the Vietnam War, roughly constant in constant dollars from 1963 to 1979 (in terms of percent GNP, it fell from 8.7 to 5 percent). At the same time Soviet military expenditures, in constant rubles, increased about 4 percent a year, or about doubled. During this period the Soviet GNP more than doubled, and the percentage of the GNP spent on national security decreased, but not as rapidly as that of the U.S. The American and NATO governments seemed relatively unconcerned that the Soviets were gaining important advantages in almost all categories of military power. The term "arms race," therefore, is a poor metaphor for the East-West competition between 1963 and 1980. In those seventeen years the U.S. and NATO nations were not racing—at best, they "walked," while the Soviets jogged and once in a while ran. The result is the present difference in the military balance.

At the present time, however, I think that the chances are good that the United States and its European allies will luck out—i.e., will not suffer any grave consequences from the failure to keep pace adequately with the military buildup of the Soviet Union—though the United States and/or its allies may be running some risks which could be almost as serious as a direct attack. Despite the clear Soviet superiority over the United States in both the European theater and strategically (at least by most calculations), given likely Soviet prudence and caution, some quick fixes in U.S. and allied defense postures such as increased long-term spending on defense, and some good fortune, the 1980s could be a decade which the United States and its allies will survive without great loss, and possibly even with a gain in security. It is unlikely that the decade will be devoid of any crisis or conflict, but the United States and European allies should be able to endure any which may occur.

This does not mean that we are sanguine about the state of U.S. defenses or unaware of the foreign policy difficulties and the many dangerous risks fostered by the decline of U.S. power and prestige. The quick fixes (e.g., increased defense spending) are useful but not adequate, since it will take several years for their effect to be felt in terms of reduced vulnerability. It takes time to amass greater numbers of weapons, ships, and aircraft, as well as more ammunition and better-trained, higher-morale, better-maintained, and more-ready forces. Until then the United States and its allies will remain vulnerable—much too vulnerable—to political coercion or even battlefield defeat at the hands of a militarily stronger Soviet Union.

We believe that the prospects for very dangerous and extreme Soviet forays are remote; that even though some aggressively minded Soviets will be able to make many apparently persuasive arguments and calculations for various adventures, the responsible leadership will judge the uncertainties and risks to be too great. But we don't think it is wise to be so dependent on Soviet prudence and caution for our security, especially since the Soviet strategic and theater nuclear-force buildup, complemented by its conventional forces, has reduced the risk that even a responsible leadership will associate with such aggressive ventures. Soviet willingness to "gamble," particularly in politically unstable parts of the world, will probably increase—perhaps more than many analysts, including myself, expect.

During the 1950s and early to middle 1960s the United States could credibly wield the threat of strategic escalation to deter potential Soviet foreign designs. The reverse is now at least partly true—the Soviet Union may be able, in an intense crisis, to limit if not paralyze many potential U.S. initiatives through a credible threat of counterescalation.

The change in the military balance could bring about a variety of scenarios, including some which are highly unlikely, but potentially disastrous—a frontal military assault by the Soviet Union against the Persian Gulf, the NATO theater, or U.S. strategic forces. The fact that the Soviets will probably be too cautious to attempt such an assault does not mean we shouldn't prepare for it; engineers do not reduce the quality of structures designed to resist earthquakes just because earthquakes are infrequent. As long as there is a low but significant probability, certain standards must be met.* Further, since the multilevel Soviet military buildup

---

* This is an important point. Assume one lived in an area which had annual earthquakes. One would then build very high-quality earthquake-proof structures. Assume now that the frequency went down by a factor of 10. One would build about the same quality of structure.

U.S. Defense Policy ■ 149 ■

is unprecedented, no references to past periods of relatively cautious Soviet foreign policies are completely convincing or comforting vis-à-vis the new strategic environment of the 1980s. In any case, confrontations that were not desired or planned by either side but which were "not implausible"* could still occur in which both sides say, "One of us has to be reasonable, and it isn't going to be me." For the moment, the Soviets would have a decisive advantage in any such confrontation.

One question that immediately arises is "Why did President Carter allow this change in the military balance to happen?" While it began in the early '60s and became quite apparent during the Nixon administration, it did not get to a crucial stage until Carter took office. The answer is simple. Neither he nor any of his staff (with the exception of some people in the office of the national security adviser) believed in the existence of genuine thermonuclear threats. They really regarded nuclear war as unthinkable—an end of history, something that cannot happen and if it does it has nothing to do with policy. At the same time, they were also completely convinced that both sides had "overkill" and hence "more" and "less" had but thin meaning.

This kind of thinking still allowed for the possibility that nuclear war could in fact happen, but nevertheless was easy to deter; all we needed was a minimum "deterrence only" force, and not what is now called a "war-fighting" capability. Accordingly, President Carter noted in his 1979 State of the Union Address:

Assume now that the frequency goes down by another factor of 10. One might now begin to take chances. Another factor of 10 and the problem would be considered minor. But you don't have to believe in annual earthquakes to be deeply concerned; once every ten or twenty years will do the trick. Of course, the scoffers will believe that the concerned person is paranoic—believes in annual earthquakes. If the earthquake were to occur in two or three years instead of in one, he would say, "See, I was right," but the damage would still be the same.

* The term "not implausible" is not a double negative meaning "plausible," but a construction technically known as a litote. To illustrate this concept, let us use the term "not improbable." "Improbable" could normally be a probability of less than .1. "Probable" would normally be a probability of substantially greater than .5. "Not improbable" is therefore greater than .1 which includes a much larger range than "probable."

The use of litotes in strategic argument is central. We are dealing with remote events which most people don't take seriously. We often try to make the point that even though these possibilities are remote, they are not *so* remote, improbable, or implausible that they should not be taken with deadly seriousness. (Our note about the need for earthquake-proof construction is most relevant.) The reader will gather that I believe we will luck out in the next decade, but he should also clearly understand that I am horrified at the degree to which we are depending on luck rather than capability. It is almost totally irresponsible.

> ... just one of our relatively invulnerable Poseidon submarines—comprising less than 2 percent of our total nuclear force of submarines, aircraft, and land-based missiles—carries enough warheads to destroy every large and medium-sized city in the Soviet Union. Our deterrent is overwhelming, and I will sign no agreement unless our deterrence force will remain overwhelming.

In the United States, and in the West and among NATO countries generally, almost the only acceptable position is that nuclear war is the "end of history" and not an "experience" which can occur and be survived. Of course, most Westerners realize that nuclear war may occur, but they don't think in terms of having to fight and survive one and then to deal with the postwar world. For Soviets, a nuclear war presents one possible, even if undesirable, path to bring about world communism (and to become the dominant power) in a postwar world (if they perform well), or to plan on a greatly diminished role for both communism and themselves (if they do badly). The "deterrent only" argument is therefore not overwhelming enough for the Soviets.

THE SPIRITUAL IS AS IMPORTANT AS THE MATERIAL (EVEN, OR ESPECIALLY, IN THE NUCLEAR AGE)

Power politics, including nuclear politics, are not based solely on rational calculations. While calculations are probably much more important than many commentators, publicists, scholars, and politicians believe, they are nowhere near as important as many systems analysts and policy researchers think they are. Thus for the last twenty years the Chinese have pushed the Russians around much more than the Russians have pushed the Chinese, even though there is no question that the balance of forces lies firmly on the Soviet side. With this in mind, we would argue it is a lot safer, as well as better from a psychological perspective, for the United States to deal with the Soviet Union as if it were doing so from a position of (relative) strength. This seems to be the policy of the Reagan administration. The president said in his inaugural address:

> When action is required to preserve our national security we will act.... Above all we must realize that no arsenal or no weapon in the arsenals of the world is so formidable as the will and courage of free men and women.

While the above rhetoric is more or less standard, it is not necessarily meaningless. In any case, the president apparently plans to make such rhetoric (and the corresponding reality) part of our military arsenal. We would argue that it is a good basis for policy, and one of the main reasons we don't expect a serious deterioration in the U.S. world position in the next decade or so. It would be a fatal error at this point to demoralize our allies further and to tempt the Soviets by the appearance or actuality of weak, uncertain, and defensive international policies—or to provoke them and our allies by excessively aggressive and bellicose policies. It is a matter of balance and situation.

In German there is a word, *Machtfrage,* which means that a given military, political, and/or moral issue is a test of the real power of a country—a question of whether a nation is in fact a great power or merely has the trappings of one. If the nation does not adequately meet the challenge of a *Machtfrage,* further testing and a serious loss of prestige and status are likely to ensue. This is dangerous because it can lead to miscalculation—the provocateur may underestimate the willingness or capacity of the nation being tested to respond; the provoked nation may unexpectedly "lose its cool" and overreact; or it may just judge it has been driven into a corner and has no choice except to turn on its tormentor.

A nation which fails a *Machtfrage* test—or appears likely to fail one—must be prepared to defend its interests by actual use of military force. The more prestige, status, reputation, and credibility that have been lost, the greater the need to rely on actual force rather than reputation and credible deterrents.

Many people believe the United States failed the *Machtfrage* test in Vietnam, Angola, and the Iranian hostage crisis. The situation was aggravated by a loss of faith in President Carter, who began to be perceived as personally undependable, even frivolous, in national security policies. (For example, he canceled the neutron bomb after Helmut Schmidt had gone out on a limb to support it. What was most damaging was that Carter did so without warning, and he consulted not his normal foreign and defense policy advisers, but only some cronies.) SALT II, whatever its merits, was considered by many to be a formal concession of U.S. military inferiority, and an agreement conceding its continuance. The loss of prestige and faith seemed likely to prompt further serious challenges to American interests; it weakened the NATO alliance in that its members wondered whether they could count on the United States in a time of crisis—or even in negotiations. Many were forced to ask if the United States knew what it was doing.

The latest proposal to upset our NATO partners involves the declaration of a "no first use" policy. Under this plan, the United States would renounce its intention to initiate the use of nuclear weapons. Our allies, and especially West Germany, see this as a further U.S. withdrawal from Europe (and from the world) and regard it as a U.S. concession to Soviet military superiority. The potential consequences of such a move are terrifying to them; it means the Soviet Union could launch a massive conventional attack on their soil without fear of any significant retaliation; it means they would have to undertake a massive conventional buildup of their own (and the West Germans have made it abundantly clear that they are unwilling to fight a conventional war); and it means that West Germany might well "go nuclear" or "go neutral."

And yet, with proper consultation and arrangements with our allies, a "no first use" doctrine seems a perfectly reasonable position for the United States to take. Primarily, it gives us a *moral legitimation* to prepare more adequately for defense.* By declaring that we will not be the first to use them, we nonetheless retain the option to correct for their use by others. Never are the warheads to be considered "just another weapons system" which can be employed in the normal escalation of a conflict; instead, a "no first use" policy would be the truest sign that the United States is categorically opposed to nuclear war except in extreme circumstances in which we are morally justified (even obligated) to retaliate against others who have initiated an attack with nuclear weapons.

The U.S.–Soviet defense issue, then, involves more than straight military capability. Political, economic, diplomatic, morale, and moral factors on both sides—and of the allies and neutrals—are also very important. The Reagan administration is seeking to strengthen the U.S. position on all fronts, an effort which would be greatly facilitated by more support and cooperation from presently disenchanted or reluctant allies. They could take up some of the slack as the United States redeploys its forces; they could buttress U.S. intervention forces; they could provide the United States with bases, staging areas, and other operating facilities; and perhaps most important of all, they could help legitimize and

---

* See *New York Times Magazine,* June 13, 1981 "A Moral Defense of Defense" by Herman Kahn.

strengthen appropriate U.S. foreign, defense, and arms-control policies. They are not likely to do any of these if we appear either too weak and uncertain or too bellicose and callous to the risk of war or the arms race; rather our allies are more likely to opt for compromise and neutralism, and the Soviets, if they can, will do much to encourage these trends.

THE NEW STRATEGIC BALANCE AND SOME POTENTIAL CONSEQUENCES

The Soviets are well aware that their military buildup has fundamentally changed the way many in the West regard them, and they are genuinely elated at being—and being thought of—as number one (and quite fearful of losing that status or having to divert enormous resources from a faltering economy to maintain it). For the first time in its history, the Soviets are not, and do not feel, militarily inferior to prospective opponents. How this situation will affect their present behavior may be less interesting than how it affects the new Soviet leadership which will almost certainly arise during the 1980s—the first generation of civilian leaders who did not come to power during the Stalin era. Many experts in the West feel that the coming Soviet struggle for succession and the current Soviet military superiority render the chances for new and more reckless Soviet initiatives and experiments more plausible than ever before. I find this unlikely, but not impossible; it is certainly one more reason for urgency in revitalizing U.S. foreign and defense postures.

Nonetheless, with the possible exception of Lieutenant General Daniel Graham (U.S. Army retired), Paul Nitze, and Colin Gray, almost all of the better-known Western analysts, even conservative ones (see Annex at end of chapter) seem convinced that Soviet leaders will continue to be essentially prudent and cautious. Soviets, above all else, are realists. They know that war—particularly nuclear war—would be risky and uncertain, almost certainly not as simple, neat, and definitive as some military planners or moralists would have us believe. Strategic advantages notwithstanding, most American and European analysts judge (we hope correctly) that the Soviets are unlikely to deliberately initiate nuclear war—even in an intense crisis—for positive political gain; they would do it only if they judge it rational and to avert an immediate disaster.

Which is not to say that the Soviet strategic buildup is irrelevant, or that it does not give the Soviet Union great advantages in its relations with the United States and others. Imagine, for example, that a very serious but unforeseen and unwanted crisis has developed to the point where it is threatening to get out of control. It could be another East German revolt (trying to get some of the freedoms recently sought by the Poles), perhaps an uprising by Czechs who are inspired by the Polish example, or perhaps a situation in which the Soviets have threatened Yugoslavia and the West has, in turn, threatened the Soviets and the situation has gotten out of hand. In any case, assume a crisis in which the Soviets feel that most of Eastern Europe may explode, that the "poison" might spread to the Soviet Union, and that they have to stop it. The Soviets might calculate that once they have evacuated their cities and given the United States an ultimatum, the United States would then almost have to stop its "interference" and the insurgents, who would now feel abandoned, would be easy to control. Or some Soviet leaders may even decide that if the United States does not back down, they will go ahead and launch a strike. Part of the reason for striking, and, in fact, for their ultimatum would be the belief that—because of their present strategic superiority, which they may feel they have to use—they can win the war and dominate the postwar world. Once an evacuation of their cities had taken place, the Soviets' confidence in their own superiority could begin to become influential and perhaps make the crucial difference in the outcome of the crisis.

At this point the United States would be in a very bad position to strike preemptively unless a great many changes had been made in its force posture and in its ability to evacuate its own cities. It should be noted that U.S. evacuation may have a destabilizing effect upon deterrence; that is, it may heighten the possibility of a first strike by either side. Thus, unless our strategic forces are adequate, then even if we have an evacuation ability we may not be willing to use it and risk the increased probability of deterrence failing. Indeed, one could argue that having a moderately protected U.S. population increases the probability of a Soviet first strike because the Soviets may then believe they may be able to limit the war and get away relatively unscathed.

In the event of such a crisis, the United States would be foolish to stand firm in the belief that the Soviets were bluffing about their intentions. Indeed, they probably would not be. Rather, the United States should start negotiating very fast, possibly making rather shameful and dangerous concessions if necessary. In any case the United States should compromise or retreat, and under some circumstances, the Soviets might be less interested in accepting concessions than in using their newly acquired military superiority. Or, even worse, the United States might be unwilling to make concessions, a misjudgment which could touch off a Soviet strike. It is at this point that the U.S. option to resort to its "launch on warning" or "launch on attack" system (in order to prevent U.S. Minutemen from being destroyed in their silos) would become more attractive. It would also be less attractive, however, because the system might be more accident-prone than usual, given the tenseness of the situation and the high state of alert. This would be particularly true if the U.S. action touched off a Soviet decision to institute a "launch on warning" posture.

There is also the question of what targets the United States should strike with its launch-on-warning capability. It would be imprudent to launch very many missiles at the empty holes from which the Soviets had already launched their missiles (unless a Soviet reload/refire capability appears likely), and it would be totally disastrous to launch our missiles against their cities. But regardless of the target, if the Soviets knew that their first strike would incur U.S. retaliation, they might be deterred at the onset from launching their own missiles—an example of what is sometimes called "the rationality of irrationality." We tend to be strongly opposed to any launch-on-warning system, especially in such tense situations in which Americans might be willing to risk briefly the possibility of accidental war rather than back down.

But the real point is that it is disgraceful that the United States might ever be in a position in which it has to consider adopting such desperate measures as "launch on warning" or "launch on attack," and equally disgraceful that we cannot balance Soviet bargaining leverage because of inadequacies in our own strategic preparations—both offensive and defensive. The final disgrace is that we have created the most dangerous of all possible situations—one in which we have allowed the balance of power to tilt so much against us that we now actually increase the danger by rearming, indicating to the Soviets that unless they use their superiority when they have it, they may lose it forever. (Yet we believe it is safe to rearm, particularly if we rapidly implement some appropriate short-term measures such as decreasing the vulnerability of our strategic forces. Nonetheless, rearmament means depending to an extraordinary degree on the extreme reliability of our intelligence and our estimates of likely Soviet behavior.)

The above-described scenario illustrates the importance of looking at systems under strain. The United States should not judge its strategic forces (and doctrine) by whether the deterrent will stand up on a bright summer day when no one is provoked or aggravated. Rather the deterrent should be judged on the basis of its ability both to deter a potential aggressor (i.e., the Soviet Union) in an intense crisis and to do so clearly and reliably enough that we and our allies can virtually depend on it to work under any given circumstances. If in spite of its adequacy deterrence in the long run failed, we would at least achieve what is sometimes called an "improved war outcome."

Finally, it should be noted that a deterrent cannot be reliable if its strategic land- and air-based forces are weak and it is left to rest only on the invulnerability of sea-based forces. This implies that if the Soviets had one technological breakthrough or some ingenious operational innovation, most likely including attacks on U.S. command and control, they could damage or unexpectedly limit the remaining leg of the triad. As we discuss later, the first two legs are almost certainly dangerously vulnerable in the early '80s, and if the Soviets even fake the possibility that the third leg is in danger, they will be in an extraordinarily good bargaining position. In any case, if the United States (but not the Soviet Union) is afraid to evacuate its cities and threaten a first strike because of fear that the Soviets will preempt, it could be in serious trouble. To put it in simple if stark terms, what the United States must be able to do is to persuade the Soviets that in an intense crisis, even though they prefer striking first to striking second, they should really prefer backing down to striking at all. Striking first is too likely to have unacceptable consequences when the United States retaliates.

This capability to coerce the Soviet Union to conciliate rather than escalate is what we refer to as "escalation dominance." Escalation dominance requires that Soviet leaders always consider conciliation and/or de-escalation to be preferable to continued conflict and escalation. It also requires that U.S. strategic forces have a much greater capability than simple assured destruction. However, U.S. extended deterrence responsibilities render escalation dominance a necessary standard for measuring "how much is enough" in strategic forces.

Some analysts (not I) believe that more than most countries, the Soviet empire depends on having a reputation for success in order to legitimize bloc or internal political control. Political retreat by the Soviets, therefore, might not be an option in some "not implausible" crisis. I believe that as long as such political retreat does not involve any concession on frontiers or ideology, or any serious concession on the control of their internal affairs, the Soviets can be made to back down by the kind of pressure we should be able, and prepared, to exert (but not if the current military imbalance is allowed to continue). Further, in estimating Soviet caution, we should be conscious that there is a difference between acting to achieve political gain and acting to prevent great (even if not intolerable) political loss. There is also a difference between the Soviets' deliberately planning a crisis and their taking advantage of a situation that has been thrust upon them. We do not believe the Soviets would intentionally precipitate a showdown based on the shift in military power; we do believe they would leverage every advantage in a confrontation. And finally, existence of large nuclear forces makes both the United States and the Soviet Union cautious, but it has by no means eliminated the human potential for mistakes, miscalculations, or pure folly—or even for daring and creative ventures that just might work according to plan.* In either case we have to worry about deterrence failing and a war beginning—i.e., we'll need "war-fighting" capabilities if only to limit damage as much as possible.

THE POSSIBLE NEUTRALIZATION OF WESTERN EUROPE

In the 1980s, the areas of greatest risk of escalation-prone U.S.–Soviet confrontations are Central Europe and the Persian Gulf. Most Western analysts have long believed that the Soviets probably have no burning

* From this point of view the United States might be relatively lucky in its choice of opponents. In both the Soviet Union and the United States there is a clear-cut concept of "war by miscalculation" and almost no concept of a "war by calculation." This was not true in prewar France, Germany, and Japan. In these three countries there was a clear-cut concept that one might make war-game calculations, go to war on the basis of these calculations, and the calculations would probably be reliable and correct. In other words, their belief in the possibility of "war by calculation" reflected their previous history. In both the United States and the U.S.S.R. no such history of war by calculation exists, and this is one reason for my estimate that in the future we will luck out. We are not dealing with a Hitler or Napoleon or even with the kind of general staff which the Germans, the French, and the Japanese once had. There are many important differences in the strategic culture of the United States and the Soviet Union, and while it is most dangerous for Americans, as they often do, to ignore or downgrade these strategic differences, in one aspect the two countries are quite similar. They do not normally and easily trust military calculations, particularly if they are complex and involve great risks.

desire to occupy Western Europe. Rather, they would like to "neutralize" it to the point where it would not be a military or political threat to the Warsaw Pact and would be committed to close economic cooperation with the Soviet bloc. Increased trade and investment (much of it based upon Western credits and loans to develop Soviet natural resources) could indeed be mutually profitable. They also like the idea of West European countries giving up a more or less automatic support of U.S. positions but being more objective (i.e., neutral) in any U.S.-U.S.S.R. dispute (one step in this "increased objectivity," which the Soviets seem to encourage, is for West European countries to try to act as a go-between in disputes between the United States and the U.S.S.R.). Such West European policies with regard to the Soviet Union are consistent with the nominal existence of a NATO alliance, but all kinds of questions are raised about the value of this alliance and the likely willingness of its members (including the United States) to continue to support it adequately.

Nonetheless, the idea of more independent policies (but along the lines of at least partial neutralization) has been gaining acceptance among many West Europeans, especially as the United States has been increasingly viewed as an inconsistent, incompetent, weak, and unreliable alliance leader—bringing Europe many problems and liabilities as well as inadequate security. Moreover, European economies are presently stagnant and are likely to remain so for some years unless stimulated by something like economic cooperation with the Soviets. Almost every advanced European country has overbuilt what might be called the early-to-mid-twentieth-century industries—steel, heavy construction, transportation, shipbuilding, and many engineering facilities. The Soviet Union is a natural customer for almost all of these and could pay for imports with energy exports and other raw materials.

In fact, one of the most obvious ways to solve Europe's energy problem as well as its economic stagnation is through closer cooperation with the Soviet Union. The Soviets have already found about 1,000 trillion cubic feet of gas (equivalent to about 170 billion barrels of oil, or an amount almost equal to official Saudi oil reserves). Potential oil and coal supplies seem equally plentiful; all that is needed is adequate development. And the Europeans are in a perfect position to supply the necessary capital and technology at terms which could appear—and perhaps be—quite advantageous to both sides.

Economic cooperation with the Soviet Union is particularly attractive to West Germany. In fact, it is difficult to draw the line between the current *Ostpolitik** and partial neutralization. We believe it can be done, though it is much easier if there is a strong United States, a strong NATO, and a strong tie between the United States and West Germany. The West Germans are working hard to extend the *Ostpolitik* even further, and would probably continue to do so even in the event of a Soviet invasion of Poland; there might be great indignation for a year or so, but eventually "cooler" heads would prevail. "After all," they would argue, "the Soviet action was basically defensive and we can't have open hostility with the Soviet Union for the rest of history." The cooling off would be even faster if the Polish government suppressed Solidarity without recourse to use of Soviet troops.

West Germany's European ties with East Germany are substantial and growing, but the human ties between the two countries are even stronger. West Germany has in effect taken the position that it is responsible for the welfare of East Germans; Chancellor Helmut Schmidt has referred to them as "our seventeen million hostages."

The distinction between "détente" and neutralization is real and important, but it may easily become blurred in West Germany as well as in the rest of Western Europe. Indeed, it is already showing signs of doing so. The West Europeans now have an enormous—and growing—economic and political stake in détente and will not give it up easily—certainly not in response to any Soviet "opportunism" outside their areas of vital interest (Western or Southeastern Europe and the Persian Gulf). As a result, it will be increasingly difficult for NATO to present a united front in response to ambivalent or complex Soviet initiatives, or to risk antagonizing the Soviets by taking the political and military steps that are now necessary for European security.

The Soviet strategic buildup has degraded the credibility of the "U.S. guarantee"—i.e., the strategic capability to deter European war or, failing deterrence, the force to limit such a conflict to one which would leave Europe viable. Europeans are not eager to do their part to prepare for limited war—much less for what they regard as a fatal level of escalation. If

---

* Politics toward the East, a policy which goes back to Willy Brandt's historic meeting in 1970 with Willi Stoph, East Germany's premier. However, the policy is usually identified with Helmut Schmidt's "live and let live" policy toward East Germany and to the extensive economic and political interaction with the Soviet Union and the East European nations.

one polls almost any European audience and asks, "Which would you choose, everybody red or everybody dead?" the answer is overwhelmingly "Everybody red." But this is not the question; the whole purpose of NATO is to prevent it from ever becoming the question. Many Europeans, however, regard the related choice "everybody red, dead, or neutral" as the real issue. Especially in West Germany, the neutralist position is being presented as the patriotic position. The antiwar, pro-ecology, anti-American, antinuclear, anti-growth, and pro-welfare movements (again especially in West Germany) are beginning to coalesce and to use patriotic arguments. Several religious and pacifist groups have joined in. Some West Europeans have even advanced the argument "We don't want to fight any more of your wars in our country"—a most extraordinary revisionist interpretation of World Wars I and II.*

Whatever the reason, increasing numbers of Europeans are becoming pacifistic, neutralist, cynical, apathetic, or just disillusioned about defense. The current West European preference is to compromise in any situation in which there would be a serious risk of nuclear war—if necessary, to compromise by "preemptive surrender." But most Europeans believe that the Soviets would never intentionally test them; in fact, almost every serious discussion of defense ends with the statement "It would be too dangerous for the Soviets to 'dare' us because they could not be sure." The Europeans then often continue, "The Soviets don't want to occupy Western Europe that strongly, if at all—and they couldn't digest us if they did." Perhaps so. In either case, while acute crises in Europe do not arise often and the question of nuclear use normally does not surface, not having a credible deterrent makes both such crises and such threats more likely—and more dangerous if they do occur.

* However, there is no use in arguing that the Americans and the Russians were not big gainers from World War II (no matter what the averted horrors of a victorious Hitler would have been). Further, a plausible case (to those who wish to believe it) can be made that the division of Europe and Germany is, in some ways, a de facto agreement between the United States and the Soviet Union to keep Europe (and Germany) weak. From this it is only a step to the position that the Soviets and the Americans do not have Europe's (or Germany's) interests at heart, that their quarrel is not of Europe's (or Germany's) making, and that the best strategy for Europe (or Germany) is to try to sit it out.

THE PERSIAN GULF

The strategic significance of Persian Gulf oil, coupled with the proximity of the Soviet Union to the region, establishes the Persian Gulf as another potential flashpoint for escalation-prone conflicts. However, both geography and the suspicion with which the United States is viewed there make the task of preparing for crises a great deal more difficult.

The hostility expressed by states in the gulf (most notably Saudi Arabia) toward the Soviet Union—a hostility based on religious opposition to communism—has tempted U.S. military and political leaders to view the region in much the same way it viewed Iran, i.e., as allies who will cooperate with the United States because of the common Soviet enemy. This attitude, and subsequent proposals that the United States be allowed to establish military bases in the region (as in Europe and Japan), show an ignorance of the most fundamental fact of political life in the Persian Gulf—that the United States, while disliked and feared less than the U.S.S.R., is disliked and feared. It is tolerated primarily because of the lack of a good alternative.

U.S. support of Israel is one reason for the gulf states' hostility. Another is that many strict Muslims consider our country to be the world's major source of decadence and permissiveness, exhibiting the use of drugs, pornography, "promiscuous" sex, weak character, and an undesirable degree of secularization of society. Leaders in the Persian Gulf states consider internal disruption by radical political or religious groups to be a much greater threat to the region than the Soviet Union is. They would not, therefore, risk too close an identification with the United States, because that would give these factions substantial ammunition in their struggle to overthrow the ruling elites.

They are also afraid of the United States directly. They can envisage many scenarios in which the United States might attempt to take over the oil fields or at least install a classic "protectorate" over them. Announcements that we will protect the country under almost all circumstances, including internal revolt, make the Saudis in particular more nervous than reassured. After all, one characteristic of internal revolt is that there are two competing groups, and the United States would have to pick the one it considered more legitimate or worthy of protection. Probably the best policy for the United States is to remain silent about potential plans for intervention. It is also probably best not to ask the Saudis to accept a disturbingly visible presence of American forces as a normal part of peacetime operations (at present there are only about 650 uniformed American personnel stationed in Saudi Arabia). And any threat of U.S. intervention against Qaddafi would be most unpopular. It is not that the Persian Gulf states support Qaddafi; they do not and will be delighted if he is replaced by a less troublesome government. But U.S. intervention would be judged a very dangerous precedent. (This is not necessarily a bad thing from the U.S. perspective. It would put many governments on notice that they do not have a free ride if they support terrorist groups freely.)

Nonetheless, the threat of Soviet intervention, even invasion, remains sufficiently "not incredible," as does the need for a force which can be quickly mobilized in the event of a crisis in the Persian Gulf. Depending on the nature of the attack and the tactics employed, the recently organized U.S. Rapid Deployment Force (RDF) could prove successful in limiting or delaying certain crises until other forces could arrive. But if the crisis were a large-scale Soviet attack the RDF would almost certainly be defeated, though not necessarily easily, and by compelling the Soviets to realize that they would have to destroy one of two American divisions, the United States would substantially raise the stakes of the Soviet action. There is deterrence value in any credible American resistance, especially if it is clear up front that destruction of the RDF might well lead to a declaration of war and/or a full-scale mobilization of at least the magnitude that occurred during the Korean War. (In June 1950, Congress was debating whether the defense budget should be increased from $13 billion to $14, $15, or $16 billion. Then North Korea invaded South Korea, and Congress gave the Department of Defense new obligational authority for *$60* billion. It was this and subsequent authorizations that gave the United States its superiority over the Soviets for the next two decades. Let us hope we do not need another such provocation before we can carry out currently necessary measures.)

THE GREAT VALUE OF THE PROPOSED MOBILIZATION CAPABILITY

The example of Korean War mobilization is useful to explain that there is a potential for a large and rapid increase in defense spending. The huge fourfold increase of 1950 was largely a response to U.S. fears that the North Korean invasion was designed to presage (by distracting U.S. attention from the area) a general war in Europe. This fact is underscored by the U.S. decision at the time to send only its unorganized reserves (mainly World War II veterans) to fight in Korea, leaving the organized reserves available for action in Europe if necessary. Similarly, the Strategic Air Command husbanded its primary resources and did not participate in what was regarded as "the wrong war, at the wrong time and wrong place." The quadrupling of the budget was less a reaction to the Korean crisis itself than to a perceived general threat to NATO. Many felt that an attack on Western Europe was imminent.

Similarly, any mobilization following a crisis in the Persian Gulf would be as likely to be triggered by concern for a future (relatively near-term) Soviet threat to U.S. vital interests as by the specific consequences of the attack itself. A U.S. defense budget of between $500 billion and $1 trillion—or more—is possible under those circumstances. Indeed, Defense Secretary Weinberger has recently suggested we should have plans to mobilize half the GNP—i.e., $1.5 trillion. And, at the moment, creating and maintaining a "mobilization base" (an ability to rapidly increase one's strength in reaction to a degraded international environment) has become a serious and high-priority national program. There is even serious consideration of the possibility of adding a few billion dollars a year to defense spending in order to procure the ability to increase the budget by several hundred billion dollars in a year or so if international relations deteriorate enough to justify it.

The possibilities for greater defense purchases and rapid peacetime mobilization are much greater than most people realize, in part because the United States could draw heavily on overseas as well as U.S. procurement. But even if the United States were restricted to domestic procurement alone, much could be done. For example, any large construction program normally takes about five or ten years, but with proper preparations it wouldn't take more than a year or so to build $100 or $200 billion worth of shelters in the United States. The construction industry is very large and very deployable. A highway contractor given the proper blueprints and materials can start building shelters within a matter of days; he might not be very competitive but he can get the job done. With standard planning, financing, and legal and other red tape, such a program is normally stretched out for more than a decade, but this is by no means inevitable.

The consequences of such mobilization would be uncomfortable for the United States but disastrous from the Soviet point of view. Suffice it to say that the U.S. "war-fighting" capabilities would be much greater than expected by anyone used to thinking in terms of overkill and mutual homicide as the only outcome of a large nuclear war. Along with the increased "war-fighting" capability would go increased bargaining power so that the United States could hope to achieve its objectives without fighting.*

A credible mobilization deterrent requires that U.S. strategic forces be capable of deterring the Soviets during a severe crisis, in which they might feel great pressure to strike the United States. Knowing that an attack on the RDF would prompt a massive U.S. mobilization, the Soviets might feel that it was less risky to strike at our Strategic Air Command (SAC). But if the U.S. strategic forces were clearly adequate to deter such an attack on SAC and were reliable to the extent that an all-out mobilization could be actualized, and if this last possibility deters Soviet attack on the Persian Gulf (or on the RDF), then SAC is playing a crucial role in that deterrence, even without the threat of any direct retaliation.

A serious program for a pre-attack mobilization base—one that is designed to be actuated and carried through after major provocation has occurred or war declared, but prior to massive attack on U.S. cities—is a new concept for most planners (at least in terms of official policy). There is still much confusion on both the military and civilian sides as to the appropriate strategic, political, and economic concepts, policies and programs. The Soviets, however, seem to be relatively clear on this because of their experience during the Korean War, when they had to double their military budget and double their army and yet accept a position of extreme inferiority. They are therefore completely aware of the danger of provoking the United States into doubling, tripling, or quadrupling its own military budget. Further, if before provocation the United States openly spent billions of dollars to prepare for mobilizing after such provocation, the deterrent to the Soviets would be even greater.

* In fact, many Hudson studies have focused on what Max Singer (formerly of Hudson) has called "mobilization war" (or a competitive mobilization) as a substitute (in some circumstances) for a fighting war. Fear of such mobilization is probably a greater deterrent to massive Soviet provocation than existing strategic forces.

U.S. DEFENSE POLICY ■ 165 ■

CURRENT PROBLEMS AND ISSUES IN REVITALIZING U.S. DEFENSE POSTURES

We have already noted that the balance of strategic nuclear forces has been shifting against the United States for over fifteen years. Soviet strategic capabilities have moved from unquestioned inferiority to parity to (at least temporary) superiority. Further, the existence of vulnerable ICBMs is dangerous in itself: during an acute crisis, the Soviet Union might attack them simply to prevent the United States from using them first itself. This in turn puts the United States, particularly if it deploys Pershing and cruise missiles in Western Europe, under some pressure to preempt on its own.

The reciprocal fear of surprise attack has been compared to the classic duel in cowboy movies; the duelist who fires first, and accurately, gets away unscathed. This obviously puts a great premium on shooting first and accurately. In practice, matters are not this simple; for example, one side can announce a "launch on warning" or "launch under attack" posture in which missiles are fired instead of left at risk of being destroyed. But such a policy, despite elaborate precautions, is likely to raise the problem of false alarm and accidental war. It also requires choosing a target system ahead of time, a very difficult task to do rationally unless one totally believes in the mutual assured destruction (MAD) doctrine of automatically concentrating one's attack on destroying Soviet cities and population. The fact that the Soviet Union could be in a position to destroy most of our ICBMs while using only a small fraction of its own arsenal puts the United States in an agonizing dilemma: while we may not be capable of any meaningful attack on Soviet military targets with our remaining forces, an attack on Soviet cities would result in a far more devastating counterattack on U.S. cities.

America's strategic bomber forces also show the effects of disparate U.S. and Soviet spending on arms. Former President Carter's termination of the B-1 strategic bomber program has left the manned-bomber mission largely to the B-52. However, according to official estimates, the steady growth and modernization of Soviet air defense has raised questions about whether the B-52 will be able to penetrate Soviet defenses throughout the 1980s, to say nothing of the 1990s. The air-launched cruise missile (ALCM), which can be launched from B-52s while still outside Soviet airspace, offers a partial remedy. But developments such as

Soviet long-range interceptors with look-down, shoot-down radar and missiles suitable to attack cruise missiles, as well as the new generation of Soviet surface-to-air missiles and the increasing vulnerability of the U.S. B-52 before takeoff, indicate that this kind of cruise-missile deployment will not eliminate the need for a new penetrating bomber. The recently revealed technology for reducing radar visibility will not benefit existing B-52 and FB-111s, though it will be of some help to the B-1.

Indeed, all currently deployed elements of U.S. strategic offensive forces will face serious problems in the 1980s. As far as we know, submarine-based missile forces will suffer least, but by putting all our defense eggs in one basket, we force ourselves to accept all the risks associated with possible Soviet breakthroughs or ingenious tactics to weaken our sea-based forces (including first attacking communications links and then using blackmail and physical attacks to degrade any eventual use of the force). This is the cumulative consequence of U.S. unwillingness to devote adequate resources to its nuclear arsenal; it is the result of an attitude that has spurned actual preparation for nuclear war in favor of "deterrence" or "mutual assured destruction" (MAD) as the solution to all strategic problems. Those who have adopted this doctrine then use the inadequacies which result to prove their theories. This is predictable. Since such a doctrine makes thermonuclear war unthinkable, even the experts and responsible decision-makers stop thinking realistically about the subject, and the neglect might lead to mutual destruction.

We might comment here on what is now called the MAD vs. NUTS controversy. "NUTS" stands for "nuclear use theorists," and it is argued that even though the MAD doctrine may seem bizarre, it is not as bizarre as the various doctrines espoused by various NUTS. I am a reasonably well-known member of one NUTS group whose own version of the doctrine goes as follows: we must be prepared to use nuclear forces to deter and correct the use or threat of use of nuclear forces by others but should not use our nuclear forces for positive gain—e.g., should not threaten nuclear escalation against conventional threats.* I am acutely aware that this position has great difficulties, albeit more technical than moral. It is not that moral issues do not arise, but the moral basis of using—or threatening to use—nuclear weapons is, according to some NUTS theorists,

---

* We have developed at the Institute a whole series of "nuclear limitation" policies that are in accord with this basic position. For some of the earlier work, see "Nuclear Proliferation and Rules of Retaliation," *Yale Law Journal,* Vol. 76, No. 1 (November 1966); and "Criteria for Long-Range Nuclear Policies," *California Law Review,* Vol. 55, No. 2 (May 1967).

eminently justifiable. There are other NUTS doctrines in which nuclear concepts might be considered less justifiable, e.g., those that accept nuclear weapons as just another weapon. But given the present global situation, I have no apologies regarding the moral aspects of maintaining large and usable nuclear forces. However, to maintain these forces just to save money, or to solve problems associated with having inadequate conventional forces, is both immoral and impractical. The crucial point is that every position—MAD, NUTS, unilateral or world disarmament, world government (or world empire)—has serious problems. I argue that the NUTS position I propose is the least unacceptable.

In addition, one especially debilitating effect of the acceptance of MAD is the absence of serious preparations to defend the U.S. homeland. The United States has a blatantly inadequate civil defense program, and an air defense system which is officially recognized as barely capable of protecting U.S. airspace during peacetime.

Here, again, the asymmetry of U.S. and Soviet defensive preparations is striking: the Soviet Union has approached homeland defense with a seriousness which is simply nonexistent in the United States. The U.S.S.R. has spent over $100 billion on air defense, with a sizeable commitment to civil defense. Not all Soviet efforts are well designed, but the net result presents a formidable challenge. An improved U.S. defense posture must, therefore, include not only the capability of waging nuclear war, but also the capacity to limit the damage that the Soviet Union could inflict upon the American homeland.

A new U.S. strategy requires accurate survivable weapons; a survivable national leadership capable of intelligently commanding the weapons; sufficient nonstrategic forces to deny the Soviets any hope of occupying Western industrial recovery assets (e.g., West Germany and Japan) or being able to commandeer or buy them in the postwar period; and, above all, a survivable United States. Weapons and strategic infrastructure are needed to improve the deterrent *and,* if deterrence fails, to improve the war-fighting capabilities of the surviving force. This requires that large investments be made to reconstitute strategic forces after the first attack and that there be an ability to use these forces effectively in continuing the war, policing a cease-fire, or backing a postwar situation. The biggest defect in doing all this may be survivable military C^4I^2 systems (command and control; see Chapter 4 for an explanation of C^4I^2).

As noted, the submarine-missile force is likely to remain relatively secure for the near term, though subject to some degradation in operational or system capability against a Soviet preemptive strike upon its communications (and its survivability in a lengthy war is also open to question). Similarly, while low-altitude satellites are already vulnerable to attack, those in synchronous (high) orbit appear as yet immune, though the immunity may well be exhausted by the end of the decade. (Both kinds of satellites are essential elements of our surveillance and C^4I^2 systems.) The level of technology available in the near term is unlikely to permit a defense of cities in the event of a surprise direct attack, but if there is no such attack then current civil defense technology should be able to preserve many millions of lives. This is not a prescription for winning or losing nuclear war, only for limiting damage if war occurs.

The immediate goal for the United States is to protect our offensive weapons as well as their commanders, up to the national (presidential) level. One important benefit of protecting the national leadership is that in the face of a Soviet attack, the president becomes part of the total strategic weapon system. This connection seems far better understood in the Soviet Union than in the United States.

The Reagan administration has begun to take steps to reduce U.S. strategic vulnerabilities, and, more broadly, to strengthen overall American military capabilities. There is currently a national consensus that approves of spending more money on defense; the Reagan administration will clearly capitalize on this consensus while it exists. Critics have already begun to argue, along typical "guns or butter" lines, that the poor and disadvantaged will be denied essential social services by the large-scale shift of federal budget priorities from domestic programs to defense expenditures. But unlike the debate in the United States ten years ago, defense efforts *per se* are not now being discredited, just the extent of the shift.

This new acceptance of the importance of national security—complete with its "militaristic" components—may not last long. There is currently a rebirth of a new peace movement which is part of the "New Class" *Zeitgeist*. The recent antinuclear rallies in Europe attracted thousands; similar protests in the United States have had fewer protestors, but their ranks are growing here too. It will be most important that the "establishment" (including members of the U.S. government both in and out of uniform) be prepared to debate effectively with both the old and the new pacifists. It means the United States must develop articulate and well-informed (morally, politically, and technically) spokespersons, but at the moment very little is being done.

THE SOVIET REACTION

Having tasted military superiority, the Soviets will probably be loath to give it up. However, because of their own internal troubles, it is unlikely that the Soviets will go to heroic lengths to counter U.S. efforts to reduce or eliminate Soviet "superiority." But they will certainly try to test U.S. and NATO resolve and endurance in an effort to preclude, or at least delay, the oncoming shift in the correlation of forces. The Soviets will probably issue a great deal of frightening rhetoric about the destabilizing consequences of increased U.S. defense spending. They may even make some implicit or explicit threats. But if the Soviets deliberately initiate large-scale war in the 1980s it will almost certainly not be a move calculated for political gain or for preventing their long-term competitive position from deteriorating, but only in reaction to a desperate short-term crisis, so desperate that they judge it less dangerous to strike than to negotiate or back down.

Because of the serious nature of various Soviet domestic problems, many of the nonmilitary dimensions of the correlation of forces will appear to Soviet leaders (correctly) to be moving in an unfavorable direction. The Soviet rate of annual economic growth has been declining since the mid-1960s and now stands at a low 2 percent. It seems likely to drop to zero or even below by the mid-1980s, in part because of a stark labor shortage and low worker productivity. Because of the lack of growth and of poor practices in maintaining existing capital goods and infrastructure, the 1980s will also witness an untimely decline in new (net) Soviet capital formation. By the end of the century, ethnic Russians will be in a clear minority because of the much higher population growth rate of other ethnic groups. Demographic trends indicate that there will be internal ethnic troubles and a drastic reduction in the size of the working-age population, and that the Soviet army and industry will increasingly be manned by less educated, less "reliable" non-Slavic Muslims and Central Asians. (A similar problem, of course, exists in the United States, where the absence of a draft has produced a barely literate, largely minority force of recruits.) Soviet demands for conscripts will put even greater strain on the inadequate labor supply.

The Soviet economy continues to be unable to cope with modern agricultural needs or to provide technological or skilled consumer services. In an overall assessment of the correlation of forces, therefore, Soviet planners must recognize that their domestic ability to compete with a generally hostile outside world is certain to decline in the near term and that they have few resources which can be allocated to any grandiose military ambitions. Soviet economic and political weakness is more likely to result in low morale and foreign-policy conservatism than in desperate foreign adventures, though these cannot be completely ruled out.

Thus, to repeat our original premise, despite current U.S. force deficiencies and vulnerabilities, the prospects for high-level, direct confrontation or conflict with the Soviet Union during this decade appear to be fairly limited. Undoubtedly the Soviets will take advantage of the shift in power to support and exploit anti-Western movements and leaders in the Third World, and they will insist on "nonintervention" by the West in Soviet "spheres of influence" or against Soviet-supported national liberation movements. But this is really nothing new; the 1970s saw several notable examples—in Angola, Ethiopia, South Yemen, and Afghanistan—of a more aggressive, forward Soviet foreign policy. And we have begun, if somewhat ineptly, to do something about these possibilities.

WHITHER THE ARMS RACE

While the 1980s are a potentially dangerous decade, the chances that this potential will be realized are not as high as they may be in the 1990s. The degree to which the 1990s become dangerous in part depends on how the United States and its allies deal with their problems, and in part on how they deal with new issues such as the potential emergence of new nuclear powers, both large and small. Looking beyond the 1990s we believe that the growing economic and political strength, as well as the military potential, of China, Japan, West Germany, and even eventually Brazil will create the potential for a more stable, multi-polar balance of power—even if in the 1990s their emergence tends to rock the boat. The present bipolar U.S.–Soviet relationship is inherently unstable because it places the two superpowers in direct competition, but it is not likely to survive much past the year 2000. The world's other major powers are simply becoming too strong to accept a subservient role in international relations. Moreover, at least some of the new strength of other nations will be gained at the expense of the United States and the Soviet Union. By the end of the century the world is likely to be dominated by four to seven "superpowers" (most likely, of course, are the United States, the U.S.S.R., China, and Japan, but West Germany, France, a Franco-German alliance, or other alliances entered into by either France or Germany might also compete). Actually, by 2000, Brazil may have a gross product of a trillion 1980 dollars and be in a position to join the great power club.

The reader may be surprised to see that we expect the Japanese and Germans (or a Franco-German alliance) to have nuclear weapons by the end of the century. Actually, given both nations' economic and technological prowess and military tradition, it is surprising that both nations have thus far not developed nuclear weapons and large conventional forces. The end of U.S. strategic nuclear superiority means that these two states can no longer rely as much on the protection of the U.S. nuclear umbrella; they will have both greater incentives and greater capabilities to provide their own deterrent and war-fighting capabilities, while at the same time the political restraints left over from World War II will recede (especially if worldwide proliferation occurs).

We would argue that the movement from a bipolar to a multi-polar world is likely to increase world stability, though it might contribute to regional instability, as various regional adjustments are made to the new constellation of forces. Primarily, multi-polarity will mean that no two countries will be such desperate rivals that they would be willing to engage in a mutually destructive war. If they did, they would likely lose out to other great powers even if they won the bipolar war (unless they did so with almost no damage at all). In any case the prize is no longer world domination.

There is a general theory in international relations that a multi-power world is stabilizing because it decreases the likelihood of escalation-prone confrontations: a bipolar world competition almost inevitably arouses intense crises and there is no structural reason to back down; in a tripolar situation there is a tendency for two of the powers to move closer together (for economic, military, political, cultural, or ideological reasons) and gang up on the third; in a four-power world the competing nations are likely to pair off into hostile groups of two and two and draw their ally into a conflict which the ally might prefer to avoid. But in a five-power world, one nation is likely to want to play a "swing" role. It can move closer to one group or the other to ensure that there is never an overwhelming advantage on either side. Or it can play arbiter. And in the world of seven great nuclear postures which we see as likely by 2000—or soon afterward—balance-of-power politics seem even more likely. Further, in the event of a war where some nations remained neutral, the warring powers, if they suffer mutual damage, would most likely end up far weaker than the noncombatants, giving those nations an undesirable advantage in the postwar world. This prospect is likely to make any power think twice before initiating a conflict, precipitating a crisis, or letting a crisis get out of control.

It is quite possible that the most important arms-control development in the next two or three decades will be the emergence of the world described above rather than any written agreements between powers. This does not mean that we do not believe it important to pursue written agreements. But in the world outlined above, where all the great powers have to be careful and nobody knows exactly where an attack might come from, basic systems will have to be flexible and tough and will have other prudential characteristics that may make the world much safer than that established by complex written agreements, which are so extraordinarily difficult to negotiate and justify.

The nuclear weapon systems of major powers will be less accident-prone, and, if activated, more likely to be targeted carefully. The widely held concept of the spasm response (press every button in the headquarters and then go home) is almost certain to become obsolete. Many of the traditional objectives of arms control which are now much neglected would now automatically be furthered, e.g., the aim to make any war, but particularly an accidental or inadvertent war, as undestructive as possible. The peacetime cost of military systems would remain high, but much less than the cost of war.

We are not suggesting that anybody will be deliriously happy with this vision of a seven-power world. We are suggesting that it is much better than the vague feeling most Americans and Europeans have that the arms race will inevitably and inexorably lead to total destruction. In fact, one real problem the West has in negotiating with the Soviets is that very often the Western negotiator is more afraid of the arms race than the Soviets. Fortunately, this asymmetry in attitude is not likely to be as much a problem with the Reagan administration as with most of his predecessors. But there will still remain great problems of this kind in the political arena. It is most important that the West develop pictures of, and policies for, the arms race which are both reasonable and a little reassuring; otherwise neutralism, pacifism, and low morale are almost inevitable—as well as more direct danger from the arms race itself. One possibility is to merge U.S. foreign and military policies with the concepts of the Great

Transition and the Emerging Problem-Prone Super-Industrial World Economy. It is quite useful to consider many arms-control measures and programs as just being part of a larger effort to make the many emerging problem-prone technologies into largely problem-controlled technologies. When one asks, therefore, what the purpose is of these forces, the answer is not only to preserve the status quo, or to prevent others from using force, but to guide and further the Great Transition. This is an ultimately much more positive concept and provides a much more useful perspective on the current problems of arms control and strategic force.

ANNEX: ON SCENARIOS, REALITY TESTING, AND VARIOUS "WINDOWS"*

SCENARIOS VS. REALITY

The reader will have surmised that much of the Hudson Institute's work in military planning is based on scenarios about which he will doubtless be suspicious and rightly so. Nevertheless, the use of scenarios is more or less inevitable—at least to a degree. We don't know any other way to accomplish the following:

1. Illuminate the interaction of psychological, social, political, and military factors, including individual personalities, and to do so in a way which permits the consideration of many other interacting elements and issues in a more or less holistic manner.
2. Force the analyst to deal with details and dynamics which he might easily neglect if he restricted himself to abstract considerations.
3. Dramatize and illustrate possibilities that might otherwise be overlooked.
4. Illustrate forcefully, sometimes in oversimplified fashion, certain principles or questions which would be ignored, lost, or dismissed if one insisted on taking examples only from historical experience. Scenarios

---

* The reader will remember that we discussed how there will be, as far as the United States is concerned, a window of vulnerability, but that as far as the Soviets are concerned, it is not likely to be considered as much a window of opportunity as many fear, though they may be able to exploit it politically.

are really quite helpful in forcing oneself and others to plunge into an unfamiliar and rapidly changing world. They are particularly useful for Gedanken experiments.*

5. Consider alternative possibilities and branching points systematically or by "sampling."
6. Overcome the current common lack of shared knowledge of military and diplomatic history and of the terra-incognita quality of much of the present and future. A library of common and well-understood scenarios can substitute (inadequately but usefully) for a lack of experience and even for a lack of a shared history and shared literature.

The use of scenarios has been criticized as being paranoid and schizophrenic. In the first case, it is argued that only a paranoid personality, unjustifiably distrustful and suspicious, could conceive of such plots. The analyst is, of course, interested in what devilish means others might contrive to destroy him; he is also interested in what they might not do. To the extent that such criticism is justified, it pertains more to the plausibility of the particular scenario than to the methodology (though the method does lend itself to paranoid fantasies).

The second "diagnosis" (schizophrenic) may be more serious but not devastating. The argument in this case is that these fictional plots and details may be so divorced from reality as to be not only useless but misleading and therefore dangerous. This can happen. The analyst is often dealing with an unknown and unknowable future. But it's less likely to go undetected with a scenario than with a more abstract presentation. In many cases it may be quite controversial that there is such a sure divorce from a reality which does not yet exist. Most bizarre possibilities never materialize, but that does not mean that the bizarre is always of low probability; it may only be unfamiliar. Imagination has always been one of the principal means for dealing in various ways with the future, and the scenario is simply one of many devices useful in both stimulating and disciplining the imagination. To the extent that scenarios may be divorced from reality, this again seems a criticism more apt for particular

---

* A Gedanken experiment (a thought experiment) is a well-known concept in philosophy and physics. Its purpose is to think through what would happen if a certain experiment (in accord with the physical laws of nature) were carried out, even though it will probably never actually be performed. Nevertheless, the process of thinking through and analyzing it can be very helpful in understanding certain kinds of issues. It can also be misleading if the assumptions behind the experiment are fallacious or the conclusion misapplied.

scenarios than for the methodology (again, scenarios often lend themselves to being unrealistic, though less so than many other methodologies). If a scenario is to be plausible, it must, of course, relate at the outset to some reasonable version of the present. In addition, it must throughout relate rationally to the way people could behave, though it is important not to limit oneself to the most plausible, conventional, or probable situations and behavior—and even more important not to insist on conventional or familiar behavior in very unconventional or apparently bizarre situations.

It is not that we believe the scenarios will reliably predict the future, or that the scenarios will include all eventualities. The very word "scenario" was chosen to put these "future-tense anecdotes" in a low-key perspective. (After all, it's only a scenario—the kind of thing a Hollywood writer might come up with.) Further, most of the time we voluntarily restrict ourselves, but not always, to what we call "surprise-free" scenarios, mainly because the number of ways surprising things can happen is unlimited. There is no way to investigate them systematically except by a kind of sampling. And yet, very unexpected things do happen—consider the historical scenario for the outbreak of World War I.* Almost all historians argue that it was basically an "unintentional war"; none of the governments concerned wanted a Europe-wide war in 1914. More important for our current purpose, a number of bizarre things occurred which would make these historical events quite unacceptable in a scenario. Yet I am reliably informed that World War I actually happened.

Still, we have to plan on the basis of reasonable and plausible circumstances—or at least "not unreasonable" and "not implausible" ones. We can only sample some implausible events and try to think through as many possibilities as we can.

This kind of program frightens many. They feel it is taking the possibility of war both too seriously and too lightly (i.e., almost makes a game or amusement out of it). But war and crises can occur if only unintentionally. In addition, we must take the dangers of being presented with a choice between a Munich (threatened or actual attacks on an ally) or other provocation and going to war. We do not believe the danger of a Munich or other war-prone crisis is overwhelming, but it is certainly high enough to be frightening. Further, we feel that having more adequate

---

* For a much more complete discussion see Herman Kahn, *On Thermonuclear War* (Princeton, N.J.: Princeton University Press, 1961), pp. 350–75; or Barbara Tuchman, *The Guns of August* (New York: Macmillan, 1962).

Figure 8-1

"Estimated" Probability (Late 1960s) of a NATO "Disaster" (Pearl Harbor, Munich or Mutual Homicide) in the Decade Ahead

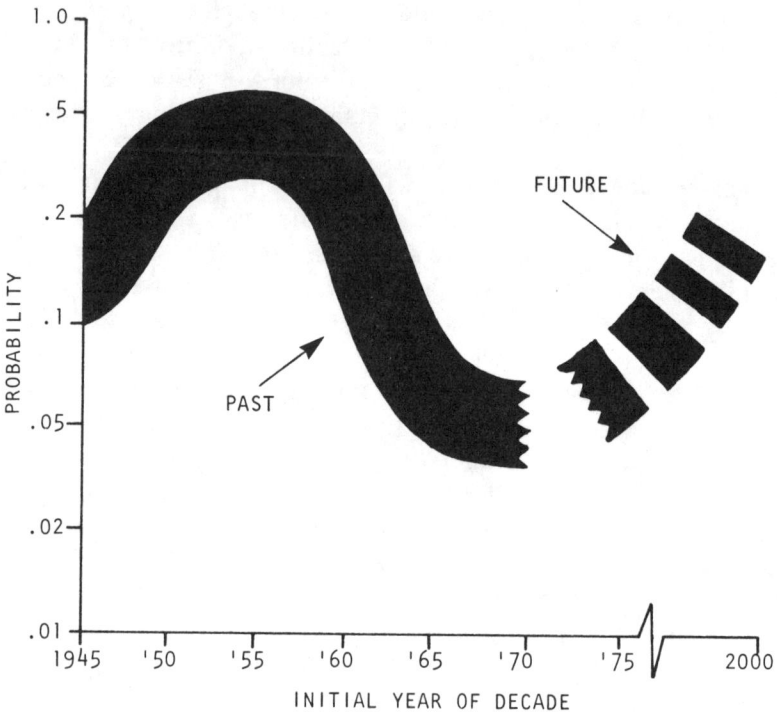

war-fighting forces improves deterrence of Pearl Harbors (direct attacks) and of Munichs.

Figure 8-1, which illustrates the "estimated" probability of the occurrence of a Munich or Pearl Harbor, has been drawn in various forms at the Institute since the early '60s. The version shown is from the late '60s, but not much changed from the earlier version. The concept presented is that in the '50s the situation was genuinely dangerous; forces on both sides were accident-prone; both sides were vulnerable; whoever launched a well-planned first strike would probably win the war and get away almost scot-free.

This was almost certainly a reasonable estimate for our side and possibly for the Soviets as well. And we felt that the situation became—or would become—less dangerous in the '60s and '70s with the advent of protected "second-strike" (i.e., more or less invulnerable) missile forces and better operating procedures that would reduce the possibility of an accidental war. We also predicted that the world would get more dangerous in the late '70s and early '80s because the NATO side, both people and government, would get careless. We didn't predict just how careless the United States and NATO did indeed become. We knew the concept "Nuclear war is unthinkable" would be very prevalent, and that as a result people would stop thinking very hard and realistically.

HOW HYSTERICAL OR PARANOID ARE CONSERVATIVE ANALYSTS?

The National Defense University holds an annual meeting on national security issues, and in 1977, I served as chairman of the panel on strategic warfare. A number of members of my panel had achieved some degree of prominence by advocating policies and estimates that were often thought of (by themselves as well as others) as being rather conservative, or even "hard right" or hawkish, on national security issues. But none of them were paranoiac in their concerns about the Soviets (as opposed to a common stereotype), or even really very hard right on nuclear war (as compared to their image). In fact, even those analysts who had been labeled "hawks" for their opinions of Soviet intentions then believed—and still believe—in the basic caution and prudence of Soviet leadership. All but one member of the panel believed that thermonuclear war between the United States and the U.S.S.R., in particular, was not likely to be initiated and fought for long-term (or even short-term) positive gains however great the temptation, because the risks and uncertainties would be judged as not worth the potential gains (large as they might be).

Thus, it is believed on the part of most analysts that if the Soviets do choose war they will do so out of desperation and not just to gain world dominance or other advantage. It is possible that these analysts could be wrong, but I share their opinion and therefore believe it to be reasonable. However, all of the analysts (including myself) believe that we as a nation should not rely as much as we do on Soviet caution and prudence for our protection, especially since Soviet leadership could change dramatically, we may overestimate Soviet moderation, or special situations may arise which overwhelm their caution and prudence or which are interpreted very differently by Soviets than by us.

In any case, the possibility of war—deliberate or inadvertent—exists. We could give many scenarios (in addition to those we have provided thus far) to illustrate just how this possibility might be realized. None of these scenarios is very plausible, but neither are they wildly implausible; they are in the "not implausible" range. Yet even if the scenarios were implausible we could not take great comfort, because history has a habit of being richer, more imaginative, and more perverse than any analyst who is concerned about credibility and plausibility ever could be.

CHAPTER 9

GOVERNANCE: MANAGING AN AFFLUENT DEMOCRACY

BASIC CONCEPTS AND ISSUES

Governance—the art of managing a society at all levels—has become a fashionable word for a complex and dynamic process. It includes the president's relations with Congress, his ability to lead his own party, and his capacity to implement policies at the grass-roots level. It includes the delivery of municipal services from fixing potholes to collecting garbage, from facilitating economic development to improving the quality of life. And often it is used as a convenient excuse for inaction or bad management as in "New York City [or "The United States"] is simply ungovernable."

Hannah Arendt once referred to the rule of bureaucracy as the rule of nobody (as opposed to "autocracy," the rule of one; or "oligarchy," the rule of the few; or "democracy," the rule of many). This is the problem exemplified by that faceless machine which travelers in the Soviet Union meet so often. It says "Nyet" with the finality of a computer which, like death and taxes, cannot be argued with, only accepted. A faceless bureaucracy has not been the problem in the United States, though it is a problem in many totalitarian countries and to some degree in France and West Germany and a lesser degree in England and Italy. The recent problem in the United States is almost the opposite—too many faces, each intensely pursuing relatively idiosyncratic, ideological, or "public-interest" objectives. For example, many young people perceive the process of governance as a kind of crusade for what we call the "New Emphases" (see Table 9-1, later in this chapter)—e.g., protection of the environment, of consumers, or of the psyche. The problem is that they formulate many of their policy demands without much knowledge or judgment.

Another bureaucratic problem in this country concerns the excessive influence of what is sometimes called the "iron triangle"—a coalition consisting of an interest group, certain elements of the civil service which may be affected by the proposed legislation, and Congressional staffs interested in the same area. Until recently, many social scientists believed that these iron triangles were almost invulnerable and that even the president of the United States would not be able to make much headway over their opposition. This is clearly not true for the current administration. For example, many of the ideas in this book were presented in a series of briefings Hudson Institute made to new members of Congress and their staffs in the last week of January 1981. At the end of the briefings we asked how many thought that all or most of the initial Reagan program would actually get through Congress. No one did. But half of them thought that a significant part of it would get through, and the other half thought that only window-dressing alterations would occur. In fact, almost all of President Reagan's initial program was passed.

This may be the start of a genuine watershed in the U.S. polity, particularly if the president is successful in sustaining the coalition of economic conservatives, national security conservatives, and social conservatives discussed earlier. We are not arguing that the influence of the iron triangle is dead, only that it is much less than absolute and that in many cases the current administration seems to be able to deal with it remarkably effectively.

One of the main problems of bureaucracy in the United States was referred to (before the Carter administration) as a kind of "guerrilla war" of neo-liberals against old-line traditionalists, i.e., relatively inexperienced idealistic types vs. hard-core pragmatists. Under Carter these so-called guerrillas became the darlings, at least initially, of the administration. The president appointed at least a hundred people drawn from public-interest groups to key positions just below the level requiring Senate confirmation (which most probably would not have gotten). I am told the president seems to have thought of these "public-interest" appointees as being relatively objective. Actually they were all members of the neo-liberal symbolist class ("New Class"), who are the exact opposite of the objective; they are crusaders for what we call the New Emphases. They think of themselves as reformers with higher and more enlightened values than most of the country. They consider opposition to their views selfish, ignorant, bigoted, or evil.

As these members of the New Class began to carry out the routine functions of their various offices, their positions often became modified (but in most cases their language more than their underlying attitudes and values changed). Many people feel that among the most important things Reagan has done is to reduce the involvement and influence of the New Class in the government. The neo-liberal symbolists are still active, many even constructively so, but they no longer dominate the federal bureaucracy.

We are not arguing that even the relatively extreme neo-liberal public interest groups are necessarily a bad influence. In fact, we think it is important to have people who are at relative extremes in order to create tension and an awareness of the interests they represent, so that their views may be investigated and accommodated when appropriate to do so. A great deal of the flexibility of a bureaucratic system like that in the United States comes from the active competing interests of its members, who are effective at getting things done when the situation allows them to, and who still remain active as critics and competitors even during periods of "nonactivity" in terms of policy-making. But when extremist groups get into power for too long, or gain too wide an acceptance among the governing elites, all kinds of damaging distortions, inequities, and counterproductive rules, regulations, and bureaucratic decisions can ensue.

But whichever group is in power, it must govern. The problematic issues of governance are those which must reflect a point of view—the environment, welfare, abortion, the distribution of the GNP, and so on. The challenge today is to develop policies which appropriately reflect the new emphases, priorities, and ground rules of the 1980s. Which of the many currently fashionable attitudes, tastes, values, or customs will ultimately turn out to be appropriate and/or durable; and how far should the administration go in one direction or another? Many of the central questions and issues of governance revolve around technical and theoretical matters involving the relations (often not well formulated or understood) between cause and effect (as in many of the tenets of monetarism and supply-side economics).

The traditional consensus, structures, and institutions which enabled our society to work fairly well until the mid-1960s have not worked as well since. In particular, the United States has not dealt effectively—at least recently—with crime, with educating our children, with energy, with "modernizing" and rehabilitating certain groups at the bottom of our society, and above all with national security and national morale. But perhaps the most serious breakdown of governance in the past two decades has been one of the most elemental and basic—the failure to provide a sound currency.

Many critical problems of governance today are traditional ones that are carried out in a healthy society without great stress and strain, e.g., managing the society so that most people can earn an adequate living and live in a neighborhood that is "a good place to raise children." The less fortunate should be adequately supported or given special opportunities, but what is adequate—or at least appropriate? And how does one do these things in a way that will facilitate the revitalization of the United States? What new trade-offs and compromises are appropriate to meet this last requirement? Which point of view—hostility, indifference, benign neglect, activism, passionate commitment, or fanatical fervor—comes closest to being the "proper" perspective on an issue? Environmentalists, anti-nuclear-power forces, pro-abortion groups, and many other "New Class" (and "New Right") advocates tend to turn issues into ideological, religious, and/or moral imperatives or believe them to be matters of national or world survival and therefore no longer subject to compromise or cost-benefit analyses.

The Reagan administration has so far exhibited what we consider a healthy "no-nonsense" attitude toward many governance issues. Good instincts and common sense plus a relatively well-tuned sense of right and wrong seem to be more prevalent in Washington now than at any time in the recent past. Many issues are now regarded as questions of cost-effectiveness or "proper" or "meritorious" behavior rather than as matters of morality or life and death. In our culture, for example, it isn't right to belch out loud after dinner. It is bad manners and it is frowned upon, but it is not legally or morally wrong; it is just not proper. Similarly, meritorious behavior in political terms is not always a moral issue, sometimes just admirable. Thus protection of the environment is now regarded, at least as far as marginal decisions are concerned, as an issue of cost-effectiveness and of proper and meritorious behavior—not as a moral, religious, ideological, or survival imperative.

Similarly, the major cuts in U.S. social welfare programs are not immoral, as some would claim, nor are they an attempt to undo all of FDR's innovations. They are, however, an attempt to make the programs—a few of which have become almost resplendent in their plushness—less plush and even austere. The United States is not suited to a paternalistic welfare system, while many European nations are. The United States, for example, is the only developed country which does not have a family allowance scheme, a national health insurance, and many other comparable large-scale welfare benefits. Rather, it has traditionally been committed to a relative emphasis on individualism and self-support, even if greatly modified by Roosevelt's New Deal. The American tradition of "rugged individualism" generally precludes the need—and for many the desire—for lifelong support systems. The fact that the United States is a country of minorities (whereas most advanced European nations are relatively homogeneous) also makes it particularly difficult to set national standards for welfare. The same benefits are often judged to be excessively generous in some states, excessively miserly in others.

There was virtually a national consensus when Reagan came in that budget cuts were needed—the controversy was over how much and from which programs. We have already noted that the budget of the federal government has not "soared" in real terms nearly as much as people think; it has only about doubled from 1945 to 1980, less than the GNP. Total government expenditures, including local and state, have grown faster than the gross national product but have not grown spectacularly in percentage terms; they were 30 percent in 1961 and about 32 percent in 1981, and are going down (unless there is a severe recession).

More to the point is that the government has been extraordinarily inefficient in the way it spends its resources. While many disadvantaged groups made enormous improvements in their status during the '60s and '70s (e.g., the blacks, the handicapped, the poor, the elderly), many of the programs had unnecessarily inefficient, counterproductive, or undesirable components. Even as worthwhile an endeavor as food stamps (which was quite successful in improving the nutrition of the poor) was badly abused; much of the money went to recipients who lived better even without stamps than the "truly poor" did with them. As New York Senator Pat Moynihan noted, "It should not be necessary to feed horses in order to get food to the sparrows."

The growth in the "reach" of the federal government has meant increased intervention into the personal and corporate lives of us all. In 1900 there were five independent federal regulatory agencies; in 1981 there were fifty-five. Regulations affect our food, clothing, homes, jobs, and environment. They affect the price we pay for energy, transportation, and communications; they affect product prices by increasing costs for producers and ultimately for consumers. One estimate places the total cost of government regulation at more than $100 billion per year.* But it is not the dollar costs of regulation that are so bothersome; it is the intervention itself (the entrepreneur no longer feels in control), the hassle and uncertainty, the time lost, and the overall debilitating effects. The innovative "animal spirits" that Keynes found so important are thoroughly subdued.

REGULATORY REFORM

Regulatory reform is one of the top domestic priorities of the Reagan administration. Vice President George Bush is chairing a commission to ease federal standards which have become especially burdensome or counterproductive. The initial changes are likely to be moderate. Congress would not accept—and indeed should not condone—the elimination of needed and cost-effective health, safety, and environmental rules. But even moderately increased regulatory flexibility and predictability would be helpful, as would an easing of overly rigid standards coupled with clearer principles and rules of the game.

Every critic of overregulation, whether businessman, academician, or policy analyst, has his own favorite "horror story." I am no exception. Here are several examples of counterproductive (and sometimes downright stupid) regulations, probably formulated by well-intentioned but misinformed bureaucrats.

The first relates to the decision by former President Carter to create a national park in Alaska, the so-called "last wilderness" of the United

---

* Center for the Study of American Business, Washington University, St. Louis.

States. The idea was basically a good one; certain areas of our nation should be preserved (even if they do contain valuable mineral deposits) for the enjoyment and edification of future generations. Ten parks of, say, 1 million acres each (about the size of a smaller state such as Rhode Island or Delaware) and one or two of 5 million acres or so (about the size of New Jersey or Massachusetts), or a total of 10 to 20 million acres, would have been reasonable. But the administration proposed setting aside *100 million acres,* five to ten times as much—an area roughly equal to the size of France, and about twice that of West Germany or Japan. (It has never occurred to anyone before to set aside so much land as a more or less unused and mostly unvisited park—it is a genuinely new if dubious concept.) The proposal to create a park of such size reflects an unreasonably pessimistic assumption that the government must save the wilderness from the consequences of any kind of private development. Such pessimism is unjustified, as is the removal of so much land from possible exploration for much-needed energy and mineral resources. The traditional U.S. policy of joint use for both recreation and acceptable private development is far more reasonable than the current rules under which all private exploration is forbidden for at least five years, and even then is discouraged. But even under joint use it is probably unreasonable, though much more tolerable, to set aside an area of 100 million acres in which development is to be severely regulated.

Another example of environmental overkill is the law governing waste disposal in the oceans. Such laws are astonishingly uniform despite the vastly different characteristics of the Eastern and Western coastlines. Since the East Coast is especially vulnerable to pollution because of its vast continental shelf (100 to 200 miles wide), stringent waste-treatment requirements are justified. But the West Coast has no shelf; often simply extending sewage pipelines a few hundred feet more into the Pacific would result in the rapid and safe breakup of treated waste products; there is so much water available that secondary or tertiary treatment is usually unnecessary. And in Hawaii, almost all environmental groups, even some of the most vociferous and militant, seem to agree that most sewage simply could be dumped offshore and perhaps spread around to prevent dead spots. As a small island group in the middle of the world's deepest ocean, it is almost impossible for the effluents from Hawaii to pollute. Yet these coastal variations notwithstanding, federal regulations require the same (expensive) level of tertiary sewage treatment in all three areas.

Moving from the land to the sea to the air, current Environmental Protection Agency (EPA) regulations require new coal-fired generators to remove 70 to 90 percent of the potential emissions in any coal they burn, regardless of whether it is the "dirty" (high-sulfur) Eastern variety or the "cleaner" (low-sulfur) Western coal. Industries using clean coal must therefore install the same multimillion-dollar scrubbers as industries burning the high-sulfur variety. They are forced into heavy expenditures to clean up emissions that are less "dirty" to begin with than the "clean" coal from Appalachia and Illinois. This results in unnecessary costs and unnecessary pollution.*

Affirmative Action rules have also brought about costly and often counterproductive results. Originally designed to create equal opportunities for minorities, the regulations have frequently resulted in bizarre examples of reverse discrimination. A Miami police officer who served for twenty years on the force as a patrolman while less senior minority officers were promoted was able to obtain a promotion only after establishing that his father was born in Cuba, thus qualifying him (legally but not really) as a member of a minority.

But these stories are only the tip of the iceberg. They attract attention and ridicule, but they cannot capture the real costs of overly restrictive rules and requirements—the man-hours and paperwork wasted in filling out endless government forms, the decline in productivity in excessively regulated sectors of the economy, the restrictions on new technologies caused by overlengthy licensing practices, and the deterrent effect on capital investment created by a regulatory environment characterized by uncertainties, contradictions, and even hostility toward the private sector.

Regulations added $666 to the cost of an average new car in 1978, $2,000 to the cost of a new house, and $38.86 per day to the cost of caring for a hospital patient in New York.† Most of this hidden "sales tax" is passed on to the consumer. How many of these regulations are cost-effective or otherwise desirable and how many are not is questionable. No one really knows for sure.

---

* The requirement was the result of a special "favor" to Appalachia and Illinois, to protect their "dirty" coal from competition by relatively "clean" and inexpensive coal from the Western United States. This kind of misuse of environmental regulations is not uncommon. However, when the energy crisis emerged, its continuation was almost unforgivable.

† See "Cost of Government Regulations to the Consumer," Hearings of the Senate Committee on Commerce, Science and Transportation, November 21–22, 1978, Serial No. 95-139.

Still, price increases and inflationary pressure caused by meeting regulatory requirements could be considered acceptable when the regulations in fact produce real benefits. Unfortunately, however, the few studies which have been done suggest that this is rarely the case for most recent regulations. Rather, many of them just don't work. The job safety program, for example, despite all the rules, inspections, and expenditures of large sums of federal money—and despite the many hassles and cuts it has created—probably has not resulted in any significant reductions in the number of work days lost because of sickness or injury. The trend lines are mostly down, but as far as can be ascertained, no more than would have been true in the absence of the regulations concerned.

A related problem arises as a result of the proliferation of regulations with conflicting goals: inherent contradictions preclude the possibility of complying with them all. This may not be the fault of the government, since the need for compromise is intrinsic, but it does mean that a deft hand is needed, and, under current circumstances, this is not the hand of government. Take the case of the butcher who was told by the Occupation, Safety and Health Administration (OSHA) that he must put down rubber skidproof mats to guard against falls caused by the blood-slicked floor. The butcher put down the mats and was promptly told by the Food and Drug Administration that the mats trapped bacteria-producing meat scraps and must therefore be removed. There is a real problem here, but it is not likely that governmental bureaucracies will solve it expeditiously. Probably the best bet is to set up reasonable performance standards and thus create incentives for the butcher or an enterprising designer to be creative in meeting the conflicting objectives.

Government agencies have wreaked havoc on the automobile industry as well. They have produced self-defeating regulations by attempting to pursue three objectives simultaneously—reduced fuel consumption, reduced emission of exhaust pollutants, and improved safety standards, some of which increase fuel consumption. All three are desirable but they conflict with each other and trade-offs would seem to be essential, but present regulations do not usually allow for them. The Department of Energy encourages companies to switch from imported oil to coal. The EPA, on the other hand, encourages companies to switch from coal to oil because it burns cleaner. There is often no coordination of these efforts nor much attempt to reconcile differences before costly, contradictory, and remarkably inflexible regulations are imposed. Regulations are needed, but they are infringements on freedom, often counterproductive and ineffective, and hard to correct, and they should be so regarded and correspondingly limited.

"REGULATION MAKERS": THE NEW CLASS AND OTHER ELITES

Many unproductive or counterproductive regulations are imposed by Washington bureaucrats who have no recent (or any) practical "hands-on" experience and no real understanding of the industries they regulate. Most of the time they are not in a position to assess the impact of their rules. Some of this lack of understanding can be attributed to an "educated incapacity," a concept which maintains that on the average—at least in most advanced countries—one's ability to understand and solve real-world, practical policy problems declines as one's level of education increases. The original phrase, "trained incapacity," comes from the nineteenth-century economist Thorstein Veblen, who used it to refer to several problems, including the inability of trained engineers or sociologists to understand issues which they would have understood had they not received their advanced education.

Increasingly, the staffs of regulatory agencies (and Congressional committees) have been drawn from well-educated elites with little or no "real-life" experience prior to joining the government. They do not know how the private sector operates and often are hostile or indifferent to its welfare, yet they are intimately involved in setting policy for that sector. One of the many reasons we are encouraged, even optimistic, about the Reagan administration's chances of improving economic conditions is that among other things, it is choosing administrators who have had practical experience, who are trying to encourage rather than hinder private-sector development, and who understand the difference.

"Educated incapacity" and "unacknowledged class interests" are manifestations of larger problems that lie behind the massive increase in regulatory activity over the past decade. The societal elites from which this country primarily draws its decision-makers were increasingly becoming emotional and ideological or religious "anti's"—i.e., opponents of economic growth, of the private sector, of nuclear power, of adequate national defense, of many traditional values and mores, and of almost any projects which disturb the environment or their own sense of priorities. The opposition can be passionate even about matters which do not directly affect them or about which they have no real knowledge.

It is true that at the moment the tide is against the anti's, and as a result the movement is more or less in abeyance. (The hard-core movement is still strong, but the general acceptance and influence it enjoyed in the late '60s and early '70s has largely eroded.) If the Reagan administration is reasonably successful, many of the excesses of the anti movement will be done away with for a long time. If it is not successful there may be a backlash which will be extremely destructive to the emergence or staying power of "the coming boom." To this extent a lot rides on the success of the administration.

To some extent, the growth of the hostile attitudes of the anti's was both natural and inevitable. As nations become wealthier and their citizens more affluent, the more successful segments (or their children) often want to work less and enjoy life more; tend to become more interested in crusades and causes than in careers; and are less practical and pragmatic about economic or national security issues.

It should not surprise us that the more affluent members of society are usually the first to "knock off" from the hard work and dedication to economic success and efficiency that accompanies economic growth; they have already obtained a substantial share of the economic pie. They have little incentive to exert themselves on their own behalf, and even less motivation to work toward general increases in affluence. Indeed, more wealth for all threatens their own privileged economic and social position.

During the early stages of industrialization and modernization, when success is still in doubt, hard work and sacrifices are not only acceptable, they are usually made willingly and highly approved by one's peers. But by the time a nation has created an industrial base and established a relatively efficient economy, sacrifices are made more grudgingly and energies are directed toward things other than just material progress (economic survival is no longer a dominating issue). Indeed, a high economic and technological standard of life is accepted as natural and inevitable, and the "quality of life" becomes a much more important concept, both in the work place and at home.

To a significant extent, affluent young people are instinctively aware of the deterioration in certain amenities which occurs as an economy becomes more highly developed and as all begin to share in the affluence.

Beaches become more crowded, highways more clogged, domestic help more scarce, access to elite colleges more difficult. As a result, they often turn away from the old-fashioned notion of progress and attempt to block further economic growth. They look for inspirational causes like environmentalism or nonproliferation of nuclear power (particularly if they stem from mainstream Protestant, *haute bourgeois* Catholic, liberal Jewish, or other relatively transcendental religious backgrounds). Since fewer and fewer workers are needed to meet the nation's basic material needs, a growing percentage become involved in service occupations or jobs which satisfy individual needs for self-expression and fulfillment. The perfect outlet for their ambitions are the so-called "public-interest" groups which have been among the strongest supporters of increased government regulation and intervention in the economy, often advocating policies inimical to economic growth and detrimental to "square" values.

We believe that in contemporary America, and more generally in the Atlantic-Protestant cultures, this disinclination toward growth and the "Protestant Ethic" has developed too quickly and rather irresponsibly. Neither the nations concerned nor the world as a whole has reached a level of affluence which would justify severe limitations to growth as a general policy. There is still a long way to go in the struggle for decent living standards for many citizens of developed nations, and even further to go for the rest of the world's population. To slow down material progress deliberately and significantly would be bad governance. It would not enhance social justice or welfare. It would deny both the poorer classes at home and the nations of the Third World many of the advantages (material and nonmaterial) that the industrialized nations have achieved—or made possible—over the past two hundred years. The progress of the poor both in the United States and in the developing nations would be slowed by a deceleration of economic growth in affluent nations. While social limits to growth will increase as the world moves from an industrial to a "post-industrial" phase, most nations have not yet achieved high industrialization, and the move to a premature post-industrial economy and culture should be discouraged.

Prudent reservations about some aspects of progress and technological innovation are justified. But the intense opposition which is reflected in both attitudes and regulations has restricted business activity, stunted productivity, and fostered a demoralizing atmosphere. Irving Kristol makes a telling point:

Here in the United States, the regulatory impulse seems to be directed against the economy itself. That is, the people who are demanding even greater regulation, even greater governmental interference in the economy, the policy of more and more costs on business activity, are not the people who will someday have to make the economy work. They are not the people who will be held responsible for economic growth or its absence. There is in this division of labor in the U.S. a built-in irresponsibility on the part of those who are arguing for more and more regulation.*

A strong case can be made that in the late 1960s and early 1970s, the humanist left and the neo-liberal members of the symbolist class either controlled or dominated the following (largely symbolist) groups and institutions:

—The humanities and social faculties of almost all leading universities (both private and public), professional schools, and teachers colleges;
—most national media (newspapers, periodicals, book publishing, commercial television networks, recording, films, and most educational media);
—the fine arts;
—the "establishment" foundations and other nonprofit institutions concerned with influencing public opinion;
—research organizations;
—staff assistants to liberal congressmen;
—the federal social welfare bureaucracy; and
—government regulatory agencies.

All of these groups and institutions have been in the forefront of the anti-growth movement which sought to replace the basic values and assumptions of American society, particularly the concept of material progress that has dominated Western culture since the Industrial Revolution.

While the influence of the neo-liberal symbolists has weakened significantly in the last few years—in large measure because of the failure of their ideas and policy recommendations—neo-liberal values and sensibilities still deeply permeate a surprising variety of other American insti-

---

* Irving Kristol, "Reasonable Aims Through Reasonable Means," in *Reforming Regulation* (Washington, D.C.: American Enterprise Institute, 1980), pp. 81–84.

tutions, including some implausible ones: business schools, state and local government bureaucracies, advertising agencies, trade unions, public relations agencies, and many long-range policy-planning groups in major corporations.

The neo-liberal symbolists have advanced the view that economic growth threatens the survival of the human race. The new societal "emphases" which they suggest are a product of affluence, technology, and relative security. They reflect the desire of the wealthy and the successful to preserve their economic and social status, to pursue gratifying crusades, and to pursue their own idiosyncratic values and pleasures.

While changes in values are natural and inevitable, they can also be detrimental, as the stagflation and overregulation of recent years attest. Table 9-1 lists some of the "New Emphases" and compares the form they take when they occur more or less naturally, as part of the evolution of an affluent society, with the form they take when pushed too far by overzealous advocates (as we believe has been the case in the last two decades).

Table 9-1

THE NEW EMPHASES

NEW EMPHASIS	A MOSTLY NATURAL AND INEVITABLE DEVELOPMENT	RESULT WHEN ADOPTED TOO SOON OR CARRIED TOO FAR
1. Selective risk avoidance	With advances in science and technology one can usually measure the risks of innovation better and both reduce and choose among them. One (and the community) must still bear some risks, however.	Innovators, entrepreneurs, businessmen, and "do-ers" generally are forced to bear all the burden of proof for innovation and action as if only they, and not society as a whole, benefited from their efforts.
2. Localism	Emphasis on protecting neighborhoods and communities against many controversial changes.	Policies clearly favor local vested interests (the ins) over the larger needs of society (the outs).

Table 9-1 (Continued)

THE NEW EMPHASES

NEW EMPHASIS	A MOSTLY NATURAL AND INEVITABLE DEVELOPMENT	RESULT WHEN ADOPTED TOO SOON OR CARRIED TOO FAR
3. Protection of environment and ecology	Repair of past damage and improvement of existing environment and ecology. The possibility of irrevocable damage or major catastrophes arising from relatively remote and implausible events (e.g., ozone-layer depletion or climate change) is taken relatively seriously—at least at the research and discussion level.	Pursuit of environmental and ecological protection without regard to economic cost or clear understanding of issues; attempts to create a risk-free world or to establish subservience to nature which often involve an almost "spiritual" disregard of materialistic objectives. Almost all frightening calculations and analyses of the most bizarre and remote contingencies are taken seriously (and elicit immediate calls for action).
4. Comfort, safety, leisure, and health regulations	Since basic survival needs can almost (but never completely) be taken for granted, there is greater interest in satisfying the next level of personal needs and desires.	Excessive and unrealistic government regulations approaching "health and safety authoritarianism." A general disregard of cost-effectiveness criteria and even the preferences and tastes of the "subject" population (the people being regulated).

Table 9-1 (Continued)

THE NEW EMPHASES

NEW EMPHASIS	A MOSTLY NATURAL AND INEVITABLE DEVELOPMENT	RESULT WHEN ADOPTED TOO SOON OR CARRIED TOO FAR
5. Happiness and hedonism	Emphasis on personal enjoyment; deemphasis on but not disregard of material achievement, self-discipline, personal responsibilities, etc.	Total immediate gratification. Do your own thing. One is obligated to oneself to seek personal fulfillment. Almost nothing except endangering life or limb is of greater priority.
6. Public welfare and social justice	Concern about greater equity for the deserving poor and the handicapped. Many kinds of welfare and social justice become a right rather than a privilege or gift.	Concern with equality of result, not equality of opportunity. Historical inequities should be compensated for as well as rectified. Welfare becomes a lifestyle for those who need it (or just want it).
7. Cultural diversity, alternative life-styles	Reduced pressures toward an excessively conforming society; tolerance or even encouragement of growth of interest and social groups with a wide variety of objectives and life-styles.	Excessive tendencies toward radical chic, trendy trends, and disastrous erosion of traditional standards and structures. Hostility toward the "classic" aspirations and values of the silent majority. Emphasis on adversary culture.

Table 9-1 (Continued)

THE NEW EMPHASES

NEW EMPHASIS	A MOSTLY NATURAL AND INEVITABLE DEVELOPMENT	RESULT WHEN ADOPTED TOO SOON OR CARRIED TOO FAR
8. General opposition to technology, economic development, middle-class attitudes	Reduced priority for economic progress; tolerance of some erosion of the work ethic and other traditional middle-class values.	"Small is better" and "limits to growth" are vital. Voluntary simplicity is the only ethical and satisfactory life-style, but enormous resources are allocated to promote emphases 1-7 above.
9. Less faith in traditional market forces	Less emphasis on entrepreneurship, "rugged individualism," and the accuracy, efficiency, and social utility of profit motivation as a guiding hand.	Increasing reliance on social control and overall planning of the economy. New emphasis on corporate social responsibility, the "public-interest" movements, and many more governmental attempts to achieve public welfare and social justice directly and not by the encouragement of private and individual efforts.
10. Modern family and social values	Deemphasis on traditional roles and values such as being a man or woman, religion, patriotism; more emphasis on happiness and personal preferences.	Almost total deemphasis on objective achievement, responsible behavior, scholarship, good citizenship, job-oriented skills and attitudes; honor, duty, and country; and other "square hangups."

Table 9-1 (Continued)

The New Emphases

NEW EMPHASIS	A MOSTLY NATURAL AND INEVITABLE DEVELOPMENT	RESULT WHEN ADOPTED TOO SOON OR CARRIED TOO FAR
11. Concern with self	Expansion of opportunities for self-expression and self-actualization; less need to sacrifice for job, success, family, and society.	An almost anarchic and narcissistic self-indulgence often accompanied by a cultist or fashionable emphasis on fulfilling oneself as an independent human being (pop psychology and self-improvement fads, and doing one's own thing).
12. New rites, ceremonies, and traditions	Under these conditions of increased affluence and advanced technology, society and culture evolve. New behavior emerges both against and instead of tradition; new standards of evaluation and status also emerge. But there is no need to hasten the erosion of old values and traditions and much need to create satisfactory syntheses.	Protest as a way of life, as a mode of socializing and entertainment. A revival of paganism, animism, superstition, and gnostic rites and religions. Status from "negative success," e.g., impeding growth and progress; the dropout hero; "small is beautiful"; back to nature. An almost total contempt for traditional middle-class bourgeois and patriotic values.

Both columns represent social limits to growth: the first in a fashion we regard as "mostly natural and inevitable" (and therefore relatively acceptable even if not always joyously so), the second in a fashion we regard as less natural and more forced and therefore causing many unnecessary problems—both personal and public—including "creeping stagnation" in terms of further economic growth. (We sometimes refer to these tendencies in affluent countries as a movement to a "prematurely post-industrial society.") At the moment many of the "creeping stagnation" phenomena are in abeyance (as are some of the "mostly natural and inevitable" trends), but the forces are mostly still there just waiting to reemerge. However, since there is certain to be some degree of synthesis between the two columns, it is likely that these phenomena will be much less detrimental in their "reincarnation" than they were originally. Again, much depends on the success of the current "conservative renaissance," "counterreformation," or the "anti-anti movement."

SOME DESIRABLE LIMITATIONS ON REGULATIONS

Given the strength of the current trend toward supply-side economics, strengthened national security, and traditional values, the future role of the neo-liberal symbolist class is in doubt. Some of its members will attempt to use current trends for their purposes. Others will simply oppose them. But, barring a catastrophic failure of the Reagan administration, their morale, outspokenness, and "excessive" influence are likely to be substantially reduced in the next decade or two—a prospect which bodes well for America's coming boom. In any case, many neo-liberals no longer regard every issue as a moral imperative. Some are even beginning to apply a cost-benefit analysis to their "principles"; they are no longer so fanatic and self-righteous; they are beginning to understand that on most of their burning issues, the appropriate concept is proper and meritorious behavior.

Cost-benefit analysis can be particularly useful as a corrective for overregulation and excessive zeal. Except in very special situations, the burden should be on the regulatory agency to document that the benefits of a proposed rule outweigh its costs. There are obviously difficulties in measuring costs and benefits, especially nonquantifiable or nonmonetary ones. But the effort alone would force agencies to recognize that many regulations have both negative and positive impacts, and that they must be examined in those terms. Recent administration initiatives to emphasize cost/benefit criteria are very much to the point.

Another alternative which is beginning to emerge is the use of federal regulatory budgets. Traditionally, federal regulatory agencies have had no effective "budgetary-type" constraints on their demands. (Some attempts have been made in the last five administrations, but they were mostly ineffective.) Standards are sometimes required to be "reasonable," but no mechanism mandates agencies to limit numbers of new regulations or to track their overall costs; i.e., if an EPA administrator decides to tighten auto-emission standards, he need not ask if that would impede his ability to spend resources on, say, toxic-waste standards or whether he is overloading the system—even if only temporarily. Since most of the costs ultimately fall on the private sector, there is often no limit to the current costs the government can require for compliance with its many goals. There is an analogy here with the cash-flow concept of private business. A company cannot do all its worthwhile projects at once; it is limited by cash-flow and credit restraints. Similarly, the regulators should not ask for too much at once, even if eventually all the demands will be met. In particular, there should not be excess demands during an energy crisis, a depression, or an inflationary spiral, even if the result of delay may be some "irrevocable" damage.

A regulatory budget would force agencies to prioritize their goals and, indirectly, assess more carefully the costs vs. the benefits of their regulations. A budget would require Congressional approval and thus facilitate review of the agency's regulations. Would OSHA be given the right to require compliance costs of, say, $5 billion this year if the agency could not establish that its rules and standards were clearly making the work place safer and healthier? Limited resources would soon prompt the search for "less expensive" standards which would leave the agency resources for other projects. Each decision would affect the regulatory options available in other areas.

In the long run the best hope for our nation (and the rest of the developed world) is to channel most forces for social limits to growth into their "mostly natural and inevitable" forms, limit their rate of growth, and develop alternative philosophies and attitudes. We are not advocating that the clock be turned back to an earlier era, but that the drift toward creeping stagnation be slowed. The prospects for the revitalization of the U.S. economy, and particularly for giving the movement staying power, will to a large extent reflect our success in limiting, deferring, and redirecting the negative influence of these social limits. Only then will our vitality and productivity be restored.

A broad bipartisan consensus holds that deregulation of certain industries is desirable; that it is important to try to balance the federal budget; that it is not only time to cut or contain the growth of both federal spending and taxes, but to do the same for the costs mandated by the federal government for the private economy. The Reagan administration is leveraging this consensus as a means of directing social limits to growth forces into positive or neutral rather than negative channels.

PLANNING VS. PLANNING

There is today in the United States, or has been, a relatively strong and vocal movement for what is called national planning. Many concerned scholars and politicians don't like what they think of as the anarchy, mindlessness, callousness, and shortsightedness of market forces. Many also feel that even if the invisible hand of the market once was a legitimate concept, it has been so distorted by business and government that it is almost useless. We would argue that except for distortions due to such things as inflation, taxes, and unwise government regulations, on the whole the market mechanism works fairly well. While government intervention may often be called for, normally the burden of proof that interference is desirable should be on the government.

The fact is that relatively high-quality planning often occurs at lower and more decentralized levels (by builders, architects, homeowners, businessmen, workers, teachers, individuals). In sheer numbers of hours this kind of planning is several orders of magnitude greater than is available in centralized government bureaus. Take, for example, a governmental zoning commission. It might have ten senior people each putting in about 2,000 hours a year (20,000 man-hours all told), most of which is focused on bureaucratic, political, and internal administrative matters. A project left to the people who are close to the relevant issues and who know the most about what's happening in their areas of interest would therefore put in a great deal more time planning and thinking than any government bureaucrat.

Local planners, it is true, may lack a global viewpoint. In most cases, however, the advantage of a global view is less useful than the harm done by distance, lack of personal involvement, and the distortions of politics and/or ideology. For example, for the first twenty-five years of its operation the Council of Economic Advisors never predicted a recession, though in fact six recessions occurred and were widely predicted by others—the stock market predicted every one of them (though it also had two false alarms). Institutional or bureaucratic shortsightedness is not an infrequent occurrence when national planning is left to national planners. And educated incapacity can also take its deadly toll. There are major virtues to decentralized decision-making, especially when decentralized to individuals and groups vitally and personally interested in the result. A good example is the housewife looking for a home for her family. Within a matter of weeks she may grow more knowledgeable about a particular kind of house than the most knowledgeable of local real estate agents. She would know exactly the trade-offs to be made between an extra playroom, a better kitchen, more storage space, and so on. She can do this because she is able to zero in on what she wants and what is available. And, of course, the depth of her personal involvement and interest is of great help.

Therefore, we should not think of national planning as an issue of planning vs. no planning but as planning by one group of planners vs. another.

I would like to make it quite clear that I am not categorically or ideologically opposed to government intervention. I've spent too much time in places like Singapore, Hong Kong, South Korea, and Taiwan, all places where there is a great deal of constructive government intervention. While these governments can make mistakes, they usually don't, and in any case they tend to fix their mistakes quite rapidly. (The same was true for Japan up to about 1970; until then government intervention on the whole tended to be very intelligent and realistic. It seems to be less so now.*)

In our own country the free market system normally operates well without additional guidance from the central government. Adjustments and innovations normally come about more or less spontaneously—i.e., by planners operating in a decentralized fashion. In principle, a wise government can improve both the choice and rapidity of adjustment or in-

---

* Lee Kwan Yew once explained to me why planning was so good in the five countries by citing Sam Johnson, "There is nothing like facing hanging in the morning to focus your attention at night." The Japanese, once rich, were no longer facing hanging in the morning.

novations by intelligent, sensible, and skillful intervention—if only by making information available and using indicative planning. There is a problem however, since in a relatively mature economy like that of the United States, with a high level of modernization and with the invisible hand of the market operating, the easy and obvious tasks are usually accomplished effortlessly and well by the decentralized planning system. If the government tries to intervene, it has to do so very competently or else it usually does not help the situation. But there is one special situation when economic policy set by the government does seem to work reasonably well. This occurs when the following three requirements are met:

—the economy is behind, so a reasonably clear idea of where one wants to go is furnished by examining more advanced economies;
—the government is sufficiently powerful and disciplined that it can resist pressures to dissipate its resources in propping up failing industries and subsidizing politically attractive but economically unattractive programs; and
—the government experts and decision-makers are and appear competent and knowledgeable (appearance is important so that the businessmen will respect them and accept their information and indicative planning).

None but the last requirement holds for most advanced capitalist nations today.

When the people making adjustments are not very knowledgeable or skillful, the intervention can be destructive, or at least more counterproductive than productive. To reiterate, the basic standard for government intervention should be that the burden of proof of need of intervention be on the government. Unless it makes a very good case, it should not become involved. If there is a basic and distorting underlying problem (e.g., the current inflation), the government must act to correct it. In that case no decentralized planning system can do it alone. Nor can a decentralized system do a good job of internalizing external costs and benefits. In addition, when the operation of "the invisible hand of the market" has been distorted by acts of government (usually by unwise regulations and badly designed taxes) it will require acts of government to correct them. And, of course, the government must do those things which only a government can do, e.g., defense, law enforcement, foreign policy.

In sum, then, government intervention, regulations, and management—in a word, governance—has a critical role in our personal and public lives. The wisdom and subtlety of that "intrusion" can foster or impede the coming boom. The kind of interference which was represented by the recent IBM and AT&T cases (which each took over ten years of litigation) is abominable. The time and attention involved in the cases simply tied up public and private resources as the original issues at stake become irrelevant in a rapidly changing economy. The quick resolution of these cases is a good example of reasonable and practical behavior by the current administration. This, indeed, brings common sense back into governance.

CHAPTER 10

REVITALIZATION: HOW TO MAKE IT HAPPEN AND GROW

A BASIC SCENARIO FOR THE UNITED STATES

A lot of things have gone wrong over the past two decades which now need to be fixed, changed, updated, or scrapped. While there are initiatives currently being taken that have great potential for revitalizing America, there are still four areas where much more could be done: (1) the promulgation of a realistic and positive ideology for the United States and for the world; (2) overcoming short- and long-term deficit problems and doing so without distorting the economy or decreasing incentives; (3) stopping the vicious deficit/stagnation/high-interest (or inflation) circle; and (4) countering the trend toward a premature post-industrial society. All of these are interrelated and should be done in ways which reinforce and complement each other.

Thus, one important step that could be taken by the government to expedite the coming of the boom and give the revitalization of the United States both depth and staying power is to carry out an acknowledged but not always accepted responsibility and opportunity of leadership—it can provide an inspiring and liberating vision of the present and future. An ideology (or scenario) which is reasonable and desirable, as well as defensible and plausible, is an important part of changing social and economic expectations, attitudes, and performance. It should also be inspiring, as per Robert Browning—"A man's reach must exceed his grasp, or what's a heaven for?"

The first task is to change short-run expectations about the inflation and the economy. (Almost everybody in the government now seems to understand this, and also that it can't be done by rhetoric or by legislation but only by results—some of the concepts in Chapters 5 and 6 could help greatly.) But equally important is to change long-run expectations about resources, environment, ecology, and the "consumer" society generally. Here rhetoric and proper educational/public relations activities can be very effective. In fact, if long-term expectations can be changed it becomes easier to change short-term ones as well. Who can be optimistic about the near term if longer-range prospects are likely to be disastrous? How can we control prices now if shortages are soon going to occur?

The president—or someone in some part of the administration (vice president, State Department, Council on Environmental Quality, Commerce Department, etc.)—should take on the task of putting appropriate current issues into a larger context, both in terms of breadth and in terms of history. The administration should be diligent in presenting as positive a vision of the future as is justified by the facts and theories available—without, however, glossing over genuine problems and risks.

We have suggested a vision which we call the Great Transition to a post-industrial society. The term "post-industrial" tells what the society is not—it's past being industrial. Despite the plethora of books on the subject we don't know much about this post-industrial society. But details on just what it will be seem neither necessary nor appropriate—few religions give all the specifics of heaven. My own belief is that we will get a kind of "mosaic" society in which the essential problems of economic allocation and distribution will lose most of their intensity, at least for most issues, most people, most of the time. The economy will to some extent be dynamic, though not highly so, and with any luck at all, this kind of society should allow for a freedom and creativity which will be unique in world history. It can be extraordinarily permissive and tolerant, not necessarily in the sense of low standards of personal behavior within any life-style, but in choosing alternatives among life-styles. Economics is not culture, but it supports and makes culture possible and in this case will allow for fascinating and challenging possibilities. National defense is not culture, but it protects—and sometimes extends—culture. And one reason the coming boom is so exciting and important is that the vitality of the culture—through the healthy functioning of that which supports, protects, and extends it—will be restored and will accelerate the trend to a post-industrial society.

In order to give readers a sense of what the vision of the future might include, Table 10-1 presents a scenario—a somewhat optimistic one—for the United States for the next 120 years. While plausible, the scenario is intended to be more illustrative than predictive—to provide a rough outline of and context for a very rich and highly technological post-industrial society.

Our optimism may turn out to be too modest in both the short and the long run. Once the economic boom is underway, and depending on the degree to which certain reforms are successful (e.g., supply-side economics, regulatory reform), the economy may become more dynamic than we expect. There may be much greater economic growth, particularly if the measures discussed in this chapter are accepted and the trends to "creeping stagnation" and a premature post-industrial society are slowed. In any case, we assume in Table 10-1 that economic revitalization will last at least two decades, during which the United States will average about 3.5 percent growth in GNP. (This is high for the early 1980s, probably low for the mid-1980s through the early 1990s, and probably high for the rest of the 1990s.) While the projected average growth is almost as high as that which the United States averaged in the 1950s and early 1960s (even higher in growth per capita), it really is not as impressive a performance

Table 10-1

A GUARDED OPTIMISTIC ECONOMIC SCENARIO FOR THE UNITED STATES IN THE NEXT CENTURY

YEAR	POPULATION IN MILLIONS	GNP IN TRILLIONS OF 1980 DOLLARS	AVERAGE % GROWTH	GNP PER CAPITA IN 1980 DOLLARS
1980	220	2.5		11,500
			3.5	
2000	250	5.0		20,000
			2.0	
2033	300	10.0		33,000
			1.0	
2100	400	20.0		50,000

as it could be, primarily because of the effects of the New Emphases discussed in Chapter 9. Without these restraints, growth would be even faster in the 1980s, considering the enormous stimulation of new technologies, a likely boom in housing, leisure, and capital goods generally, the impact of defense spending, and so on. While the slowdown in the growth of the work force will tend to slow down overall growth, this will be more than compensated for by the changing composition of the work force. The greater experience (and therefore output) of the baby boom generation, working women, and members of minority groups will especially contribute to increased productivity. By then, these "new" workers will be an experienced part of the labor force.

Most of this will not be due to Reaganomics. But Reaganomics should help and will in any case get (or take) credit for almost all of the success if it occurs. If it does, Reaganomics will attain a status and prestige that is likely to increase its effectiveness—both politically and economically. It is difficult to estimate how far this might go. It might even develop a charisma associated with a "wave of the future" movement. (This would be especially likely if Margaret Thatcher achieves even partial success in England.) The converse is also true. If Reaganomics fails, there is likely to be a spectacular backlash against all the ideas associated with it, including those which had little or nothing to do with the failure.

If the United States could attain a 3.5 percent average growth from 1980 to 2000 it would double its GNP to about $5 trillion from what it was in 1980. Assuming a population of about 250 million Americans in the year 2000, this would mean a per capita income of about $20,000—not quite double that of 1980, but still very impressive. While all of this is calculated in 1980 dollars, in relative terms the cost of most personal services will go up and the cost of most material goods and products will go down so that the market basket of what people choose to buy may be somewhat different from what they would buy with $20,000 today. By the year 2000, poverty, as defined by current criteria, except as pathology or voluntary choice, should have disappeared in the United States.

Table 10-1 also assumes that the growth for the thirty-three years after 2000—i.e., during the first third of the twenty-first century—drops to an average of 2 percent; this is a more or less arbitrary number but seems reasonable. It implies a doubling of the GNP over thirty-five years. Assuming only a 20 percent increase in population, the United States gets to $33,000 per capita, a level of affluence very few people have ever dreamed of as feasible for any large country. This would imply a median income of about $65,000 per family (as compared to the current $21,000 or so). Most of the country will be, at least by current concepts, upper-middle-class or rich. Unless there is very large-scale importation of labor, there will be a growing, even desperate, shortage of workers for low-paid and unskilled jobs. Some hardships for those used to having low-paid services available will result, as will the intense use of robots and automation, the erosion of industries that still depend on such labor, and pressure for both legal and illegal immigration—all of which are in evidence now and will become even more apparent in the future.

Finally, we assume that in the last two-thirds of the twenty-first century, the average growth rate drops by a factor of 2, but the GNP still almost doubles. We are also assuming a relatively large increase in population, to 400 million people (in part as a result of immigration). This results in a per capita income of about $50,000, or about the level we associate with being genuinely post-industrial. While we know very little about the motivation and cultural patterns of such a country a century from now, it is clear that in this context 1 percent economic growth is not really stagnation, though now it would seem so. The point is that while various social limits to growth bring about a slowing down, there can still be moderate rates of positive growth (say 1 percent) which still lead to a factor of almost 3 in a century. Or the growth as normally calculated could be negative. In any case, the very concept of GNP gets to be a less useful economic aggregate as it includes mostly relatively low-priced goods produced by largely automatic means and more and more high-priced services performed by individuals. (It should be noted that if we ever get back to the thirty-year 3 percent bond discussed in Chapters 5 and 6, the capital cost of automation will go way down, and so therefore will the cost of the goods produced in automated factories.)

All the numbers in the tables and text could in fact be too low if the social limits to growth are curbed. But because it is highly possible that these forces will not be curbed, the numbers are more likely to be somewhat optimistic from the viewpoint of those who favor economic growth. Yet even growth enthusiasts will agree that most of the need for economic expansion will probably have been pretty much satisfied by 2100. Barring some new challenges or opportunities, a society with $50,000 per capita income should and will turn many of its energies away from economic development and increasing affluence and take up other objectives instead. (This may not occur if there are compelling or exciting challenges such as those to national security, or those that come out of large-scale exploration and "settlement" of the solar system, or out of other dramatic departures from our "surprise-free" scenario.)

We believe that the United States (and the world) would have little trouble finding, more or less indefinitely, the raw materials needed to sustain an assumed eventual $25 trillion gross product (about $250 trillion for the world).* There will certainly be temporary shortages, and adjustments will clearly have to be made from time to time, but barring mismanagement (particularly political) and bad luck, no crisis such as the recent energy crisis is likely to occur again in the foreseeable future. Also, given future high technology and the will to use it, there should not be any dramatic issues that arise concerning clean air, clean water, the environment, or ecology in general. What might be of greater concern, however, are such issues as expansion of the population into exurbia, the endangered-species problem, and massive increases in tourism and leisure.

It should also be noted that we think of world population as more or less leveling out in the mid-twenty-first century (at about ten billion people) and gross world product leveling out somewhat later (at about $250 trillion). In other words, the United States will eventually go from having 5 percent of the world's population and about 20 percent of its gross product (1980) to about 4 percent of its population and perhaps 10 percent of its gross product. This represents a loss in relative standing of a factor of about 2.5 (in terms of being richer than average), but the loss is inevitable: at the end of World War II the United States had about 50 percent of the gross product of the world, but there was no way it could maintain this position (nor should it have tried). As the world achieves advanced industrialization, the relative loss in U.S. ranking cannot be reversed. However, the country could still be first among equals according to many economic and technological criteria.

In addition, the relative (and absolute) loss in U.S. status and prestige, and especially in domestic morale, can be reversed. The coming economic boom will do a lot; proper leadership and educational programs will practically guarantee it.

---

* See discussion in Herman Kahn et al., *The Next Two Hundred Years* (New York: William Morrow, 1976).

REFORMING THE TAX SYSTEM TO ENCOURAGE ENTREPRENEURSHIP, SAVINGS, AND INVESTMENT

In order to counter, to some degree, the tendencies toward "creeping stagnation" described in Chapter 9, it would be most useful to redesign the tax system to discourage consumption and encourage savings, investment, and entrepreneurship (again in both the short and the long run, though probably different programs would be required for each). If the initial exposure to Reaganomics turns out to be successful, there should be a significant opportunity to do this and much else.

One obvious possibility is an 8-12 system—a value-added tax of around 8 percent or so accompanied by a flat income tax of 12 percent or so—with the only exception being a low standard deduction. By keeping both taxes low the pressures to evade distortions are minimized and there is little need for special tax exemptions. I would guess that while the numbers suggested are low they are probably high enough if there is restraint on the federal budget. This guess includes even more revenue aid to states and cities than today. The value-added tax has the great virtue that it is probably the least distorting tax of all. It is also one of the most easily enforced. (It requires a lot of accounting, but this is not difficult given the widespread availability of computers.) Because usually only a small part of the value-added tax is absorbed by businessmen and most of it is passed on (hidden in the purchase price), it has very little political impact. Finally and perhaps most important, the value-added tax is a tax on consumption and therefore encourages investment and savings.

With a flat rate of 12 percent the income tax would be low enough so that there would be no great incentive for large-scale tax avoidance and tax evasion—or great pressure for legislated deductions and tax shelters. In fact, just the opposite would occur: many of the billions of dollars lost by the government and society because of the great pressure on almost all income groups to look for tax shelters could be virtually eliminated. Further, much of the underground economy would disappear or pay taxes.

The flat 12 percent income tax might easily end up collecting about as much in taxes as the current income tax, and much more fairly and acceptably. (Despite its high rates, the current system collects less than 12 percent of the national income.) There would also be an enormous improvement in the morals and morale of the taxpayers.

Some will feel the 8-12 system is regressive (i.e., taxing too heavily or unfairly the lower income groups), but given the high level of prosperity, the many opportunities for advancement, and the adequacy of welfare, the regression is probably not critical. If it is, then adjustments can be made to the basic scheme; the deductions for tax-free income can be increased, there could be some degree of negative income tax or a similar measure, or the income tax can be made moderately more progressive. (This last is probably not desirable because it is important to keep the principle of a flat rate intact, to avoid "creeping progressivity.")

In addition, political support for the 8-12 system would increase if some of the proceeds of the two taxes were used to pay for the welfare portion of Social Security taxes and to eliminate or reduce state sales taxes. Indeed, a revised and simplified tax system that did not discourage incentives and encouraged savings and investments without distorting tax shelters would go a long way toward deepening economic revitalization and extending it well into the twenty-first century—and to some degree indefinitely. While analyses of the complexities and ramifications would require a separate book, we simply note here that a basic tax reform ought to be seriously considered within the next few years.

SOME OTHER USEFUL IF MORE LIMITED (BUT MORE IMMEDIATE) TAX REFORMS

According to recent poll data the current administration is viewed as favoring the rich over the poor. This seems largely incorrect in terms of ultimate objectives, i.e., "fixing" the country and bringing about a better vision of, and better actual prospects for, the future. The poor and many minority groups will benefit more from these objectives than from many welfare or reverse-discrimination programs. But the accusation is accurate in that many programs will benefit the richer more than the less well-off in the short run and therefore will *appear* to favor the rich. However, it's quite likely that income distribution in the United States, which has remained remarkably constant before taxes and welfare (and changes in favor of the poor when tax and welfare effects are included), will continue to remain constant. This implies that there will be a considerable "trickle down." Nonetheless, as a matter of good politics as well as equity, the administration should bend over backward not to favor—or even appear to favor—the rich, and especially not at the cost of the general welfare.

A number of obvious examples come to mind, for example the unlimited deduction of interest on mortgages from local, state, and federal income taxes. There is practically no other advanced country which permits this except Sweden, and the practice there is to be changed in the near future. Many countries allow a deduction of the interest for low-income homeowners in order to encourage home ownership by them, a policy we consider desirable for the United States too, but no other advanced country allows deductions of interest payments of many thousands of dollars a year. The United States might therefore initiate a program that limited deductible interest. However, it would be a mistake to start too drastic a program and thus both disrupt the housing industry and create great political opposition (84 percent of the voters in the last presidential election were homeowners).

If the ceiling on deductible interest were set initially at $10,000 (in 1980 dollars) and then gradually taken down over ten or twenty years to $5,000 (still in 1980 dollars), it would not have a great impact on the home-building industry. Eventually, it should have almost no impact on the housing market for any but the upper class, assuming that inflation has been dealt with and that interest rates are back to 4 percent or so. But it would rectify an important inequity and also a serious problem: it would lessen the expense of subsidizing housing for the rich, which should lead to better investment choices by them, as well as resulting in an appreciable increase in income to the government.

We would also argue that property taxes on personal real estate as well as interest payments on consumer loans should not be a deductible item on one's income tax. We realize that the following suggestions on additional tax reforms may be judged politically impractical or technically difficult, but they are important (and many reasonable things once considered politically impractical have recently turned out to be perfectly feasible).

Perhaps most important is the concept that the inflationary component of interest should not be allowed as an expense to the borrower (and no longer considered as income to the lender); it is really repayment of capital. We have already described how this practice distorts financing and encourages borrowing even in tight money situations, and suggested that if one does index the principal of loans by the MCI or other index, it would also be a good time to change the taxes as well. (Of course, disallowing deduction of the inflation component of interest on mortgages would cause a major increase in the real cost of mortgages for as long as the inflation continues and thus may not be supported by homeowners.) This change should be in addition to the limit on interest deductions, but the latter would no longer be as necessary.

Similarly, it would be reasonable to consider any interest paid on a consumer loan to be part of the cost of consumption and therefore not deductible; there is virtually no ethical or economically rational reason for allowing this interest to be deducted from anyone's income taxes, rich or poor—it only encourages borrowing and as a result discourages savings. Another example involves property taxes, paid to buy things which are good for the quality of life or standard of living of the local people and are therefore part of their consumer expenditures. These, too, should not be deductible. One could do it gradually by setting a limit on the deductible amount and gradually decreasing the limit.

I live in Chappaqua, N.Y., a town which recently built a magnificent library for use by its ten thousand citizens. The library is equivalent to one you could find in a city of a hundred thousand or more. I'm delighted that we have it, but I feel a twinge of guilt that about half the costs were borne by the state and federal governments because the (relatively affluent) residents of Chappaqua were able to deduct their local property taxes. This really is hard to justify.

A FINAL NOTE ON TAXES

The country's immediate need for tax revenue might be at least partially met by some new but relatively acceptable taxes on energy, cigarettes, and perhaps liquor, some of which seem fully justifiable, some less justifiable, but all probably politically feasible and in accord with basic Reaganomics. One fully justifiable tax would be on imported oil (and perhaps on imported natural gas, though the argument there is much weaker in terms of improving our energy posture). Any large importation of oil by the United States interferes with programs to decrease U.S. dependence on foreign oil and thus raises security problems. This is particularly true if, as seems likely, the downward pressures on oil prices continue and relatively expensive domestic sources are abandoned or no longer developed. There are, in effect, external costs associated with importing oil which a tariff would internalize. It could make a great deal of sense to have such a tariff; it could also "incidentally" raise a great deal of revenue that would help lessen the deficit. For example, a tax of $1 a barrel could raise almost $2 billion annually, and one can easily justify a tax five or ten times larger. Such a tax had been considered by the Ford and Carter administrations, but was unpopular in a period of rising prices and increasing inflation. High energy prices are very sensitive politically, but this tariff should become a reasonable political option in a period of falling oil prices that both lessen the political impact and bring about a need to protect domestic sources of energy from "cheap competition" by foreigners.

A less justifiable but probably still worthwhile tax would be a true windfall tax on decontrolled gas. By the term "windfall" we mean that the tax should only be on old gas rather than on all gas (which would then be an excise tax and probably discourage exploration and production as much as consumption). Under current circumstances, it seems particularly important not to levy such a tax on future sources of gas. Actually the United States government should also move away from the concept of levying heavy taxes whenever there are "windfall" profits, but a windfall tax on old gas might be a relatively justifiable and certainly a popular exception. There are more than 200 trillion cubic feet of "old gas" in known reserves today; an increase in the price of $1 per 1,000 cubic feet automatically implies an *eventual* "windfall" profit of $200 billion. If gas is fully decontrolled the price rise on old gas will almost certainly be more than $2 per 1,000 cubic feet—a major fraction of a trillion dollars. A tax of $1 could easily contribute—at least initially—another $20 billion or so annually to the U.S. Treasury. I would guess that something like this will be done in 1982 or 1983 to help solve the current deficit problems.

There are many important open issues which have to be settled in devising a tax restricted to old gas and many difficulties in enforcement, but we believe a reasonable bill could be drawn up. Indeed, such a tax will probably be forced on the president by Congress if he chooses to decontrol gas, and this might be his optimal strategy, since he campaigned against such a tax and has said he would veto one. Having Congress force it on him could solve that problem, and it would be politically impossible to have accelerated decontrol of gas prices without some such tax.

A tax on gasoline might also be considered. Every cent per gallon would raise about $1 billion annually. (There have been suggestions that this tax would go to 50¢ or so and raise about $50 billion if there is not too great a decrease in the consumption of gasoline.) If the tax were instituted it would probably be necessary to share the proceeds with the states. It should be noted that there are limits to how high state excise taxes can go because they are so easily evaded by motorists importing gasoline across state lines, but this is not as true for federal taxes because it's harder to cross national borders.

Similarly, one could justify a heavy increase in the tax on cigarettes purely on health grounds. The evidence indicates that while existing smokers will not be discouraged very much by the tax, new smokers will. While I am against persecuting existing smokers, it could be an important contribution to public health to discourage new smokers. And the "incidental" contribution to the U.S. Treasury could easily be $5 to $10 billion a year.

The point is that there are several politically and economically practical and justifiable ways, in addition to those we suggested in Chapter 6 on unconventional financing, to reduce the federal budget deficit. If combined, these methods could more than solve the problem of a dangerously large deficit and without any fundamental compromise with the basic Reagan tax/budget program.

GLOBAL 2000 PLUS

Tax remedies for short- and longer-term revenue problems are extremely important for unburdening the economic atmosphere. An oppressive or inequitable tax load is bad for a lot of reasons, not the least of which is that it eventually undermines morals as well as national morale. But tax reform or other technical fixes can go only so far in revitalizing a sagging outlook. Psychological fixes are also needed.

We have already described some of the current and continuing harm that has been done by the pessimistic forecasts of official government publications like *Global 2000*,* and in particular by its much quoted conclusion:

* *Global 2000*, Report by the Council on Environmental Quality and the U.S. Department of State, 1980.

REVITALIZATION

> If present trends continue, the world in 2000 will be more crowded, more polluted, less stable ecologically, and more vulnerable to disruption than the world we live in now. Serious stresses involving population, resources, and environment are clearly visible ahead.... Barring revolutionary advances in technology, life for most people on earth will be more precarious in 2000 than it is now—unless the nations of the world act decisively to alter current trends.

Other widely quoted sections are not helpful either:

> If the fertility and mortality rates projected for 2000 were to continue unchanged into the twenty-first century, the world's population would reach 10 billion by 2030 and nearly 30 billion before the end of the twenty-first century. [We believe the 10 billion figure is the topping-off point.]
>
> The largest existing gap between the rich and poor nations widens.
>
> The quarter of the world's population that inhabits industrial countries will continue to absorb three-fourths of the world's mineral production.
>
> Extinctions of plant and animal species will increase dramatically.

All of the above statements are either largely misleading or basically irrelevant. The United States government now has a responsibility to correct or at least update the *Global 2000* report, and to present a more unifying, edifying, and justifiable vision of the future of the world. And it should especially promote more inspiring perspectives on the role that the United States is playing in world economic development. The administration should seize these opportunities.

Some changes have already been made that help to substantiate the argument against the *Global 2000* report. One important change is in foreign-aid policy. The United States now emphasizes the role that free markets should begin to play in breaking the grip of poverty on the poorest countries. Most aid programs have tended to encourage centralized government planning. In fact, in many cases, centralized planning is forced on the government or it cannot get the aid. In a few instances this pressure is productive because it can focus attention on neglected issues, but in most cases the policy is unnecessary. It simply ensures that the recipient country will continue to discourage free markets and free enterprise. One reason why these countries are poor is they don't have many entrepreneurs, and centralization discourages the ones they have. A perverse characteristic of many developing countries is their use of socialist techniques to further economic development. This could work well only if they had very efficient and competent planners and implementers—precisely the resource they lack most; they need systems which economize on this resource, not ones which maximize the need. Nor do they understand how dynamic capitalism can be. Karl Marx understood this well, as is clear from the *Communist Manifesto,* written in 1848 (the reader can substitute the word "capitalist" for bourgeoisie; the use of the term "capitalist" was not common until later):

> The bourgeoisie has been the first to show what man's activity can bring about. It has accomplished wonders far surpassing Egyptian Pyramids, Roman aqueducts, and Gothic cathedrals; it has conducted expeditions that put in the shade all former Exoduses of nations and crusades.
>
> The bourgeoisie, during its rule of scarce one hundred years, has created more massive and more colossal productive forces than have all preceding generations together.... What earlier century had even a presentiment that such productive forces slumbered in the lap of social labor?

Capitalism has done even better in the last hundred years. Despite this, many of the poorer countries are still not aware, as Marx was, of the incredible dynamism and proficiency of capitalism in improving productivity in almost all cultures. Of course, as noted in Chapter 2, the Industrial Revolution did not really spread (trickle down) from the sixteen advanced capitalist nations (ACNs) and the Soviet Union until the end of World War II, but capitalism and rapid industrialization have worked well almost everywhere they have been seriously tried. The poor countries also don't realize that in most cases a good deal of the increased productivity will be shared by most of the nation, even if unevenly. In countries such as South Korea, Taiwan, Singapore, and Japan, increased income at the top trickles down to the bottom. This trickle carries along with it some income redistribution (e.g., the creation of a middle class); mostly it apportions the new income in much the same way the old income was apportioned (but often to new people). If the top 20 percent get 50 percent of the national income and the bottom 20 percent get only 5 percent, much the same distribution will usually hold after the trickle down—at least for a while. In countries such as Mexico, India, and Brazil the trickle does not go down as deep; it varies from about two-thirds to four-fifths of the population. These countries have to design special programs to aid the bottom, if it is to share proportionately (or even at all) in the general increase in per capita income.

But the fact that special programs may be needed for the very poor is no reason to preclude the possibility of improving the condition of richer but still poor groups—or even of the rich. And in the long run, what helps any percentile of the population will probably help almost everybody.

We would argue that for most cultures, the poorer a country is, the more beneficial it is, at least economically, for that country to use freemarket price mechanisms and both local and foreign entrepreneurs and capitalists. Even when modified and restricted, if not too much so, capitalism really is an extraordinarily effective system for creating and allocating resources in an economically efficient and dynamic way.

It is also important to stop stressing the importance of "closing the gap" between the rich and the poor. Of the 3.4 billion people we normally include in the Third World, 2 billion now live in middle-income countries and are beginning to close their gap with the richer countries; to wit, the middle-income countries are growing faster than the rich ones—in fact, almost twice as fast in GNP, though less fast in GNP per capita (their more rapid population growth slows down the increase in per capita income). The emergence of this group of middle-income nations is the most extraordinary change which has occurred in the last twenty-five years. Before this, the world really was divided into the rich and the poor. Now it must be increasingly thought of as middle-income with extremes of rich and poor.

But the very existence of the gap has been the most important single force toward creating economic upward momentum and redefining economic classifications. Consider a middle-income country such as Mexico. It is generally not realized that Mexico has sustained an average growth of more than 6 percent for almost half a century—one of the great economic success stories in world history. Furthermore, about two-thirds of the Mexican population have shared appreciably in this growth, and in another half century this upper two-thirds could be about as rich as Western Europe is today, or richer. Without the gap, the model and resources of the United States, U.S. tourists and investors, the entrepreneurial efforts of Mexican businessmen selling to the United States, and the income provided by Mexican workers in the United States (all products of the gap), this growth would not have been possible. As expressed in the *Communist Manifesto,* Karl Marx understood the capitalist capability of "trickle down" very well (he refers to it as "breaking down all Chinese walls"), much better than most of his followers; while it is still somewhat of a mystery why it did not work better earlier, it clearly has been working well recently.

The United States has difficulty in helping its own lowest-income groups. It can subsidize them, but getting them to adopt constructive attitudes toward life, work, family, and so on is much harder. It is more difficult still to reform or vitalize similar groups in foreign countries. We believe it is impractical for the United States to pour resources into, or to feel guilt for, conditions which are really basically beyond its influence. Far more reasonable is the attitude which it seems recently to have adopted and which emphasizes private enterprise, trade, and much self-help supplemented by some outside aid.

But all this is not enough. Not only does the United States need to focus on practical, tough-minded, pragmatic approaches to economic development (which it is now beginning to do), it must also promote an exciting, plausible, and realistic vision of the future—e.g., something like the Great Transition.

One way to do this would be to undertake another *Global 2000* type of study, but from a larger perspective and by different people (also incorporating new data which have become available). A renewed discussion of the future might well be connected with a White House conference to which participants from all nations and with all points of view are invited, thereby giving any consensus which emerges both credibility and wide distribution.

The main point of the conference might be to focus attention on the "Emerging Problem-Prone Super-Industrial World Economy," on how to make it largely "problem-controlled" by the year 2000 or so, and on how both increased affluence and current and emerging technology can help. It would involve looking at all the difficulties and growing pains within an overall framework of basic guarded optimism. The conference would make clear that it is unreasonable to expect a great transition in which the world goes from poor to rich, from primitive to technological, from parochial to cosmopolitan, from life expectancies of a few decades to perhaps a century or even more, and from less than a billion people to about ten billion without difficulties and problems. Some of the problems of the Emerging Problem-Prone Super-Industrial World Economy could be disastrous unless they are dealt with properly; one purpose of the conference would be to make sure they are. Another would be to make clear that the problems are not increasing exponentially but grow more like an S-shaped curve, that the gains from economic and technological progress are great, and that even though technology and affluence caused the problems, more technology (of the right sort) and further economic growth, while not panaceas, can be very helpful.

Indeed, the conference should stress that most current trends (short-, medium-, and long-term) are positive, and that the better future is worth the attendant pain and risks. The "upbeat" vision which could emerge could be an important tool for the American media and U.S. educational system and for U.S. foreign policy—particularly if this view of the future survives critical and hostile scrutiny as well as we believe it will.

There are enough documentable facts to support a positive long-range outlook, but if they are to become part of the conventional wisdom in the near future, the facts have to be demonstrated more clearly than they have been and given a full-scale, multimedia, all-American public relations treatment. Without such exposure, the facts are all but lost to the public. Thus, even though the leaders of the Club of Rome have publicly "recanted" on the position that the world is running out of resources, few know about this. (Few know about the "spike" graph—Figure 2-1 in this book— or that David Ricardo has been historically wrong about his law of diminishing returns.*) It's time to promote an atmosphere conducive to the coming boom and to American and world interests generally. It is particularly important to have this "new" vision of the future fully reflected in the school system and the media, which, given the change in American politics, may in large part eventually happen anyway. But if left to itself without appropriate programs, the promulgation of these views will be unnecessarily slow, incomplete, and uncertain.

Many will still remain unconvinced of a U.S. revitalization or a better future for the world as a whole. For some, this position will result from a pardonable skepticism or a reasonable pessimism; for others, it will be

---

* Of the four basic resources—(1) something in the ground; (2) technology; (3) capital or investment; (4) skill and organization—only the availability of the first (e.g., unimproved fertile land) diminishes over time. The others all become more productive and available over time.

less an issue of documentable facts than of values and preferences. For still others, it will be just a matter of ignorance, of being misled, of having ideological blinders. But most of the world can be persuaded that optimism is in order; at the Scotch-verdict level, the case for a more sanguine prognosis is almost overwhelming—at least in economic and technological terms. Further, except for some special groups—mostly upper-middle-class elites—most people want to hear good news for a change. This is especially true of schoolchildren.

THE NEED TO REINSTITUTE TRADITIONAL EMPHASES AND VALUES

At present, almost all schools in the advanced capitalist nations teach that the world is running out of resources, that our grandchildren will not live as well as we do because of the reckless use of nonrenewable resources for frivolous purposes, that the environment is being polluted beyond repair and the ecology being destroyed, and that industry is increasingly producing products that give consumers and workers cancer.

All of the above are either completely or largely false. One might well ask what kind of a price these countries will have to pay for teaching this kind of insidious and invidious nonsense to the younger generation. We would argue that the price is nowhere as high as one might suspect, but too high to let the current situation continue. We need to return the school system, and the country, to a sense of pride in its successes, an interest in treating its problems constructively, and a recognition that affluence and high technology make good citizenship and a good national character more important than ever—and we need to do so rapidly and effectively. Despite the emergence of neo-conservatism in the academic and political world, to let events just take their course might take a generation or so to make a significant difference.

It has, of course, always been a function of government to promulgate the concepts, attitudes, and morals judged desirable for the proper functioning of society. Thus the U.S. educational system has traditionally had the following priorities (minimal literacy being a given): (1) to turn out good citizens, (2) to give students an ability to earn a living, and (3) to raise their level of cultural knowledge and awareness and increase their ability for self-fulfillment and self-actualization. At the present moment these traditional priorities seem to have been reversed. Yet in the relatively unstructured and unpressured world in which the next generation is likely to find itself, there is a particularly strong need for internalized structures, good ideology, and a proper education in character and reality testing.

We would argue, along with such people as Michael Novak and George Gilder* (and others who have recently put forth a variety of forceful cases), that the traditional picture of capitalism normally presented, even by its supporters, has been unnecessarily harsh—especially the U.S. version of capitalism. Novak, for example, makes the point (we believe correctly) that the American system is not just a capitalist economic system based on the invisible hand of the market and individual attempts to aggrandize or promote individual selfish ambitions, but first and foremost a democratic political system which has a culture based on the Judeo-Christian creed and (we would add) on what David Potter has called being a People of Plenty.†

The American system is very attractive to most people. It includes an emphasis on charity and philanthropy, combined with a tradition of religion (whether transcendental or orthodox) and the pioneer spirit and rugged individualism. And this combination—political democracy, American culture, and the capitalist economic system—has worked superbly. It has encouraged and supported an extraordinarily high level of personal freedom, spontaneity, and initiative, as well as created and maintained a high general level of affluence. It has worked incredibly well. Even if it has not worked so well in recent years, it has been a city on a hill and the last great hope of humanity and can be again.

The United States is now a society in which there is heavy use of drugs. It publicly displays and sells pornography in a way which most citizens find offensive. It fails to educate large numbers of young people and educates others less well than it once did. It emphasizes rights and privileges too much, responsibility and duty too little. Much is said about personal

---

* See, for example, George Gilder, *Wealth and Poverty* (New York: Basic Books, 1981); or Michael Novak, *The Spirit of Democratic Capitalism* (New York: Simon and Schuster, 1982).

† See David Potter, *People of Plenty* (Chicago: University of Chicago Press, 1954). The Potter thesis has basically replaced the so-called Frontier Hypothesis by Frederick Turner on what has molded the character of the American people. It's part of Potter's thesis that the relative economic abundance of the United States as well as the open area of opportunity represented by its dynamic economy generally (including the frontier) created the special kind of culture that we have in America. Many of the traits that were once attributed to being an American are now spreading to the rest of the world (along with the "consumer society").

freedom and needs, little about self-discipline and self-restraint. It is an excessively permissive society in which we are told that happiness is virtually an obligation—to seize the moment and not be burdened by or "hung up on" guilt, responsibility, or duty. It is a society which tends not to honor those who defend it, nor to castigate those who attempt to debauch, weaken, or even destroy it.

Some of the more dogmatic, doctrinaire, and/or evangelical sects have done much better on most or all of the above "failures" than U.S. society as a whole. For example, in the 1960s, young black dope addicts picked up by the official system had a cure rate of about 5 percent. But young black dope addicts who got involved with Black Muslims had a cure rate of about 95 percent. (The Black Panthers, though also against drugs, had no such record of success. The difference was largely because the Black Muslims were religious and doctrinaire, the Black Panthers political and secular.) Upper-middle-class elites don't really approve of Black Muslim orthodoxy, but the Muslims are allowed to operate their own schools and educate their children. We did not agree with the content of much of what they were taught, but they were taught well. Many whites have similar needs in terms of a more disciplined learning process.

If there is to be a moral revitalization in the United States it might begin with a more doctrinaire and systematic inculcation of "traditional" American values. Many "mainstream" children (and the country as well) would have much better prospects if they were educated more as some of our more doctrinaire/evangelical children are. Consider the recent appeal of fundamentalist groups to so many upper-middle-class dropouts. I asked one girl who had become a Jesus freak, "How come?" Her answer was graphic and to the point: "I have been sleeping around and using drugs since I was fifteen; I have now decided to try God and decency for a change." There is a lot to be said for introducing these options into the total educational experience, if not into the public schools.

There are great differences between upper-middle-class elites and other groups of Americans such as certain ethnic groups which come from the mainstream and transcendental religions, those which come from more doctrinaire sects, and those who have little or no religious background. In fact, one of the most interesting trends going on in the United States today is that membership in the transcendental religions is on the decrease, and membership in the doctrinaire and orthodox sects is on the increase. Both trends go back about twenty years. (This has largely gone unnoticed because U.S. figures on religious affiliation are usually presented in such categories as Jewish, Catholic, and Protestant when they should be presented using the more interesting and more relevant taxonomy of transcendental, ecumenical, and/or mainstream vs. dogmatic, doctrinaire, traditional, and/or evangelical.) The reasons for the shift are similar to the reasons the social conservatives voted for Reagan in the first place. While they represent a plurality of Reagan supporters, the social conservatives won't see as dramatic a change in the educational/moral area as economic and defense conservatives will notice in the areas they are interested in. It is more difficult to work on behalf of social conservatives because their political goals seem to violate current interpretations of constitutional principles (bussing, prayers in school, abortions, pornography, sex and violence in TV, etc.); the issues in defense and economics are mainly questions of money and traditional governmental policies. For the moment, social conservatives will have to settle more for presidential rhetoric and example than for legislation and governmental action, but whatever can reasonably be done for them should be.

While it is clear that "turning the system over to the moral majority" is not the answer, it must be recognized that most of their concerns are both legitimate and shared by many other Americans. While it would not be desirable to teach creationism as good science, it is important for the American school system to reinforce, or at least not to attack as outmoded, the "square" indoctrination put forth by the moral majority and others. It is unfair to neglect the needs of the social conservative and the lower-income groups in favor of the needs and attitudes of the more "fashionable" upper-class and upper-middle-class elites and the transcendental and mainstream sects, even if some judges have reinterpreted the Constitution so as to almost force such discrimination. How this compromise can be accomplished and carried out represents one of the greatest challenges to the Reagan administration and one which is likely to involve some of its greatest difficulties. But it is also a splendid opportunity to serve the needs of the majority and to strengthen the country militarily, politically, and socially.

In any case, President Reagan's unique historical opportunity to create a new coalition among the social, economic, and foreign policy/national security conservatives still has great potential. The right kind of ideology and vision of the future—with special attention and creativity given to social issues—could be very helpful.

Apart from the suggestions scattered throughout the book, we have a lot of other ideas which we hope to pursue (even knowing that events will not wait for the outcome of current Hudson studies). In the meantime, we suspect that the president and his various constituencies will turn out to be fairly creative. Some of the necessary compromises and initiatives will arise out of the political process, but the leadership will almost certainly have to come from the commander-in-chief. To a much greater degree than most people realize, the strength and depth of the coming boom is dependent on the man at the top. It is still the president of the United States who creates, expedites, and manages the American opportunity. And we believe he will do quite well—with a little help from his friends.

SOME CLARIFYING THOUGHTS ABOUT MY PERSONAL POSITION

Over the years I have variously been described as an inhumane and unfeeling warmonger (after *On Thermonuclear War*) as well as a naive and misinformed optimist (after *The Next 200 Years*). My own assessment is that I am a reasonably realistic observer whose imagination and logic often lead to unfamiliar (sometimes apparently outrageous) conclusions and speculations. I almost always make clear the basis of those conclusions or speculations so that the reader can judge on his own how much credence he wishes to place in them, and I try to do so in a way which makes him more open to unfamiliar and sometimes (apparently) bizarre concepts.

I almost never say things simply to be perverse or iconoclastic, though I have been accused of being both. I don't think it's perverse to think about surviving a nuclear war. Rather, I think it's dangerous and foolish not to. I don't think it's iconoclastic to expose a "budget deficit" as a largely nominal concept. Rather, I think it is useful to note this largely nominal character if one is to address the real problems effectively (including that of having a large nominal deficit).

The United States has now reached an unprecedented stage of economic and technological development in which the basic issues of safety, security, and survival are rarely regarded as primary. At the same time, social issues, "self-actualization," and the quality of life have grown in importance because most of us can take the basics for granted. As a result, some have become complacent or apathetic. But I believe the people of this country are at least potentially as concerned, dynamic, and resourceful as is needed to meet our current problems, and with some margin to spare.

Our current resolve to try for revitalization is itself a very positive and documentable fact, even if there will be controversy, mistakes, and lost motions. If at certain points along the way Reaganomics doesn't work as soon or as well as some would like, or if it temporarily appears that the administration really is trying to balance the budget "with mirrors" or "on the backs of the poor," it is still not reason enough (or not late enough in the experiment) to cry defeat. Instant gratification is an option in so many aspects of our lives that it becomes increasingly more difficult to accept time lags. Affirmative action can't instantly correct deeply entrenched problems; quick fixes won't do away with deeply embedded inflation overnight; a greatly increased defense budget won't mean much in practical terms for five to ten years. But we—individually as people and collectively as a nation—are taking steps to do what needs to be done. Not to recognize, acknowledge, and even flaunt this is to do ourselves a disservice. In the same way that the United States no longer issues many long-term (thirty-year) bonds, we no longer issue many long-term prognoses for a better future.

Similarly, the point of this book is not that the United States has passed through two decades of malaise and it's time it did something to get out of it—or that after all the United States has coped with harder problems before and can cope with them again. Rather the main point is that there are strong indications that both boom and revitalization are on the way, that we are already doing many of the things that need to be done. There are some problems which we should fix; if we don't fix them the boom may come anyway but is less sure. If we do, both the boom and the revitalization are going to be more nearly certain, stronger and deeper, longer-lasting, and more productive. We should do the best we can, and we can do a lot.

It's highly unlikely that this will ever be the best of all possible worlds. But all things considered, we may be living in the best of all existing countries—at least by the value systems of most Americans (and of many others as well). Despite all of the negativism and recent criticism, the United States really is a good country. Those who spelled America with a *k* were mostly spoiled children being petulant and striking back at their parents, symbolic or real.

I have recently been spending a good deal of time at Arizona State University, which has about 35,000 students. Nobody thinks of it as a Harvard or a Sorbonne, but in its own way it is a great university or at least a great institution. The students and faculty are proud of it, and they get out of it most of the things that they need and want. I would guess that the parents of more than half of the student body did not go to a university. The university has a fantastic campus; the people and state of Arizona (despite a recent cut in the budget) have lavished love, affection, and care on it. The students are not naive country bumpkins. They are "with it" but at the same time they have a genuine interest in their studies, their careers, and in making something of themselves. And I think most will.

One of the really important things about the United States is that it is not dominated by the graduates of a small number of elite universities in the way Japan, France, and England are. We do not have a Tokyo University, a *Grandes Ecoles* system, or an Oxford/Cambridge clique. The elite universities in the United States do have greater than their proportionate share of influence in government, academia, and prestige professions—but not as much as they think; they definitely do not dominate the mainstream of American life, including politics, business, and public discussion. If you want to finance a big project today you are as likely to go to Los Angeles or Houston as to Wall Street. Even during the current recession about half the country is still likely to be doing well—particularly in what we call the "quality of life" zone (the term "Sunbelt" is misleading). In other words, the United States is a dynamic country; it will prosper, and it deserves to.

That the long-term prospects of mankind are very favorable in terms of resources and technology is not based primarily on my belief that man has often risen to the occasion and will probably rise again (though this would have been my premise had I attempted the same discussion twenty or thirty years ago). The prognosis is instead based on existing modern technology and recent trends. By 1975 we knew roughly how many resources we would need, where they were or how to find them, and, barring unexpected pollution effects, how to exploit them with current technology or technology that would be on the shelf by 2000. At the level of a Scotch verdict, we "know" today how to maintain ten billion people at roughly twice the standard of living of the United States today—at least in terms of food, construction, manufactured goods, and most services. It is not an issue of rising to the occasion in an extraordinary burst of creativity, energy, and/or discipline but only of being reasonably competent (and, as always, barring some perverse combination of bad luck and bad management). There will be some new problems (some of which may be caused by new technologies or other innovations), but this prospect should be the exception as far as just meeting resource problems is concerned.

Whether or not we do well in the long run is both complex and conjectural. Probably the most important issues revolve on how well we deal with wealth and apparent safety—and who is doing the judging. Will we become soft, decadent, and/or hedonistic? Will we reject technology, discipline, and sacrifice? Will we maintain what we need, including national character, morale, and resolve; will we deal with inevitable strains and stresses, as well as crises?

I believe that even with all the problems we now have, mankind in general and the United States in particular are still likely to have a great future. There are no guarantees that all of the problems brought on by the Emerging Problem-Prone Super-Industrial World Economy—or other problems which fate or luck may have in store—will be solved satisfactorily. There are no guarantees that having high technology and wealth will bring happiness. But they do bring two important things: improved security and more choices.

For example, the world has had almost a century of probably the best agricultural weather on record. Many climatologists feel there is a greater probability of a shift to cold weather than of excessively warm weather (as the people worried by the greenhouse effect expect). Whether we get cold or hot, the problems that stem from either climate will be better dealt with if we have the ability to face them. And by "ability" I mean greater affluence and advanced technology. Both provide the kind of economic surplus and mechanical flexibility that make the difference between a disaster that causes immense human suffering and just a problem that is difficult but solvable. Historically the motivation for economic development has not been to improve the standard of living or the quality of life but to improve security. And I would argue that one great virtue of affluence and advanced technology is that by giving us the knowledge and ability to deal with whatever problems may come up, they are indeed a source of improved security.

But they do more than that. They provide a range of choices for individual self-actualization and self-fulfillment as well as for national prestige and national ambition, and they provide many paths to getting there. The kinds of things we Americans, and much of the world as well, will be able to do in the year 2000 would have been associated with miracles or magic two hundred or three hundred years ago. It will be an exciting world—fulfilling and challenging—a world of opportunities, glamour, options. In the twenty-first century, we should come very close to eliminating most disease, most ignorance, most poverty, and most of the grinding isolation that human communities have always lived with. I cannot tell if this will be for good or evil. Traditionally, philosophers have told us that the way to happiness and virtue is through asceticism, or aestheticism, or religion, or spiritual values and/or ethics; i.e., through the good and/or simple life. Perhaps this very wealthy and technological society will also choose some such path, but for reasons other than economic and technological necessity. Or the future may see a creative and splendid new synthesis of what man and society are about. Whatever that future society chooses to do, it has the kinds of opportunities that no human group has ever had before; clearly we are—and should be—willing to work for this. We have made a Faustian bargain but we are much more likely to be the Goethe Faust than the Marlowe Faust—we are, in short, more likely to ascend triumphantly than to be condemned to eternal damnation.

INDEX

abortion, 59, 62
accounting, 92–94
   historical-cost method of, 92–94
   inflation-indexed method of, 92, 93
   inventory evaluation method of, 93
   replacement-value method of, 92, 93
advanced capitalist nations (ACNs):
   economic planning in, 201
   graph for aggregate output of, 33
   growth rates for, 33–34
   Industrial Revolution in, 28, 32n, 216
   malaise in, 34–35, 53, 129
   public-interest groups in, 45–46, 48
   and stagflation, 34–35
   value systems in, 47
Affirmative Action rules, 186, 225
agriculture:
   productivity of, 31, 68, 69
   revolution in, 28
Alaskan Gas Pipeline, 125–26
all-savers certificates, 115
Anderson, Chris, 119
anti-growth movement, 188–92
Arendt, Hannah, 179
Arizona State University, 226
AT&T, 75–76, 77, 202

baby boom, postwar, 51, 206; *see also* birth rates
Bell, Daniel, 48
biotechnologies, 68–69, 70, 71
birth rates, 30–31, 37–38, 47
Black Muslims, 222
Black Panthers, 222
bombers, 165–66
bonds, 91–92, 100–101, 124–25, 207
bonds, commodity, 113, 116–24
   and federal deficit financing, 121–122
   and front-end loading, 117

bonds, commodity (*Cont.*)
   futures market created by, 119
   and gold, 120–21
   in government, 120–24
   high-discount, 119–20, 123
   and inflationary expectations, 117
   and oil bonds, 116–19, 120, 122–24
   repayment of, 116
   shared risk of, 118, 119
   strategic stockpiles marketed through, 120
   in "two-for-one" plans, 122–24
boom, economic:
   causes of, 15–16
   and cultural vitality, 204–5
   de-industrialization in, 41–42
   growth rates in, 205–8
   inflation as threat to, 86
   in Kondratieff cycle terms, 39–41
   long-term capital in, 16
   potential obstacles to, 16–17, 189, 225
   raw materials for, 208
   and Reaganomics, 206
   scenario for, 205–8
   timing of, 11
   and "vision of the future," 52, 219
Brandt, Willy, 159n
Brazil, 170, 171
Brock, Bill, 54
Brown, William M., 128n
Bruce-Briggs, B., 48
bureaucracy, 179–80, 181
Bush, George, 184

Canada, 135, 136
capitalism, dynamism of, 216–18, 221; *see also* advanced capitalist nations
Carter, Jimmy, 17, 42, 56
   defense policies of, 58, 149–50, 151, 165
   energy policies of, 129, 213

Carter, Jimmy (*Cont.*)
  loss of faith in, 151
  and national park plan, 184–85
  political vulnerability of, 62
  public interest appointments by, 180–81
Central Intelligence Agency (CIA), 136
C^4I^2 technologies, *see* communications technology
classes, socioeconomic, 31–32; *see also* New Class
Club of Rome, 17, 63–64, 219
coal, production of, 130, 131, 144
communications technology, 72–74, 77, 79, 80–83, 167
Communist Manifesto (Marx), 216, 218
computer networks, 72–79
  "big systems" in, 72
  in C^4I^2, 72–74
  cottage industries promoted by, 82–83
  dangers of, 72
  in GEISCO system, 75
  government restrictions on, 77
  in information processing, 76–77
  and man's self-image, 81–82
  possible applications of, 78–79
  and "quality of life," 84–85
  technological advancements in, 77–78
  time-sharing systems, 75–77
Congress, U.S., 162, 180, 184, 213
Congressional elections of 1982, 9, 17
conservatism, 50, 54, 58–63, 197
  see also economic conservatism; social conservatism
consumer price index (CPI), 15–16, 57, 105, 115
Copernicus, 82
cost-benefit analyses, 197–98
cost-of-living index, 100
Council of Economic Advisors, 200
counterculture movement, 66
creative destruction, 31, 39, 40, 41, 47
currencies, stability of, 91–92

Darwin, Charles, 82
Deeming, Edward, 43
Deeming Award, 44
defense, U.S., 146–78
  arms race in, 172–73
  budgets for, 13, 58, 162–63, 168
    Carter's policies on, 58, 149–50, 151, 165

defense, U.S. (*Cont.*)
  and civil defense, 154, 167, 168
  conservative analyses of, 177–78
  crisis scenarios for, 154–56, 175–77, 178
  current budgets for, 163, 164
  "deterrence only" arguments for, 150, 166
  deterrent strength of, 156, 164
  "escalation dominance" in, 156
  evacuation plans in, 154
  in Korean War, 162–63
  "launch on warning" system in, 155, 165
  loss of confidence in, 151–52
  MAD vs. NUTS controversy in, 166–67
  and mobilization bases, 163, 164
  "no first use" policy in, 152
  Persian Gulf and, 161–62, 163
  procurements for, 163
  psychological aspects of, 150–52
  and "quick fixes," 147–48
  Reagan's policies on, 58, 147, 150–51, 152–53, 168, 172
  SAC's role in, 164
  satellites in, 168
  Soviet superiority over, 146–47, 148, 153, 165, 169, 171
  spending for, *see* budgets for, *above*
  strategic offensive forces in, 165–66
  "war-fighting" capabilities, 164, 167, 175–76
  Western Europe's role in, 158, 159–60
  "window of vulnerability" in, 146, 173*n*
Defense Intelligence Agency, 136
deficit, federal, 21–26
  commodity bond financing for, 121–22
  definition of, 23
  European deficits compared with, 21, 23
  financing of, 24
  GNP in relation to, 21, 23
  graph of, 22
  inflation as cause of, 24, 25–26
  interest on, 21, 22
  measurement of, 21
  monetizing of, 25
  for 1982, 9
  as nonexistent, 21, 23–24
  private borrowing affected by, 24, 25
  in vicious circle, 24–26
de-industrialization, policies of, 41–42

INDEX ■ 231 ■

Democratic Party, 54–55, 56, 57
dollar, devaluation of, 103

Easterlin, Simon, 38
economic conservatism, 60–61
   and government regulation, 60
   influence of, 18–19
   pro-business sentiment in, 61
   social conservatism vs., 61
economic growth:
   in advanced capitalist nations, 33–34
   in coming boom, 14–15, 205–8
   conservative reactions to, 49
   creative destruction in, 47
   in Japan, 43
   long-term perspectives for, 92
   malaise in, 34–35, 53
   in middle-income countries, 34, 37, 217
   opposition to, 47–49, 189–90
   peaking of, 53
   phases of, 32–33
   in poor countries, 34
   through Reaganomics, 206
   as recent phenomenon, 47
   of service sector, 79
   social limits to, 24–25, 30–31, 47–49, 53, 190, 197, 198–99, 207
   in Soviet Union, 169
economic output, world, 29
economies, 89–92
   "invisible" adjustments in, 90–91
   "real" aspects of, 89–91
   socialist vs. capitalist, 89, 90
   stable currencies in, 91–92
   supply-side issues in, 90, 91
   symbolic aspects of, 89–91
educated incapacity, concept of, 188
Eisenhower, Dwight D., 50n, 55
Emerging Republican Majority, The (Phillips), 55–56
energy, 128–45
   conservation of, 130, 140, 141
   in economic boom, 16, 128
   environmental regulations on, 131–32
   financing for developments in, 139, 140, 141, 145
   and government intervention, 143–44
   government policies on, 129–31
   from natural gas, 137–39
   oil crisis (1970s), 29–30, 139–40
   outlook for, 140, 145

energy (*Cont.*)
   scale for price of, 129n
   self-defeating prophecies in, 140–41, 145
   from synthetic fuels, 141–43
   technological innovations in, 67–68
   welfare economics argument for, 144–45
   see also oil
Energy Department, U.S., 187
environmental problems, 44–45, 63–64
   in energy production, 131–32
   regulatory overkill in, 185–86
   technological solutions to, 68
Environmental Protection Agency (EPA), 186, 198
Europe, Western, 157–60
   détente in, 159
   economic stagnation in, 158
   neutralist position in, 158, 160
   Ostpolitik policy in, 159
   Soviet policy on, 158–60
   Soviet trade with, 158–59
   U.S. as viewed by, 158, 159–60
Exxon Corporation, 139

Federal Reserve Board, 9, 25
Financial Times, 103
financing, unconventional, 113–27
   Alaskan Gas Pipeline as example of, 125–26
   with commodity bonds, 113, 116–24
   and downward rigidity, 113
   for energy development, 139, 140, 141, 145
   and gold standard, 111–12
   with indexed government bonds, 124–25
   indexing for, 115–16
   for natural gas facilities, 139
   variable-rate mortages as, 113
Fisher, Irving, 90
Food and Drug Administration, 187
food stamp program, 183–84
Ford, Gerald, 56, 129, 213
foreign-aid policies, U.S., 215–16
Forrester, Jay, 35, 37
Franklin, Benjamin, 31
Franklin Bank, bankruptcy of, 114
Freud, Sigmund, 82
Friedman, Milton, 18, 26, 90

■ 232 ■ INDEX

gas, natural, 137–39, 145, 213
   government controls on, 130, 131, 137
   increased production of, 137
   sources of, 138–39
   in Soviet Union, 158
   tax on, 213
Gedanken experiments, 174
General Electric, 93
General Electric Information Services Co. (GEISCO), 75
genetic engineering, 69
Germany, East, 159
Germany, West, 152, 159, 160, 171
Gilder, George, 221
global status, U.S.:
   challenges to, 16
   decline in, 13, 18, 208
   Reagan administration policies on, 18, 108
   revitalization of, 14
   and worldwide economic recovery, 17–18
Global 2000, 17, 214–15, 218
Gold, Thomas, 138*n*
Gold Commission, 109
gold standard, 109–112
   arguments against, 110, 111–12
   arguments for, 98, 110–11
   cultural attitudes toward, 109–10
   flexible use of, 109
   supply-siders' support for, 98
Goldwater, Barry, 55, 56
governance, meaning of, 179, 180, 181–82, 201–2
Graham, Daniel, 153
Gray, Colin, 153
Great Society programs, 55, 108
Great Transition, 28–32
   and arms-control measures, 172–73
   phases of, 28–29, 31
   and population growth, 29–31
   social limits to growth in, 30–31
   spike graph for, 29–30, 219
   world economic output in, 29, 30
gross national product (GNP):
   in agricultural revolution, 28
   in coming boom, 205, 206, 207
   concept of, 207
   deficit in relation to, 21, 23
   environmental technology in, 68
   in European countries, 24

gross national product (GNP) *(Cont.)*
   government spending in relation to, 24
   growth of, 24
   of middle-income countries, 217
   in monetarist theory, 94–96, 97
gross world product, 29, 30, 208
growing pains, economic, 17

health care, 69–70
home financing, *see* mortgages
Hudson Institute, 14*n*, 17, 20, 21, 164*n*, 166*n*, 173, 176, 180
Humphrey, Hubert, 61

IBM, 75–76, 202
ICBMs, 165
ideologies:
   anti-growth, 66
   of progress, 64
   purpose of, 64
   in Reagan administration, 57–58, 144–145
   in revitalization, 203–4
immigration, 207
"impoverishing events," 15
   pure monetary inflation vs., 104–5
   as "supply-side shocks," 95*n*
income transfers, regulatory, 107
indexing, economic, 99–106, 115–16
   in accounting methods, 93
   ad hoc, 99–100, 101
   in bonds and mortgages, 100–102
   on both sides of ledger, 115–16
   with commodities, 116–17, 119
   with CPI, 105, 115, 116
   with GNP deflator, 115, 116
   of government bonds, 124–25
   of government payments, 102–3
   impoverishment vs. inflation in, 104–5
   improvements in, 15–16
   inflation in, 15–16, 57, 99–105
   with MCI, 102, 105, 116, 124, 211
   preset, 99–100
   of principal in loans, 115–16, 211
   proposal for, 106
   reforms needed in, 57
   of Social Security payments, 104–5
   of wages, 104–5
individualism, tradition of, 183

INDEX

Industrial Revolution, 28, 32n, 216
inflation, 86–89, 94–99
   acceptance of, 87, 88
   in accounting methods, 93–94
   and bond indexing, 124–26
   bonds and mortgages affected by, 100–102
   dangers of, 87, 88
   decline in rates of, 14–15
   deficit caused by, 24, 25–26
   "embedded," 9, 10
   expectations of, 15, 25, 88–89, 204
   financial gains from, 88–89, 100, 102
   government benefits from, 103–4
   government spending as spur to, 107–8
   "impoverishment" vs., 104–5
   income transfer by, 88
   in indexing, 15–16, 57, 99–105
   Keynesian view of, 95, 97–98
   monetarist theory of, 94–98
   monetary, 15, 104
   money policies and, 9–10, 95–98
   and oil prices, 95–97, 129
   as political and moral problem, 99
   premiums to correct for, 15, 100–101
   preset indexing of, 99–100
   Reagan administration policies on, 87–88
   residual, 15
   as self-propelled, 25
   shortage of goods in, 103–4
   and social programs, 108
   supply-side view of, 98
   and tax treatment of interest, 103
   unconventional financing as curb on, 111–12, 113, 117, 124–25
   and unemployment, 52, 97–98, 99
   vicious circle initiated by, 24–26
   and wages, 98
   after World War II, 86–87
intelligence, artificial vs. human, 81–82
intelligence data, 72–73
interest rates, 16, 23–26
   deficit financing as influence on, 24
   inflationary component in, 23
   monetary policies affected by, 9
   on national debt, 21, 23
   in vicious circle, 24–26
   see also mortgages
investment:
   horizon for, 40n, 92
   inadequate levels of, 25

Iran:
   hostage crisis in, 58, 151
   revolution in, 133
   U.S. view of, 161
Iraq-Iran war, 133
"iron triangles" of bureaucracy, 180
Israel, 161

Japan, 42–44, 83–84, 171, 200
job safety, 187, 198: *see also* regulations
Johnson, Lyndon B., 54, 55, 108
Johnson, Samuel, 145, 200

Kennedy, John F., 10, 11, 50n, 54, 55, 108
Keynes, John Maynard, 90, 91, 184
Keynesian theory, 90, 95, 97–98, 109
Kondratieff, Nikolai D., 35, 38
Kondratieff cycles, 35–41
   archetype long cycle in, 39–41, 86
   downswings in, 37
   peak wars in, 38, 86
   and population growth, 37–38
   and technological innovations, 37
   utility of, 38
   variations on, 35–38
Korean War, 162–63, 164
Kristol, Irving, 48, 190–91
Kuznets, Simon, 38

Labor Department, U.S., 51
labor unions, 98
Lecht, Charles, 65n
Lee Kwan Yew, 200n
Levenson, Irving, 86n
Limits to Growth, 17; *see also* Club of Rome
liquidations, 114

McGovern, George, 56
"MAD" doctrine, 165, 166–67
Maddison, Angus, 33
management, role of, 80–81
management information systems (MISs), 74, 79–81
Marx, Karl, 48, 66–67, 82, 216, 218
mass transportation, 70, 107–8
materials, developments in, 70
Mencken, H. L., 54
Mensch, Gerhard, 35
Mexico, 217–18

INDEX

middle-income countries, growth rates of, 34, 37, 217
minority groups, 183, 186, 206, 210
monetarists, 61, 90, 94–98, 182
monetary correction indicator (MCI), 102, 105, 116, 124, 211
money, theories of, 94–95, 97
money illusion, 88, 96, 99, 104
money policies, tight:
  in inflation control, 9–10, 95–98
  of Reagan administration, 9, 98
  reduced efficacy of, 9–10
  and tax treatment, 103
Moral Majority, 58, 223
mortgages, 16, 100–102, 211–12
  fixed-rate, 115
  indexing principal of, 115–16, 211
  variable-rate, 113
Moynihan, Daniel Patrick, 48, 184
multi-polarity, 170–73
  and arms-control developments, 172–73
  and superpowers, 170–71
  world stability of, 171–72
mutual assured destruction (MAD) doctrine, 165, 166–67
MX missiles, 45–46

National Defense University, 177
National Transportation Act, 107–8
NATO, 14, 18, 147, 151–52, 158, 159, 160, 177
natural gas, *see* gas, natural
neutron bomb, 151
New Class, 40, 47–49, 66, 168, 181, 182; *see also* symbolist class
New Deal coalition, 54–55, 56–57, 58
New Emphases, 180, 181, 192, 206
New Left, 56
New Right, 19, 182
Next 200 Years, The (Kahn), 224
Nitze, Paul, 153
Nixon, Richard M., 55, 61, 129
Novak, Michael, 221
nuclear theories:
  MAD, 165, 166–67
  NUTS, 166–67
  spasm response, 172
nuclear power, 130–31
nuclear use theorists (NUTS), 166–67
nuclear war, attitudes toward, 149–50, 153, 154–56, 160

Occupation, Safety and Health Administration (OSHA), 187, 198
O'Connor, Sandra Day, 62
oil, 14, 118, 128–37, 212–13
  bonds for, 116–19
  boom in exploration for, 135–36
  cartel, *see* Organization of Petroleum Exporting Countries
  decline in consumption of, 139–40
  decline in OPEC prices for, 132, 133
  domestic prices for, 130, 131, 213
  and energy crisis (1970s), 129–30
  government policies on, 130–31
  and inflation, 95–97, 129
  non-OPEC production of, 134, 135, 136, 137
  peak price of, 143
  and Saudi Arabia, 133–34
  scenarios for developments in, 134–35
  self-defeating prophecies in use of, 140–41, 145
  in Soviet Union, 136–37, 158
  taxes on, 212–13
  see also Organization of Petroleum Exporting Countries
On Thermonuclear War (Kahn), 224
OPEC, *see* Organization of Petroleum Exporting Countries
Organization for Economic Cooperation and Development (OECD), 21
Organization of Petroleum Exporting Countries (OPEC), 123, 128–29, 132–35, 140, 143
  as cartel, 132, 133–34
  declining influence of, 128
  discounting by, 132–33
  in 1970s energy crisis, 129
  price increases by, 132, 133
  products purchased by members of, 133
  real income of, 133
  Saudi Arabia's leadership of, 133–34
  world reliance on, 134–35, 140–41

Pavlov, I. P., 82
Pepper, Thomas, 39*n*
Persian Gulf, 157, 159, 161–62, 163
pessimism, 17, 18, 63
Phillips, Kevin, 55–56
planning, national, 199–202
  decentralized decision-making vs., 200
  market forces vs., 199, 200–201
  successful intervention in, 200, 201

INDEX ■235■

Poland, 159
Ponzi schemes, 40
population, 29–31
  historical perspective on, 29–31, 208
  of U.S. in coming boom, 207, 208
pornography, 59, 60
post-industrial society, 31–32, 204–8
  culture in, 31–32, 204–5
  economy of, 91, 204, 207
  as "mosaic," 204
  per capita income in, 207–8
  scenario for, 205–8
Potter, David, 221
poverty, 190, 206, 216–17
power politics, 150
precious metals, 109n
producer price index (PPI), 122
product codes, 73–74
productivity:
  advanced information systems in, 79–80
  of agriculture, 31, 68, 69
  capitalism as spur to, 216
  in Great Transition, 31
  improvements in, 16
  investment and, 25
  management's role in, 80
progress, ideology of, 64
protectionism, technological, 77
Protestant Ethic, 190
psychology, commercial, 42–43
public interest groups, 45–46, 48, 180–81, 190
public opinion:
  anti-big-business sentiment in, 62
  pessimism in, 63
  on Reagan administration, 10–11, 210

Qaddafi, Mu'ammar al-, 162
quality control, 43
"quality of life" concept, 226

Rapid Deployment Force, U.S. (RDF), 162, 164
Reagan, Ronald, 51, 52–53, 56, 58, 62–63, 181, 223–24
Reagan administration:
  anti-inflation policies of, 87–88
  conservative coalition in, 50, 54, 56, 57, 58, 62–63, 223
  conservative policies of, 19

Reagan administration (*Cont.*)
  criticisms of, 51
  cynicism of, 10–11
  defense policies of, 58, 147, 150–51, 152–53, 168, 172
  economic problems inherited by, 10
  energy policies of, 144–45
  and global status, 18, 108
  and governance issues, 182–83, 202
  ideological intensity of, 57–58, 144–45
  intellectual shifts in, 18–19, 49
  legislative achievements of, 87, 180
  money policies of, 9, 98
  and New Class, 181
  optimism of, 10
  practical experience of, 188
  priorities of, 108
  public opinion on, 10–11, 210
  and regulatory reform, 184, 199
  in revitalization of U.S., 14, 27, 63, 223–24
  rich vs. poor under, 210–11
  social welfare program cuts under, 183
  tax cuts under, 10, 26, 87, 98
  technical issues in, 57–58
  as watershed, 54, 63, 180
Reaganomics, 16, 206, 209, 212, 225
recovery, cyclical, 15
regulations, government, 184–88, 197–99
  budgetary constraints on, 198
  and conflicting goals, 187
  cost of, 184, 186, 198
  cost-benefit analysis of, 197–98
  and economic conservatives, 60
  "educated incapacity" reflected in, 188–89
  and environmental overkill, 185–86
  growth of, 184
  "horror stories" about, 184–86
  ineffectiveness of, 187
  rationalization of, 25
  support for, 190
reindustrialization, 41, 42
religion, 221, 222
Republican Party, 9, 10–11, 54, 55–56, 57
resources, availability of, 219, 226–27
revitalization, U.S., 218–28
  cyclical phenomenon in, 53
  in education, 222
  ideology needed for, 203–4
  long-run expectations in, 204

INDEX

revitalization (*Cont.*)
  prospects for, 11, 53–54, 219–20, 225
  range of, 14
  Reagan administration's role in, 14, 27, 63, 223–24
  technology in, 84–85
Ricardo, David, 219
robots, 71
Roosevelt, Franklin D., 54, 55, 108, 183
Rostow, Walt W., 35, 37

SALT II, 151
satellites, 69, 168
Saudi Arabia, 133–34, 135, 140, 161–62
savings and loan associations (S&Ls), 113–15
scenarios, purpose of, 173–75
Schmidt, Helmut, 151, 159
school system, pessimism taught in, 63, 64, 220–221
Schumpeter, Joseph, 31, 35, 37, 47, 110–11
Scotch verdict, 20, 21, 41, 226
seismic detection, 67, 136
service sector, technological developments in, 79–80
Sharp, I. P., 82–83
silicon chips, 71
Singer, Max, 164n
Skinner, B. F., 82
Smith, Adam, 90
Smith, Roger B., 71
Smithsonian reevaluation of 1971, 103
social conservatism, 58–60
  anti-big-business sentiment of, 61–62
  critics of, 59–60
  economic conservatism vs., 61
  growth of, 59
  as middle- and lower-middle-class movement, 58, 61
  political goals of, 223
  public/private distinction in, 60
  in Reagan coalition, 58
  traditional values of, 58–59
Social Security payments, 104–5
social welfare programs, 183–84
South Korea, 43n
Soviet Union, 13, 18, 136–37
  in arms race, 172
  bureaucracy in, 179
  defense system of, 165–66, 167
  demographic trends in, 169

Soviet Union (*Cont.*)
  domestic problems in, 169–70
  economic stagnation of, 169
  and European neutralization, 157–60
  European trade with, 158–59
  Industrial Revolution in, 216
  internal political control in, 156–57
  in Korean War, 164
  military calculations of, 157n
  military expenditures in, 147
  military prudence of, 148–49, 153, 157, 170, 177–78
  military superiority of, 146–47, 148, 153, 165, 169
  NATO view of, 152
  natural gas in, 158
  new leadership of, 153
  and nuclear war, 150, 153, 154–56
  oil in, 136–37, 158
  Persian Gulf policies of, 161, 162
space colonies, 29, 69
spasm response, concept of, 172
special drawing right (SDR), 110
spending, government, 23–24, 107–8, 183
stagflation, 24–25, 34–35
stagnation, economic, 53, 197, 205, 209
Stockman, David, 50
Stoph, Willi, 159n
Strategic Air Command, U.S. (SAC), 163, 164
structural problems, 25
Sunshine Mining Corporation, 119
super-industrial economy, 44–46, 227
  proposal for conference on, 218–19
supply-side economics, 61, 98, 182
surprise-free scenarios, 20, 21
Sweden, 211
symbolist class, 48–49, 181, 191–92, 197; *see also* New Class
synergisms, 83
synthetic fuels, 67, 116–17, 141–43, 145

tax cuts:
  anticipated effects of, 10, 26, 87–88
  and income distribution, 10–11
  monetarist criticism of, 98
taxes, federal, 209–14
  on cigarettes, 214
  collection of, 26
  "creeping progressivity" in, 210

INDEX ■237■

taxes, federal (*Cont.*)
  8-12 system for, 209–10
  on gasoline, 213–14
  on imported oil, 212–13
  on interest, 103, 120, 211–12
  and mortgage interest deductions, 211–12
  property tax deductions in, 211, 212
  receipts from, 115
  reforms for, 209–14
  on unearned income, 26
  value-added, 209
technology, 65–85
  in agriculture, 68, 69
  and anti-growth ideologies, 66
  in automation, 71–72
  as biotechnology, 68–69, 70, 71
  and coming boom, 16, 17, 65–66, 67
  in computer networks, 77–78
  crisis in, 17
  and energy, 67–68
  for environmental protection, 68
  in Great Transition, 29
  in health care, 69–70
  in Kondratieff cycles, 37
  lead times for, 65
  man's self-image affected by, 81–82
  in mass transportation, 70
  and new materials, 70
  in oil exploration, 135–36
  and "quality of life," 65, 66, 84–85
  security improved by, 227–28
  of silicon chips, 71
  in space and satellite developments, 69
  in super-industrial economy, 44–46, 65
  values applied to, 46
television, cable, 73–74
Thatcher, Margaret, 206
Third World, 67*n*, 217
Three Mile Island, 130
tight money, *see* money policies, tight

Truman, Harry S., 54
Turner, Frederick, 221*n*

unemployment, 51–52, 97–98, 99
universities, elite, 226
U.S.S.R., *see* Soviet Union

values, traditional:
  in American system, 221–23
  anticipated revival of, 14
  erosion of, 14, 182
  in productivity, 16
  in social conservatism, 58–59
Veblen, Thorstein, 188
Vietnam War, 13, 50, 54, 108, 147, 151
"visions of the future," *see* ideologies

wages, 98, 104–5
Wallace, George, 61
wars, economic effects of, 38
Warsaw Pact, 158
Watergate, 54, 56
Weinberger, Caspar, 163
welfare economics, 144, 145
Wheeler, Jimmy W., 39*n*
wholesale price index, 36, 100
word processing, developments in, 71–72, 77
work force:
  changed composition of, 51–52, 206
  discouraged workers in, 52
  low growth rate of, 51, 206
  from postwar baby boom, 51, 206
  supervision of, 83
  women in, 51, 206
World Economic Development (Kahn), 38
World War I, 160, 175
World War II, 160

youths, affluent, 189–90; *see also* New Class; symbolist class